Making God
Laugh

An autobiography
By ELLEN JAMESON

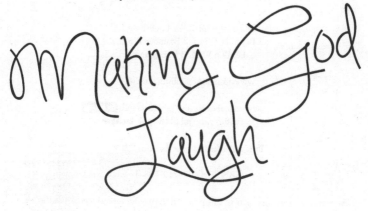

The most beautiful true story of love and
loss you will ever read

JOHN BLAKE

Published by John Blake Publishing Ltd,
3 Bramber Court, 2 Bramber Road,
London W14 9PB, England

www.johnblakepublishing.co.uk

www.facebook.com/Johnblakepub facebook
twitter.com/johnblakepub twitter

First published in paperback in 2014

ISBN: 978-1-78219-758-4

British Library Cataloguing-in-Publication Data:

A catalogue record for this book is available from the British Library.

Design by www.envydesign.co.uk

Printed in Great Britain by CPI Group (UK) Ltd

3 5 7 9 10 8 6 4 2

Papers used by John Blake Publishing are natural, recyclable products made from
wood grown in sustainable forests. The manufacturing processes conform to the
environmental regulations of the country of origin.

Every attempt has been made to contact the relevant copyright-holders, but some
were unobtainable. We would be grateful if the appropriate people could contact us.

CONTENTS

ACKNOWLEDGEMENTS

"If you write only one book in your life,
make it your autobiography" – Anon

Popular wisdom would have it that writing is a lonely pursuit. That has not been my experience in writing this autobiography. Instead, my life has been populated by a rich tapestry of ghosts from the past, long forgotten friends and best forgotten enemies.

There has also been a host of publishing professionals who have guided, supported and encouraged me. John Blake Publishing are a joy to work with, as I already knew from the book I co-wrote with my late husband Derek Jameson, *Siobhan's Miracle*, which was published by Blake. Led by the charismatic John Blake and the super class act Rosie Virgo, they made me feel valued, inspired and special throughout the whole publishing process. They gave me the opportunity to work with a team of motivated and experienced editors headed up by Executive Editor, Toby Buchan, who took time to send poems about bleak November days while I languished in Miami Beach; Editor Rodney Burbeck, a past Fleet Street colleague and friend; and the insightful freelance editor, Judith Forshaw, who I worked with for the first time but I hope not the last. I love editors, having been married to two of them. The good ones reassure you that the creative output is all yours while skilfully steering the entire project towards a seamless and magical version of the author's highest vision.

Grateful thanks also to Sarah McMahon at Random House UK for facilitating the extracts from Derek's own book *The Last of the Hot Metal Men* in Chapter 13.

Chief cheerleaders through the dark days of my new widowhood were my wonderful god-daughter Michelle Ruger and honorary god-daughter Kerry Smith, plus unflappable office assistant, Jo Dean.

In Miami Beach, my dear friend Jude Parry of Gold Coast Theatre Company was a constant companion and, having cast my husband Derek as the king in one of her Florida pantomime productions, she was able to commiserate with me when I was overwhelmed by sadness at his passing. And thanks also to my super-talented actress friend, the South American soap opera star Pilar Uribe, who was always there for me. You can't beat girlfriends when you need a good cry!

The only member of my birth family who is still alive, William, is the best big brother I could ever ask for; I can't begin to list all the different areas in which he helped me. I am delighted to be 'Great Auntie Ellen' to his loving family – wife Mary, children and partners, and grandchildren.

The family of my late husband, Derek, have always been supportive and caring; they will not mind my sharing this story of my life with their beloved father. Derek never concealed anything about himself or his life.

ACKNOWLEDGEMENTS

And last, but never least, I thank Derek himself. I miss him dreadfully but I also know that his spirit and love are all around me, urging me on to greater endeavours. In one of the last greeting cards he gave to me he wrote, 'Follow your dreams'.

Thank you to everyone who has walked into my life and left footprints on my heart.

Ellen Jameson, Miami Beach, Florida,
December 2013

INTRODUCTION

If you want to make God laugh, tell him your plans

Speaking from the pulpit of a crematorium in Birmingham, I delivered the eulogy at my brother James' funeral. He had dropped down dead in the street during a routine police traffic stop.

James was in his early fifties and I had been due to go with him the following day to an appointment with a cardiovascular consultant at Queen Elizabeth Hospital. During a scan, an embolism had been discovered in his right thigh and the consultant was to give us information on treatment options.

Finishing the eulogy, emotional and in tears, I said, 'If you want to make God laugh, tell him your plans.'

After the funeral, I travelled from Birmingham to my home on the south coast. Letting myself in, I dropped my overnight bag and walked down the hallway, calling out to my husband: 'Derek, I'm home.'

Derek didn't answer. He was lying on the floor of his

downstairs bedroom. Dying. Just two weeks after my brother James' sudden death, Derek suffered a fatal heart attack and died in my arms.

As if the shock of all that wasn't enough, in one of the most powerful dreams I had ever had – so powerful and disturbing I had written it down at the time – while he was still very much alive I dreamt that Derek had died and I had not told anyone.

The dream had occurred just days before I had been to Birmingham registry office with my other brother Billy to collect the death certificate for James and arrange his Co-op funeral. In the dream, I told myself, 'I can't cope with this. I'll deal with it when I get home.' Well, I hope God was enjoying the joke – when I got home I *did* have to deal with it.

James' death had unleashed unchannelled energy: strong, dynamic and purposeful.

'He will not die in vain,' I repeated over and over in my head like a mantra. 'God let me live, abundantly, joyfully, with passion, without fear.'

I then had to get through my brother's funeral – delayed by the need for a post-mortem – and deliver a fitting eulogy for my little brother, the baby of the family. Surely God is not so cruel that he was laughing at me, knowing that less than two weeks later my husband would die days after we celebrated our twenty-fourth wedding anniversary?

'God, are you enjoying the joke? Is that why we are here, to make you laugh?'

In my eulogy to James, I told the congregation that his leaving this world without warning shouldn't have come as too much of a surprise: he had also entered this world unexpectedly, on 26 February 1954.

'The scene was set for a home birth,' I continued, 'but after waiting all night, the midwife told mum and dad (Mamie and Gerry) that their fourth child would not be arriving for several hours. She was going home to get a few hours' sleep and would be back later. With great timing, as soon as the midwife was out of the door, James chose to make his entrance.

'My dad became the hero of the hour, and of the RAF camp in Norfolk where he was stationed and where we lived at the time. He delivered his first baby – his own son, James – using techniques he'd learned in his medical training. By the time the midwife returned several hours later – we didn't have mobile phones in those days for instant communication – James had been born, bathed, and fed.

'The last time I saw James was a couple of weeks before he died. Over lunch he said, "I feel happier and more hopeful than I have for a long time. When I get my health problems sorted out, I'll have a chance for a fresh start and to get my life back on track."

'It wasn't to be. You know what they say. "If you want to make God laugh, tell him your plans."'

A little later, I delivered my eulogy to Derek. Here is an edited extract:

My husband Derek Jameson has been described as a Fleet Street legend, a larger than life character, the second most famous man in Britain (after Prince Charles), a superb communicator, an inspirational East End lad made good – a phenomenal circulation and audience builder in newspapers and broadcasting, a best-selling author and an incredibly well-loved public figure.

Yes, he was all those things, and over the years of our marriage I was in turn inspired, educated and awed by him. When we shared a radio programme together on BBC Radio 2, I struggled to get a word in edgeways – Derek always knew more than me, projected himself more forcefully and expressed his opinions without fear or favour.

He was an incredible character and even though it is hard to be a prophet in your own land or a hero in your own home, I never forgot that Derek was an extraordinary man and a true one-off.

Derek is the perfect example of an individual having lived life to the full. Now he has passed from this earthly plain, I can honestly say that his was a life well lived and a life completed. He was a communicator, a teacher and he was supremely self-confident. All you had to do was put a microphone or camera in front of him or sit him down at the computer and the stories, anecdotes and devastating observations would pour out.

Derek really was a 'man of the people'. He was looked up to by many but I never saw him look down on anyone. Life with Derek was never dull; nor was it as exhausting as some people seem to imagine. Derek liked to have an audience but he also liked his own company. He was at ease with himself and did not burden himself with existential questions about who he was or why he was here.

His passing was as close to the ideal as you get. Over 80 years of age, at peace with family and loved ones and safe in the warmth and comfort of his own home. Derek truly was touched by angels and I believe that the angels that surrounded him all his life bore him safely to heaven before he had time to protest or even know that his day and time had come.

I am comforted by the fact that I truly believe Derek's life was completed. Unfortunately, the same cannot be said for that day's crossword puzzle. He left many unanswered questions but that may have been deliberate because there were messages in the clues he left blank. One you would have thought he could have completed: three words, first one six letters, followed by 'Island Discs'.

INTRODUCTION

His luxury item when he appeared on the Radio 4 programme Desert Island Discs *was a word processor, so I am confidently expecting some reports from 'The Other Side'. Watch this space.*

His happiest moment this year was seeing the Olympic torch pass the gate of our house in Worthing. Derek had covered the last London Olympics as a trainee reporter in Fleet Street back in 1948; he was working for Reuters, the global news agency, at that time.

Derek was strong, dependable and non-judgemental. Never once in all our years together did he ever let me down, though my frailties were often on show. Derek rarely acknowledged his own accomplishments but he did have a deep sense of his own worth and value, and the snobbery and prejudice he was subjected to because of his humble beginnings and East End accent never got him down for long. As he would say without a trace of irony, 'You can't blame them. Those public school types didn't have the benefit of my upbringing.'

Days before his fatal heart attack, Derek watched the televised Olympic parade through London and treated me to a running commentary on all the places he knew and loved along the route. The Olympic Stadium had transformed the Hackney Marshes where he was born.

He grew more and more energised and nostalgic as the parade passed down Fleet Street. 'Look, Ellen, there's Reuters where I started my journalist career as an outdoor messenger boy, and there's the old Daily Express *building where I became editor of the most famous newspaper in the world; the Punch Tavern where I had my first drink; the law courts where I lost all my money in a disastrous libel action against the BBC. Mind you, they did then give me the breakfast slot on Radio 2.'*

I listened to the commentary of his life and, as we watched and

he shared his memories, I have a feeling Derek already knew he
was nearing the end of his own parade.

'Don't forget,' he said, 'I wrote my final instructions in my
autobiography, Last of the Hot Metal Men: "Scatter my ashes
in Fleet Street – who knows, the breeze might carry my mortal
remains to an unseen crevice, some forgotten ledge, where my
spirit will hear again the laughing voices in the night…"'

Then he said generously and unusually: 'You can finish my
crossword puzzle if you like.'

Derek's life is complete, the crossword puzzle sadly still is not,
but I do know what the legendary newspaperman would have
told me: 'Now it's time to write the last words. Two words, three
letters each. The End.'

I hope you enjoy this story of my life, spanning my eventful
childhood and teenage years, my entry into show business
journalism, my first marriage, partying, meeting and marrying
Derek Jameson, our radio days, overcoming alcoholism, travels
in the USA, and an unexpected late stage career as an actress.
It follows a mostly chronological thread, but not slavishly –
there are diversions. Please stay with me and share the journey.
Where I judged it would cause unnecessary disclosure,
embarrassment or pain, I did change some names but mostly
my intention was to tell the story of my life as honestly, openly
and blamelessly as possible. In retrospect, I am grateful for every
person, experience and challenge that shaped me.

As Derek loved to say, 'Ain't life grand?'

CHAPTER I

BRIGHT EYES

'Hello, bright eyes,' said the midwife as she held the newborn baby girl.

Twelve hours before, my mother Mamie – a strangely naive and unworldly 19-year-old – had not known where the child was going to appear. Her own mother had to tell her. But she was happy as long as she had a little girl with black hair and blue eyes. Her wish was granted.

During the birth, her husband Gerry, my father, just 21 years old, had been banished from the small one-bedroom apartment in the romantic-sounding Bluevale Street, a Glasgow tenement block, to the communal stairway outside. All night long he had waited on the freezing concrete steps. The pair, often described as one of the best-looking young couples in Dennistoun, stars of the local dance hall, had been married exactly a year.

Now, as dawn broke on Friday 14 October 1949, Gerry heard his firstborn cry. He would claim later that it was a ladylike little whimper. No screaming at the harsh reality of birth. Simply a soft cry to announce his daughter's arrival and the expectation of a welcome party.

'Most beautiful baby you ever saw,' he always boasted. 'Not a mark on her. She arrived in the world with her best face on and hair newly brushed.' My 86-year-old grandfather, Old Jimmy, a former coal merchant with his own fleet of horse-drawn carts, ran down the busy high road declaring to all who would listen: 'We've got a new wee lassie. Her hair is so long you can hang it over the back of a chair and comb it.'

I was his eighty-sixth grandchild; he had had a family of 22 and my dad was the youngest, the first boy after a long line of girls. His mother died when he was just two years old and dad was brought up and spoiled by his older sisters, many of whom already had families of their own.

Dad had always been an adventurer and his dreams were too big to be contained for long in Scotland. Shortly after I was born, he re-joined the RAF, where he had previously served just after the war. He loved the life and being stationed abroad; his last tour of duty had been in South Africa.

He was intelligent and enthusiastic, and he had quickly completed many of the training courses and educational opportunities on offer in the forces. It didn't take long for him to acquire his second stripe as a corporal.

When he signed up again, this time for 14 years as a volunteer after his three years of National Service, he spent most of his time in various postings in the south of England, although he also worked in Norfolk where bomb disposal teams were still clearing the wartime defences on the beaches.

Soon he achieved his ambition of an overseas posting. We moved to RAF Wunstorf, outside Hanover, and lived in RAF married quarters in the small German town. Our modern second-storey flat soon became home to visiting neighbours and lonely airmen.

Dad was a social animal, and he and mum, still in their twenties but with four children under seven, loved the forces' life which revolved around socials, ladies' nights and dinner dances at the camp-based Malcolm Club.

My beautiful, laughing mum was as much a centre of attention as dad, the handsome Mr Fixit who always seemed to secure himself the job as entertainment secretary. At weekends they would dress up and go out looking like 1950s film stars – mum in gorgeous off-the-shoulder satin and taffeta dresses that showed off her slim figure, smelling of Evening in Paris perfume, and dad in his best Brooks Brothers' suit. They would come home late and we kids would excitedly look forward to the following day when they would tell us all about their adventures – the dance band music, the laughter, the party games and the spot prizes. Mum and dad were both great dancers. Mum had gone dancing five nights a week in Glasgow ballrooms as a teenager and Mamie and Gerry would take centre stage on the dance floor and could beat the competition in everything from the waltz to rock 'n' roll.

They shared the prizes they won with us four children and they often brought home trays filled with the remains of a generous Social Club buffet supper. My brothers and I would tuck into sausage rolls, miniature sandwiches and tiny pieces of cake while they tested our ingenuity in working out the correct answers to the spot prizes.

'The first gentleman to bring me a pair of ladies' stockings wins the prize,' the compère would announce. While other couples tried to figure out how to retrieve the ladies' stockings while preserving their modesty, dad would sweep mum up, her nylon-clad legs over his arm, and rush to the front of the stage to claim the prize.

In elimination dances, where the judges gradually whittled down the dancers by asking couples to leave the floor, mum and dad would often be the last pair still dancing. At the 'excuse me' dances, dad would carefully vet anyone who asked to cut in; on the ladies 'excuse me ', mum would generally only intervene between a couple who were best friends of her and dad.

After a night out at one of the many German funfairs, mum and dad would return with shooting gallery prizes for us children. One of the most memorable of these – and a favourite toy that was to accompany us all over the world – was a giant blue teddy bear complete with pink bow, a gift to me. I promptly named him Chiefy after the Chief Engineer aircraftsman who had won him for me.

Mum and dad had a wide circle of friends and, when not at mess events or visiting German beer cellars, there was always a party at home. Thanks to the services of a maid, supplied by the RAF, mum had been freed from housework and she didn't work outside the home, so she would spend all day – usually at weekends – preparing for the party. Mum would do the buffet and dad was in charge of buying and collecting the alcohol and setting up a bar. They would push back all the furniture and stock up on records.

Their friends and acquaintances all agreed that Mamie and Gerry knew how to throw a good party. We kids would usually be sent to bed before the guests arrived, but, as the laughter and music filled the front room, we would sneak out of bed, hover by the open door and wait to be invited in.

My brother James, the baby of the family and then about four years old, was a star attraction. His nickname was Gentleman Jim because, before he would oblige the admiring crowd with a song, he had to borrow a man's tie – any tie would do. Suitably attired, he would launch into his Johnnie Ray impersonation: 'Ju-usta walk-k-ing in the rainnnnn …' followed by 'Cry', hanging his head down and 'cry-y-y-y-ing'.

Brothers Gerard, William and I would be raised from our

beds by the knowledge that James was getting all the attention...
not forgetting the lemonade and crisps, and sometimes even
money from tipsy guests.

Gradually we would all manoeuvre ourselves into the party
and the guests would make a fuss of us. It was a delicate
balancing act between being visible and entertaining and not
being so disruptive that we were put to bed.

After the dancing and chatter there would be a sing-song. In
those days most people had a party piece and we would all join
in on favourite songs. Mum always sang 'Mr Wonderful' but she
would get annoyed when dad interjected with 'Mr Wonderful,
that's me', preventing her singing the line to him.

Dad serenaded mum with hits of the 1950s, like their favourite,
Connie Francis's 'Little Things Mean a Lot'. They duetted
together on 'True Love' and 'Que Sera, Sera', and later on the hit
by husband-and-wife singing team Steve Lawrence and Edyie
Gorme, 'I Don't Want to Go to the Party with You'.

It was during preparations for one party that all the boys –
Gerard, six, William, five, and James, not yet at school – disgraced
themselves. Dad had made a huge fruit punch; it was one of his
specialities and, although the actual recipe was a closely guarded
secret, he would reveal some of the ingredients just to get the
guests' taste buds salivating.

Give or take a couple of bottles of extra alcohol, it went
something like this: equal parts (or bottles) of gin, vodka and
whisky, liberal helpings of Dubonnet, a splash of lemonade, and
a fruit cocktail of apples, oranges and lemons.

The highly potent concoction in an oversized glass punch
bowl was put in the fridge to chill while mum and dad went
shopping. A cheerful German maid who had come in to help
with the party and to babysit kept us generously supplied with
large helpings of 'lemonada' from the fridge.

By the time mum and dad came home laden with party food, the three boys were staggering around the flat, giggling. It seems I had refused the fruit drink after the first one made me feel sick. The boys were put to bed and slept right through the party. Next day, they appeared not too worse for wear after their experience.

On subsequent party nights their intake of alcohol was severely restricted and guests were warned that the children were not to be rewarded with sips of beer or allowed to mix their own cocktails from the remains of people's glasses. But mum, who had drunk only lemonade as a toast at her own wedding nearly a decade earlier, was turning out to be a match for dad as far as drinking was concerned. 'If you can't beat them, join them,' she would say.

The war had been over for just over 10 years but the reaction of the German people to us was mixed. Some were friendly and tried to initiate us into their German way of life and customs. On the whole, the maids who worked for us were good natured and efficient. They would encourage me to sing the Elvis classic 'Wooden Heart', with which I serenaded them in English and German. Elvis was serving at that time in Germany with the US Army.

The caretaker of our block of flats generously shared his lunchtime rations of black German bread and apple strudel. I made friends with a German woman who taught at the local school and she would invite me to the home she shared with her elderly mother to hear her play the piano.

My baby brother James, the party animal, turned out to be accident prone. He cheated death spectacularly on at least two occasions during our stay in Germany. The first time he very nearly started an international incident. At the local children's playground, a teenage boy started to bully James, demanding to know 'Who won the war?' The childish game became dangerous; he held James down in the sandpit and became more and more aggressive until my little brother conceded 'Germany won the war.'

James was frightened and crying, so I ran the few blocks home to get mum. By the time we got back, the teenager had overpowered James and buried his head under the sand. As we approached, the boy ran off. James was coughing and choking with sand when we finally rescued him.

A few months later he fell out of the second-floor window of our apartment block. It was dad to the rescue that time. Dad was in the doorway of the bedroom and saw James overbalance on the window ledge and fall out. He raced down two flights of stairs, lifted James into his arms, gave him the kiss of life and cleared his airways, all before the ambulance arrived.

James was taken to hospital for a check-up, but he had just a couple of cuts and bruises – no broken bones and no lasting effects, though he did demand large amounts of ice cream to aid his recovery. However, in the annals of family history the story became embellished somewhat – probably by dad – and we chose to believe that dad caught James before he hit the ground, like Superman.

When not abroad or in school, I spent much of my early childhood years with my gran and granddad. They lived in a picturesque Scottish village, in a terrace of stone-built cottages rented by mineworkers from the National Coal Board. Communal gardens ran along the then active steam railway line.

Granddad McGhee kept chickens; the story goes that one day (I was about three years old) I asked him: 'Do you want your chickens let out?' He didn't, but by then it was too late as they were already running all over the village. He also cultivated a small vegetable plot; to this day I have never tasted tomatoes as sweet and firm as his, straight from the vine. We ate them by the pound like fruit.

My granddad worked down the mine at a small colliery outside Dollar, generally on the night shift. As they had no showers at the mines in those days – the early 1950s – he would come home covered in coal dust and strip to the waist as he washed himself in the kitchen sink. 'We might be poor but we're clean,' was a mantra of my gran. 'Anyone can afford a bar of soap.'

Every Monday, gran and a couple of friends – wives of other miners – would tackle a huge communal wash in the outhouse. They first boiled large quantities of water in kettles on the hob and transferred it to a big, brass cauldron. It was back-breaking work and children were definitely not to be heard or seen on Monday wash day. The women worked together to boil up the white clothing, poking and prodding with big wooden sticks to get every last trace of coal dust out of the white linen. Then they would manhandle the heavy sheets, which would be put through an old hand-turned mangle and hung on the washing line before being laboriously folded and ironed with an iron they heated on the hob.

They did not have the luxury of electricity in the outhouse, although there was a supply in the cottage itself. The friends worked from first thing in the morning to late in the evening. My gran would be dropping with exhaustion by the time she was finished. She was a tiny woman – just over 5 feet tall with size 2 feet – but she was always a leader and never flinched from the hard work that, over her lifetime, had made her as strong as an ox.

To her, the wash house in her own garden was a step up: when she lived in Glasgow, she would carry all her clothes to the local wash house and spend the day working hard while gossiping and laughing with the other women.

Once, as a toddler, I got so fed up waiting for her to finish her wash and take me home that I wandered off on my own towards the docks on the Clyde. A kindly stranger took me back but the women at the 'steamie' hardly seemed to notice I'd been gone. In those days, most people in and around those working class streets and tenement buildings were compassionate and neighbourly.

The women helped each other; if one had already completed her own wash and loaded it into a pram ready to be pushed home; she would always stay and help the others. For a gregarious child like me, it was mostly a happy, warm place to be; safe with the women and entertaining with their chatter and singing. What I remember most about those days, and about later times living in a female community, was good-natured banter and laughter. The source of the amusement would usually escape me but the women laughed until the tears ran down their faces.

When my dad went into the RAF, mum moved to join the family in Dollar. My granddad had transferred to the local coal mine, and gran and her friends managed to recreate their laughter-filled days at the steamie. It is clear to me now that gran felt isolated from her Glasgow roots, and so, along with her two daughters still at home, Ella and Mattie, and my visiting mum, I was a welcome companion – even though I was a chatterbox who followed her like a shadow, asking a hundred questions.

My gran had been a carer all her life, having been the last child left at home to take care of her blind mother. She never had a bad word to say about anybody and she never complained about her life. She had worked hard – in the mills as a weaver as well as at home – and protected her family like a tigress.

Gran's greatest sadness was that she had buried her first two children, who both died just months old. A Sihk Indian door-to-door salesman had told her after the death of the first one,

'Bury one baby, bury two.' Gran was deeply superstitious – throwing salt over her left shoulder, covering mirrors in thunderstorms, not walking under ladders, not cutting nails or hair on a Sunday – and she lived with the dread of the turbaned Indian's warning for years, until it came true.

My mum – the third child – was always treated as someone special. Her parents were just so happy to have a healthy child, and they then went on to have another two daughters.

Gran and granddad had a strangely polite and rather distant relationship. Perhaps not so unusual in those days when the working man was very much the breadwinner and the wife stayed at home.

Granddad liked his whisky on a Friday and Saturday night – often too much of it – but gran never complained when he came home after the pubs shut. His Friday night ritual was always the same: he would come home from work, wash and change, have his tea, give gran her housekeeping money for the week and disappear to one of the half-dozen village pubs. It would be unthinkable for her to accompany him; women just did not go into pubs in those days, and certainly not in Scotland.

When he rolled home drunk, often singing at the top of his voice (especially if any of his drinking cronies were with him), gran would patiently humour him, help him into bed and leave him to sleep it off.

In the morning when he had a raging hangover and was drinking milk with a raw egg whipped into it, gran would get her revenge. While he sat in the armchair pretending to read his newspaper, she would give him a tongue-lashing about 'showing her up' in front of the neighbours and wasting all his money over the counter of the pub.

She would draw herself up to her full 5 feet 2 and wag her

finger in his face. He was a foot taller but he was as meek as a lamb. After the telling-off, and as granddad's hangover receded, they would again resume a companionable and largely silent relationship with her putting three meals on the table every day and him reading his paper and going for a daily walk. The walks would be on his own or with his namesake, my brother William; the two walked together for hours exploring the local countryside – and as I understand, enjoying each other's company but not saying much. William, now usually known as Billy, is still a man of few words.

As a child, I was fascinated by my gran's large collection of boxes of Black Magic chocolates. Every week he would buy her a box the day after his night out. She rarely ate them and laughed as she explained, 'He only asked me the once what were my favourite chocolates. I told him Black Magic but I didn't bother to tell him I don't really like chocolate.' Luckily, I did!

Only on her birthday – she had been born as the century began on New Year's Eve 1900 – would we ever see my gran drunk. The rituals of New Year's Eve were strictly enforced. The house had to be cleaned from top to bottom, including washing windows, changing curtains and bedding and finishing any outstanding tasks. Even knitting was not allowed to be left unfinished or a book unread when the bells struck at midnight.

A meal of steak pie with puff pastry, gravy and vegetables followed by platefuls of shortbread, Dundee cake and black currant bun would be laid out, but not a mouthful would be eaten before 'the bells'. Nor would drink be taken.

Gran would put on a new apron a few minutes before midnight and stand ready to turn over the new calendar after despatching the tallest dark-haired person outside to 'first foot'. No self-respecting Scot would ever venture out of the door in the New Year until a 'first foot' guest had been welcomed into the house, and they had to come bearing food, generally black bun, a dram of whisky and some coal for the fire. All these rituals ensured that the family would have food, warmth and companionship for the coming year.

Fortunately as granddad – we called him Grample – worked for the coal board there was always plenty of fuel for the fire, and as gran was an accomplished if plain baker, we would have plenty of pies, scones, shortbread and huge slabs of suet pudding which had been cooked for hours in a pillowcase in a huge saucepan and filled with sixpences.

As midnight struck, there would be toasts, gaiety and hugging and kissing accompanied by shouts of 'Happy New Year'. In our Sunday best – tartan kilts or white dresses with sashes – we joined hands and sang 'Auld Lang Syne' and then danced jigs as we enjoyed our rich heritage of Scottish songs, usually accompanied by Andy Stewart's *White Heather Club* Hogmanay party on TV. Once a year, on this auspicious occasion, gran would be persuaded to have her annual glass of port and sing her party piece, 'Barefoot Days'.

New Year's Eve was one of the happiest nights in the calendar and for many years after – living abroad or in England – our family upheld all the Hogmanay traditions. It was a joyous, emotional night full of hope and anticipation for a prosperous and happy New Year.

Gran made just one trip abroad in her life. She came to see us in Germany. Marking the historic visit, mum had a request played for her on the British Forces' Radio Service the day she arrived from the UK. Granddad didn't come. As a boy soldier in the First World War, he had been a prisoner of war in Germany where he had worked down the mines.

He always assured us, his grandchildren, when we pressed him to tell us war stories, that he had been treated well. 'No miner would ever be bad to another miner,' he insisted. 'The Germans shared their food with us and we worked alongside them as fellow miners.' I wasn't so sure; I always wanted to know how he had got his little finger bent back, never to return to its former position. He wasn't telling.

Gran had never been in hospital in her life; she was suspicious of modern medicine and always said, 'If they take me out of the home on a stretcher, they'll bring me back in a box.' She was right. At only 63, during her first hospital stay, she developed pneumonia and was brought home from Stirling hospital to be laid in an open coffin for three days awaiting the funeral.

Only men went to the funeral; women and children stayed home and prepared the funeral tea. Ham salad, hot steak pie, mashed potatoes and turnip followed by black bun and endless cups of tea. And for the men whisky and the women a 'wee' sherry.

Until gran died, when I was 15, all holidays were spent in Dollar, wherever we happened to be living in the world. My three brothers would take it in turns to visit, but as the only girl and the eldest, I would be there for the duration. After gran died and Grample had been presented with a gold watch 'in recognition of 50 years' loyal and faithful service to the National Coal Board', Dollar continued to be a place of pilgrimage for myself and my brothers. Our happy childhood memories of a carefree life in the village and day-long unsupervised walks in the Ochil Hills, climbing up to the small cairn of stones at the top beyond Castle Campbell, meant that it held an enduring place in our hearts.

Long after Granddad McGhee had been persuaded to move to a house in Kirkham, Lancashire, a few streets away from his daughters Ella and Mattie, we still visited the graveyards in Dollar, where now the family of gran, granddad, the three sisters and our brothers Gerald and James are buried. My dad's ashes are scattered in the glen, and I plan for mine to be scattered there too one day.

Please don't laugh, God.

Although I have always claimed not to feel Scottish – I left Scotland as a toddler and have lived all over the world – Dollar and my proud Scottish family gave me golden roots in that unspoilt, rugged countryside. On the day of my wedding in Arundel cathedral, as well as throwing a bouquet from the back of an open-top Rolls-Royce into the crowd of 3,000 well-wishers, a Scottish cousin took a second bouquet to place on my mum's grave in Dollar churchyard.

My mum left Dollar to move to England following my dad's RAF postings, and both of her sisters married men they met when visiting our family on RAF stations. Mum's youngest sister, Auntie Ella, married a Dundonion who was stationed in Germany when she lived there with us for a year. She moved to Dundee, and I lived with her and her husband Frank for a time while a pupil at the local academy – one of 22 different schools I attended during my primary and senior school education. They then moved to the small town of Kirkham outside Preston. Her other sister, Mattie, had married a Lancastrian she too met while visiting my mum during an RAF posting.

It was at the local school there that I had my best-ever teacher, Mr Singleton, and had the distinction in my last year of primary school of being head girl. Mr Singleton encouraged me through the 11-plus and I became a grammar school girl. It changed my life forever.

Granddad died in his terraced house in Kirkham in 1976 at the age of 76. But I didn't attend his funeral – I was too busy in London enjoying my new love affair with the managing editor of the *Daily Mirror*, Derek Jameson.

CHAPTER 2

THE PARTY'S OVER

Singapore was to be our most exotic and life-changing overseas posting – a tropical island paradise where we arrived full of eager anticipation but left full of despair when our lives disintegrated.

Many years of studying and career training within the RAF had taken dad to a position of trust and responsibility which he relished; in his capacity as a pharmacist, he was in charge of medical supplies for the forces in the whole of the Far East. We were all proud of him because we knew how hard he had worked.

We first lived in the east of the 12-mile-long island, close to the infamous Changi jail where the Japanese held European prisoners in brutal conditions during the Second World War, but one year after our arrival we moved to an area called Seletar, in the north-east.

Our white bungalow was comfortable and modern, shaded with large banana palms and with a fair-sized garden in a quiet suburb. Again, the RAF kindly provided maids for the British servicemen as well as a visiting gardener and daily laundry and grocery delivery services.

It was a pampered and exclusive lifestyle. My brothers and I travelled to school in taxis, as did dad on his way to and from the RAF camp where he was stationed. As the school day finished at lunchtime, we spent almost every afternoon at the beach or in the swimming pool. All my clothes, including school clothes, were made by the local dressmaker. A real colonial lifestyle.

On Sundays our longest-serving maid, Gussie, a spirited Malayan in her mid-twenties, had a day off from cooking, cleaning, washing and ironing for our family of six. She would get up early, dress in her Sunday best and set off to visit her own family. The journey took several hours by local bus, but, if she was very lucky, a taxi driver friend would drive her the last couple of miles to her village. She was always conscious of her limited time: she had the long return journey to her employer's home, where she would be expected back by 6.30pm or 7pm at the latest.

Gussie would try to persuade my father to let her stay out later. He was worried about her safety and mindful that, while she was in his service, the RAF expected him to exercise a duty of care towards her but I am not sure she fully appreciated that. Gussie complained to me and asked me to intervene on her behalf with 'The Master', and she did have my sympathy as sometimes she spent less than an hour with her family before she had to start back.

A solution was for her to take me along. I made many visits with Gussie to her village before realising that she had a child and it was mainly with her that she wanted to spend more time. She also had a boyfriend, who may or may not have been the father of the child. Her dream was to be able to spend the night with her child and boyfriend much more regularly than the agreed once a month when she was allowed an overnight stay but this seemed a forlorn hope.

Gussie was always willing to have me accompany her on her day visits, which may have been because she was less likely to get into trouble if she was late home, which she invariably was. At least I was able to confirm how long the bus had taken.

At first mum and dad were reluctant for me to go with her – locals (especially the hired help) and service personnel did not mix socially – but eventually they relented, under pressure from me and assurances from Gussie that she would see that I came to no harm.

I loved visiting the traditional Malay village where her large, extended family lived. There were no streets, just mud- and water-filled alleys between the houses, with dogs and children running about. Washing arrangements were primitive and showers were often just a large can with holes punched in it suspended over a canopy and operated with a rope pulley contraption. The toilet was literally a hole in the ground covered with a piece of wood.

The atmosphere was friendly and, although there was obviously not a lot of money around, it was a colourful and lively place to visit thanks to the cheerfulness of the villagers and their constant hard work to keep themselves, their clothes and their homes clean; Gussie would spend hours squatting on her haunches, washing, sweeping and mending.

Gussie was treated as something of a celebrity because she worked for the armed forces – a good, relatively high-paying job – and she told me that her welcome from the villagers was never warmer than when she was accompanied by me, an honoured guest.

The simple house she shared with her extended family was built of wood with a roof of huge banana fronds. Inside, the well-swept dirt floor was covered with rush matting and the walls were hung with swathes of material and shelves full of religious statues, candles and flower offerings. For afternoon tea we had sweet sticky puddings and tea made with condensed milk, or we drank coconut milk through a straw from the green shell. After we had been called upon by a whole succession of smiling visitors, all too soon – for Gussie certainly – we would make our way back through the village to the rural bus stop.

The Malay ladies stepped daintily, holding up the hems of their brightly patterned skirts, which they wore with a smart starched white or coloured short-sleeved blouse. They almost always carried an umbrella made from banana leaves to shade their faces from the sun. The white skin of Europeans was highly prized, and Gussie would insist that I too shelter under her umbrella as we walked along. She could not understand why any pale-skinned person would want a tan.

Gussie liked to spoil me, always insisting that I was much too ladylike for the household tasks my dad delegated to me. On one memorable occasion, we got into serious trouble when dad came to see why the electric floor polisher was noisily whirring away for such a long time in my bedroom. He found Gussie stretched out on the double bed, guiding the polisher with just two fingers, and me fast asleep beside her. 'Missy Ellen tired,' she told him. Dad saw to it that she and I had little opportunity to spend time together after that incident. When she left our employ, I was sad to see her go as she had become a good friend to me.

Another of our staff who made a lasting impression was Chow, a middle-aged Chinese maid. She could hardly speak a word of English but she was always smiling, sweet natured and hard-working.

However, she felt the wrath of dad's temper when she chopped down a huge bunch of bananas in our back garden and put them in a dark cupboard to stop them ripening too much. Dad had been planning to take a photo and send it to our family in England and was not impressed when Chow suggested tying the bananas back on with a piece of string. Eventually seeing the funny side, dad tried to explain to her in his best mime language: 'I could buy a bunch of bananas and tie them to a tree in my garden in England.'

Chow realised that dad had gone past being angry and now regarded what she had done as a good story to retell to his friends. She giggled for days about the idea of tying a bunch of bananas to a tree in England.

For some time after she left our service, Chow returned to visit the family. She would bring us large quantities of oranges and we would all sit in a circle in the living room, nodding politely to each other and smiling. It came as something of a relief when she had to leave to get her bus home. There are only so many times you can say 'Nice to see you. Work good? Family well?'

My other main cultural interaction was with Cynthia, a schoolgirl whose family came from Ceylon; she was a couple of years older than me and lived on our street with her parents and an older sister.

She adored Elvis Presley and had seen all of his films many times over. She also loved Indian movies. In her company, I was allowed to go to the local cinema. She would also show me how to wear her jewel-coloured saris and adorn me with flamboyant gold jewellery.

Cynthia valiantly tried to teach me to dance Bollywood-style but I was used to dancing the Twist and couldn't manage the subtle hand movements and exaggerated neck and head movements, each of which has a distinct meaning. However, she and I were on common ground when it came to jiving to Elvis records.

My parents' party lifestyle continued and increased thanks to the cheap booze and cigarettes available from the NAAFI at the RAF camp. My job was to help plan the more formal events. I was particularly proud of my efforts for their fourteenth wedding anniversary.

I had gone to not inconsiderable trouble and some expense to have an aunt ship 'The Party's Over' from England. Mum loved Shirley Bassey and this was her latest single. The small Chinese record shop in the market, which specialised in the Mandarin hit parade, carried a small stock of popular British hits, but not this one. So in great secrecy I'd arranged for a special delivery.

Mum was thrilled and dad was always pleased when anyone went out of their way to make mum happy. There was never any denying that he loved her very much, even though he had a funny way of showing it, and now they were celebrating their fourteenth wedding anniversary by throwing a party. Far from being over, the party had just started.

Having assumed responsibility for the choice of music, I commandeered a seat beside the Dansette and filled the automatic stacker. A new favourite of mine, the aquamarine twin-speaker record player had been a present for my birthday earlier that month, October 1963. The blue or baby pink Dansettes were a real status symbol among us teenage girls.

We were extremely isolated and got most of our pop music news from newly arrived Brits. News of home was always many months behind, and the only radio programmes we heard were on the BBC World Service. Singapore television was still in its infancy and mainly showed home-grown Chinese serials and Malaysian music programmes – we were lucky to get one hour of TV a week in English. My Auntie Ellen sent regular updates about the goings-on in our favourite soap opera back home, Granada's *Coronation Street* (then a new series).

There was something about the new group The Beatles that caught our imagination, though none of us knew of the huge impact they were having in Britain. Even the grown-ups seemed to be singing along to 'Please Please Me' or 'Love Me Do'.

My personal 'top of the pops' with which I helped keep the party going that night also included Skeeter Davis with 'The End of the World', Lesley Gore singing 'It's My Party', Sarah Maughan with 'Bobby's Girl', and Chubby Checker's 'Let's Twist Again' – a guaranteed dance hit.

But perhaps I sensed that a darker side had crept into mum and dad's socialising since the early days in Germany. Mum had developed serious medical and mental problems since our arrival in the Far East, including a phobia about 'chit-chats', the little lizard-like creatures that inhabited our equatorial houses and were useful in controlling the flying insect population. They walk across the walls and roof, and mum would become hysterical, thinking that one would drop on her head.

Within a few months of joining the colony of ex-pats in Singapore, she had started to have epileptic fits. The first one had occurred while we – mum and the children – were playing a game of Monopoly early on a Thursday evening. Dad was in the bathroom getting ready for his boys' night out. This had been a ritual for years, as Thursday was a lodge night for the Royal Antediluvian Order of Buffaloes, the Catholic version of the Freemasons.

As the fits increased in frequency (sometimes several times a day, in quieter periods several times a week), mum spent a great deal of time as both an inpatient and an outpatient undergoing tests and treatment at the new forces hospital in Changi. Her condition was frightening; without warning, she would go into convulsions, foaming at the mouth and rolling around the floor. Afterwards she would be exhausted, bewildered and frightened, and would tell us that while having the fit she saw bright flashing lights.

The doctor showed me how to put the handle of a teaspoon in her mouth to prevent her biting off her tongue. She wasn't to be left alone and, apart from dad, I was the one who assumed responsibility for her. While dad was at work and I was at school, friends and neighbours would reluctantly take it in turns to sit with her.

As if the fits weren't scary enough for us all, the medication produced even worse symptoms. Mum was a different person from her usual laughing, easy-going self. Regulating the dosage was bad enough, but her abuse of the drug was worse. She developed an obsession that I now identify as addiction. At the time, we had no idea why she behaved the way she did or why the effects of the drug were so devastating. Nor did her taking the phenobarbitones guarantee that she would not have an epileptic fit.

She would hide bottles of tablets and then take the lot. No doctors ever seemed to check the dosage or question how she got through so many. Often, after she had taken a whole bottle in a couple of days, they would prescribe more and she would have the prescriptions filled without us knowing how or where. Perhaps the doctors believed her increasingly elaborate stories about losing them or dropping them down the toilet.

My lovely mum was losing her mind. I never knew when I came home whether she would be on a manic high, talking non-stop and unable to stay still, or like a zombie. It was not unusual to find her passed out for hours on the bed, fully clothed and white-faced, or incoherent for days at a time. When she mixed the barbiturates with alcohol, the fireworks really started.

For the anniversary party, I helped her dress and do her makeup. She looked beautiful in a midnight blue satin dress with a low-cut V at the back and a straight, tight skirt. The style was one she favoured and a local dressmaker had tailored several for her in different materials. For jewellery, she wore the anniversary present dad had taken her into the heart of Singapore's gemstone quarter to buy: matching earrings, necklace and bracelet in a pale blue moonstone that, when held up to the light, showed an image of a white pagoda.

Mum had bought dad a gold Omega watch and he was wearing it that evening, although he had sworn he never would. Earlier that week mum had ventured out alone to buy dad's gift. It was very rare for her to go out alone, so the assumption was that she must have been emboldened by drink or drugs – or both.

At the end of the school day, I found her in a hysterical state. Her dress was on back to front and she was making no sense. Getting more and more agitated, she tried to tell a garbled story about the Asian shopkeeper where she had bought the watch. In her version, he had become over-familiar with her. Sadly, there was something about her vulnerability that meant certain men would try to take advantage of her.

We never did get the full story. When he came home, dad was all for calling the police, but by then mum was fast asleep. Unconscious. We endeavoured to piece together the story but the next day she could hardly remember going to buy the watch, never mind any details about what might have happened, and mum was too ashamed and embarrassed to let us go back to the shop to find out. Dad had slung the watch in a drawer, determined never to wear it. On the night of the anniversary party he obviously had second thoughts.

Chinese tailoring is of superb quality at a reasonable cost in Singapore, and dad had his uniforms and most of his casual clothes hand-made. For the party he chose an open-necked, short-sleeved shirt in a pale blue that complemented mum's dress and a pair of beige trousers with a knife-sharp crease down the front. As a serviceman, he was always smartly dressed, hair neat, shoes shined.

They were a handsome couple who delighted in looking good, and before the guests arrived I insisted that they pose on the patio for photographs. The camera captured them beautifully. Dad was still three years off 40; mum was just 34. A young, happily married couple, successful parents to four children ranging in age from seven to 14. In the early hours of the next morning they would both take near-fatal drug overdoses.

In Singapore, because of the intense afternoon heat, most people start work early, at around 7 to 7.30am, and finish by 2pm. So, being a mid-week party, most of the guests had an early start the following morning and went home long before midnight.

Instead of retiring to bed quietly, mum and dad started rowing. I could hear them shouting from my bedroom, where I'd been asleep. I tried to ignore them but one or the other would always come and wake me to intervene, take sides or keep the peace. On this occasion it was dad.

Just before he knocked on my bedroom door, I heard him shout something about the 'bloody watch'. Then he came in and sat on my bed, which wasn't unusual. Often, after he and mum had argued, he would come and sit for hours talking about his life, his problems, and mum's erratic behaviour. If I started yawning or giving any indication that I would rather be asleep, he would get angry and hurt, complaining that no one cared about him.

Mum would often come storming into the room too, demanding that they continue the row. Whereas she was a noisy drunk, he was a maudlin type. Between the two of them, I didn't get much sleep.

The younger boys slept together in one room at the other end of the house, and although they were sometimes dragged into the rows, as the three responsible adults (me included) we would try not to wake them.

So, dad plonked himself on my bed, glass in hand, and started to ramble. Mum was strangely quiet. Presuming, or perhaps hoping, that she had gone to bed, neither of us made any attempt to check up on her. That was a mistake.

Dad staggered off into the living room to play some music. He was a night owl and often stayed up all night listening to the BBC World Service, a glass of alcohol always within arm's reach.

When I got up to go to the bathroom in the early hours of the morning, the door was jammed. Mum was lying behind it. On the still made bed, empty pill bottles told the story: she had taken an overdose.

'Mum, open the door,' I shouted as quietly as I could. I put my shoulder to it and tried to push. It was impossible to budge her. After several unsuccessful attempts to rouse her, I had to go to dad for help.

'Dad, mum's sick,' I told him. 'I can't wake her. She's behind the bathroom door.'

By now my brothers had appeared, asking 'What's happening? Why can't we get into the bathroom?'

Dad started raging. He ran into the bedroom and began kicking the door. I was crying and screaming and trying to calm him down. The commotion must have woken mum or brought her to her senses because all of a sudden she got herself up and opened the door. She was so unsteady on her feet that as she did so she dropped to her knees and hit her head on the side of the bath. Instead of being sympathetic, dad, drunk and angry, started pulling at her and shouting.

'Leave her alone,' I screamed. 'I'll look after her.'

'This is the end,' he shouted at me. 'I've had enough. I can't take it anymore. I'm finished. It's over. I won't live like this anymore.'

I was trapped between the two of them while mum, slurring and incoherent, taunted him. In her drunken state she had no fear, no sense of how angry she was making him.

Finally, I persuaded dad to go back to his drink in the living room and I half pulled, half carried mum into the bedroom. Fortunately the bathroom was en suite and the bed was only a few yards away. Without any cooperation from her, I half undressed her and tried to put her to bed. I sat with her for a while and she gradually dropped off into a drunken stupor, rendered all the more potent by the sleeping pills.

Hiding sleeping pills was a national sport in our house and dad always knew the many ingenious places mum had found to secrete her supplies. He wasn't averse to self-medication himself, either.

I settled mum and made myself a cup of tea; I didn't realise that the drama was far from over. When I went into the living room to bring dad up to date with events, he was slumped in the chair, a bottle of pills by his side and 'The End of the World' playing over and over again on the record player.

My first instinct was to get the hell out of there. Pretend I didn't know what had happened. Go to bed, pull the covers over my head and leave someone else to sort out the mess. But I knew there was no one else. Besides, what if it were a sick joke? What if he were pretending to have taken an overdose? What if

I walked away and then he went mad because I hadn't even tried to save him?

'Dad, dad, wake up,' I whispered urgently. 'Go to bed. You'll be more comfortable. Mum's asleep.'

No response. I shook him. No response. I prised open his eyelids – I'd done it often enough to mum. Not a flicker.

'My God. He's dead. Really dead,' I thought.

In a panic I started pushing and pulling him, willing him to wake up. Still no response, not the usual 'What is it? What d'ya want? I'm alright where I am.' This time he really did seem to be beyond rousing.

Frantic, I went to wake up mum. She seemed to take in what I was saying but instead of helping me she gave her considered opinion – 'Let the bastard die' – and then promptly fell asleep again.

Back to dad. No response. Back to mum. No sense.

I was only 14, yet already I had been taught various techniques for reviving people from drink- and drug-induced comas. I poured salt water down dad's throat, trying to make him be sick, then I pulled him out of the chair and tried to drag him to the bathroom. Sometimes with mum we would be able to make her sick and then walk her up and down the room, up and down for hour after hour, refusing to let her lapse into a coma in case she didn't come out again. But there was no way I could get dad to his feet, no way could I get him to drink the salt water, no way I could bring him back to consciousness.

The sun rose on another day and I made a decision. Putting on a coat over my nightdress, I ran across the garden to our next-door neighbour. We were not on the phone. She was.

It took the ambulance about half an hour to respond to our emergency call. Dad was lying in the middle of the living room floor where I'd left him and this time I was able to impress upon mum the seriousness of the situation.

'The ambulance is coming,' I told her.

'I don't need an ambulance,' she said. 'I'm alright.'

'It's not for you, it's for dad,' I explained.

The neighbour, a good friend of ours, said she would take care of the boys. Amazingly, they were still asleep.

Mum and I went in the ambulance with dad. Blue lights flashing, siren wailing, we drove past my grammar school on the coast road from Seletar to Changi hospital.

'If my friends could see me now,' I thought. 'Wonder if I'll have to go to school today.'

At the hospital, they pumped dad's stomach while mum and I waited anxiously for news. By the afternoon he was sitting up in bed, glaring at me.

'Why didn't you let me die?' he scowled. 'It wasn't a cry for help. I wanted to die. It's your fault I'm alive.'

It was also my fault that he was in serious trouble. In those days attempted suicide was a crime. Inevitably, his position within the hospital, and particularly as a pharmacist, made it a disciplinary offence and a breach of trust that he should have misused or even misappropriated prescription drugs.

Within three weeks the whole family had been shipped back to the UK. Dad's career in the RAF was in the balance. They flew us from Singapore to RAF Lyneham in Wiltshire, a reality shock after the tropics as we arrived back home during the Big Freeze of 1963.

Dad was put under medical escort and taken straight to the local psychiatric unit, while the other five of us – mum, me and my brothers, Gerard, 12, William, 11 and James, 9 – were put into a reception centre.

After dinner in the canteen they allocated us two bedrooms. Mum and I shared a bedroom with my little brother James and the other two boys were next door. None of us knew what would happen next or when we would see dad again. Mum and I cried ourselves to sleep that might after reassuring the boys that everything was going to be fine. Poor kids, they often seemed to be left to figure things out for themselves – it was a form of emotional neglect and a denial of their need for stability and security.

Dad was kept under observation for some weeks. We weren't allowed to visit him, or rather he had requested that we didn't see him in the mental hospital, so mum gathered us all up after a few days and took us by train to stay with her mum and dad in Scotland.

Dad joined us there when he came out of hospital. It was 22 November 1963: the iconic day when everyone remembers where they were. I heard the news listening to Radio Luxembourg in the small front bedroom of my grandparents' house overlooking the Ochil Hills in Dollar, Clackmannanshire.

I went downstairs and told the family: 'President Kennedy has been shot.'

'Of course he hasn't,' said dad. 'It would have been on the TV news. Is this your idea of a joke?'

At that moment, a sombre voice interrupted the television programme they had been watching to say: 'We interrupt this programme to bring you a news flash. President John F Kennedy has been shot in Dallas, Texas.' American newsman Walter Kronkite had made the legendary announcement to the American public.

No one's life would ever be the same again.

The day the music died.

My only thought was, 'Please God, don't let anyone from my new school see us', as I tried to look as if I wasn't with the rest of my family and their motley collection of bags as we waited at the local bus stop outside the railway station.

In fact, I had no idea whether my new school was even in the vicinity, but that didn't matter. I didn't want anyone from any school to see me. There were five of us – the three brothers, mum and me – plus an assortment of suitcases, holdalls and carrier bags.

Dad had formed an advance party and was to meet us at our new home in the stockbroker belt between Leatherhead and Dorking in Surrey. The exact location was the picturesque village of Box Hill, a local nature and beauty spot perched high on the North Downs overlooking the A24 and surrounding countryside.

We had travelled down by overnight train from our grandparents' home in Scotland where we had been living since our return from the Far East a few months before. On a freezing March day, dad met us at the end of our long journey and proudly escorted us to our new home.

'Fall in. No talking in the ranks,' he called out jovially as he began to march us up a narrow pathway beside a hedge just off the main thoroughfare. Our new home was to be a surprise – and it was. Out of season, he had managed to rent at reasonable rates a six-berth holiday caravan.

Full of enthusiasm, he showed us around. There were two small bedrooms as you entered the caravan from the rear, then a tiny WC and well-equipped kitchen that opened out into a large living area. The furniture was ingenious, slotting together and coming apart to form two double beds and a dining table. Every available inch of space had been maximised.

Bedroom one had three bunk beds where the boys would sleep and tiny bedroom two had just one single bed and a small mirrored wardrobe. This was to be my personal space for the foreseeable future.

Dad didn't see the funny side when I asked where the maid

was going to sleep. The family had effectively, and (to my knowledge) without any consultation, been downsized. To give him his due, dad's task of finding somewhere for us all to be together had not been easy.

After his initial hospitalisation on our return to the UK, medical reports and observations had shown that he wasn't mentally impaired. They should probably have stated: 'Temporarily rendered insane by reason of over-consumption of alcohol and sleeping pills.'

The RAF had allowed him to continue working, under supervision, in a medical capacity in a pharmaceutical clinic. Dad had been seconded to the Officers' Rehabilitation Centre at Headley Court in Surrey; he loved it there and the amazing work they did aiding the recovery of injured servicemen.

There were no married quarters on camp, nor any available in the immediate area. He had been left to accommodate us as best he could. For lack of any other transport options, dad would ride his trusty old bike, which he called the Winged Arrow, the five miles to and from the rehab centre every day, except for those occasions when the chain broke and he would be forced to push the bike all the way home, up the hill and along winding country lanes. It was unwise to be around when he arrived home after that ordeal.

Schools in the area were said to be of a high academic standard, and after various discussions it was agreed that I would accompany my brother William, who had recently passed the 11-plus, to the local grammar school. I couldn't help feeling that I was being punished for my decision to save dad's life back in Singapore. Although the social implications may not have been immediately obvious, I had been awarded a scholarship at three different private schools, so settling for a state grammar was a definite change in my social circumstances.

However, like Dickens' Mr Micawber, dad was confident that 'something would turn up'. At his insistence, and with much laughter and forced jollity, we all agreed to make the best of our new home – henceforth to be referred to as a 'mobile home', not a caravan – and try to pretend that we were on an extended holiday. Dad had a tremendous sense of fun and was the eternal optimist, except when he was drunk, depressed and maudlin. Welcome to the world of the active alcoholic.

As the showering facilities were in a communal block halfway down a muddy field, the joke wore a bit thin on cold, dark winter mornings as we queued up for our ablutions before setting off to catch the school bus.

Our neighbours were a mixed bunch of leftover holiday makers, rugged outdoor types and friendly OAPs. They made us welcome, and although there was no communal singing around the campfire, we did socialise and come to feel like part of the rural community.

Life took a temporarily exciting turn when we learned via the national news that proceeds from the Great Train Robbery of 1964 had been found in a caravan at Box Hill. Perhaps there was a pot of gold to be found at the end of our rainbow.

The wider world of Box Hill held unexpected delights for an adventurous teenage girl. On Tuesday evenings there was the local youth club, held in a wooden hut that on Mondays belonged to the scouts, where we danced to 1960s chart records. On Sundays, the folks who lived on Box Hill were galvanised into action by the arrival of hundreds of backpackers, ramblers and motorbike riders – popularly known as Hell's Angels. Their meeting places were the café at the bottom of the hill and the Wimpy Bar at the top, which had been where these mavericks gathered for as long as the locals could remember. There was never any trouble to speak of, unless you count noisy arguments over the long pool games that sprung up as the leather-clad lads and lasses descended to eat burger and chips, drink Coca-Cola and play Elvis on the juke box.

There were two distinct young tribes in those days: the mods and the rockers. The motorcycle riders were rockers and their allegiance was to black leather clothing, rock 'n' roll, American 1950s music and greased-back hairstyles. Mods rode Vespas, wore parkas (a forerunner to anoraks) and had short, modern hairstyles. Mods favoured British music and a clean-cut style. The rockers were rebels, like The Rolling Stones; mods, obviously, were modern, like The Beatles, The Who, Small Faces and Rod the Mod himself, Mr Rod Stewart.

Seaside battles between the two opposing cultures were a regular Bank Holiday occurrence in towns such as Brighton. As Box Hill was between London and Brighton, every Sunday we local kids were in a state of high excitement fuelled by whispered rumours that there would be a showdown between the mods and rockers at the top of the zigzag – the mile-long narrow road that ran between the top of the hill and the bottom.

The showdown never materialised. There were plenty of rockers, but I don't recall the mods ever showing. I sometimes pass that way now on Sunday afternoon drives, and the ritual gathering of motorcyclists still takes place. I guess they just like a ride out into the countryside, and the high noon confrontation was all a figment of our adolescent imaginations – wishful thinking to liven up a sleepy Surrey village.

However, there had been some action on the home front. We had moved into The Lighthouse – not a real lighthouse, though we kids all hoped it would be – but a bungalow of that name on the main road of the village.

We were going up in the world. Our home was a local landmark – unsurprisingly, as it was painted bright yellow and had a 3-foot model lighthouse on the front lawn.

Summer 1964. Beatlemania swept Britain and America and 'I Want to Hold Your Hand' was at the top of the charts. I wasn't just a Beatles fan – I was an obsessed disciple. John, Paul, George and Ringo: every waking minute was devoted to finding out as much as possible about them. I devoured fan magazines, TV shows and radio programmes. I ate, slept and breathed The Beatles.

A diary entry from that time reads: 'I shall be a virgin when I marry, unless a Beatle wants me.' Paul McCartney had said he always fell in love with the blonde in the third row of their concerts. Their Christmas concert was coming up at the Hammersmith Odeon and my most prized possession was a pair of tickets – for row nine. How was I going to make him fall in love with the brunette in row nine?

Mum, dad and the rest of the family humoured me in my obsession with The Beatles. They were all delighted for me when dad managed to secure the tickets through someone at the Officer's Rehab Centre. He arranged for me – along with my friend Sarah – to be taken from Box Hill to London for the day and escorted home.

Mum bought me a new outfit – a royal blue suit with alligator skin shoes and handbag – and treated me to a visit to the local hairdresser.

I counted the days.

The trip to London was exciting enough but the concert itself was one of the best nights of my life. Competing with thousands of teenage girls in the audience, I screamed from the moment the Fab Four appeared on stage until the end when they rocked their way through yet another encore of 'Long Tall Sally'.

At one point a few of us rushed the stage; after being held back by security and caught up in the crush, I fainted. Smelling salts were held under my nose by one of the St John's Ambulance team. Realising that I was missing the concert, I pleaded until they agreed to let me go back into the theatre, but the best moment of the concert had already happened for me: George Harrison had looked down into my eyes and called to the security team, 'Leave the kid alone!'

After the show, I was physically and emotionally drained. All the way home in the car I sat in total silence, staring out into the blackness. If I uttered a word it might break the spell, so I stayed locked in my world of exhilaration and excitement.

It was almost midnight when I arrived home. Mum and dad were waiting up, eager to hear all about my first Beatles concert. 'So how was it?' they asked expectantly.

'Fab,' I said in a dream and promptly fell asleep on the settee.

The Beatles were more real to me than any boyfriends. At school we endlessly discussed the merits of which one we loved the most. Paul was sweet. George looked cheeky. John was very grown up (we didn't know at the time that he was married with a son). Ringo was the clown.

The Beatles' first feature film, *A Hard Day's Night*, was released on 6 July 1964. It opened in Leatherhead the same week and, before it closed some six weeks later, I would see the film a record-breaking 32 times. I could play every part and remember every word of every song. I still can. I loved it.

The phenomenon of Beatlemania was a heady mix of adolescent sexuality and hero worship along with a genuine love of their extraordinary talent, and it swept us into a world of passion, emotion and 'All You Need is Love'.

Who could have dreamt that years later I would be in the company of Paul McCartney on numerous occasions at press receptions and music events? Derek and I even sold our beach house in Hove to Paul McCartney and his then wife Heather Mills. I would have thought I had died and gone to heaven.

I got to know Ringo Starr and his wife Barbara Bach on visits to the south of France. As for John Lennon, he and I did bump into each other once in the early 1970s at the Revolution Club in Bruton Street, Mayfair, early in my journalistic career. At the crowded bar the ash fell off the top of his cigarette and he turned and apologised, saying: 'Sorry, love, I didn't see you there.' I stopped in my tracks.

I never did meet George Harrison, though I went to his Surrey home, which was used as a recording studio, on several occasions to interview other bands.

Meanwhile, back in my adolescent days of active Beatlemania, the sixties were beginning to swing and nothing was going to stop me from joining in. Youth was on the march.

Dad was enjoying his new posting, mum seemed to be getting physically stronger now that we were back home, and I was, wherever possible, starting to live an independent life. My younger brothers were mostly a nuisance, but I tended to be wrapped up in my own world of The Beatles, music, clothes and spending endless hours talking to friends of my own age – and generally my own sex.

We developed quite a social life and there was usually a parent around willing to drive us to the cinema or to let us stay over at each other's houses. Through the youth club, we also had coach outings to places such as the stock car races or the Streatham ice-skating rink, as well as travelling to dances in neighbouring villages.

It was at one such dance that I nearly lost my virginity some years before I intended to. And it wasn't to a Beatle. Naively I had gone outside from the dance with a local boy I had just met. A bit of kissing was probably on the agenda but what followed was a warning to be very careful and not trust anyone in trousers.

We were holding hands and walking in the gardens outside the hall; the rest of my friends were still inside, enjoying the live music and dancing. The soft, romantic kissing suddenly turned hard and aggressive and this Jack the Lad started to pull me down into the grass. If he had asked nicely I might have consented; instead, he turned rough, tugging at my clothes and holding me down. I was frightened and struggling and tried explaining that the coach was ready to leave and my friends would be wondering where I was.

Luckily that was true. At that moment one of my friends appeared in the open doorway calling my name.

'Here I am, here I am,' I called back anxiously. 'I'm just coming. Wait for me.'

I broke free and ran to join my friend, who looked at my dishevelled clothes and asked, 'Are you okay? What was going on out there?'

'Let's go. I'm alright,' I assured her. The relief when I got safely on the coach was immense and it was only then that I realised I was shaking. I had had a lucky escape and promised myself that I wouldn't put myself in that kind of danger again.

But I did – and only a few weeks later.

A school friend was having a barbecue at a village some miles away from my home and I was determined to go. I wasn't going to miss what promised to be a good party.

My gran was visiting from Scotland and I enlisted her help to persuade dad to let me go. I agreed to the usual conditions about being home by 10 o'clock, though I knew there was no way I could get back from a party that didn't start till 8. Perhaps if I had been honest from the start, arrangements could have been made for me to be collected or allowed to stay overnight.

The barbecue was held in woods at the bottom of my friend's garden. We were all having great fun and I resented having to leave – the party was just getting into its stride and I had met a very nice boy who was flirting with me. As time wore on I began to get anxious about how I was going to get home in time for my curfew, especially as I was about 20 miles away without any transport.

Without telling anyone I was leaving, and at least giving the grown-ups an opportunity to see me home safely, I set off up the road after saying thanks and goodbyes. By the time I got to the centre of Leatherhead, I had missed the last bus to Box Hill. I started to walk.

A 15-year-old girl walking home alone in her party clothes. Whatever was I thinking of? By the time a car stopped on the lonely, badly lit country road to offer me a lift, I felt only gratitude. I got into the back seat and realised there were four young men in the car.

They were joking with each other the way young men do. All expressed surprise that I was alone and so far from home. I hadn't even been walking in the right direction. Still, they offered to take me to Box Hill and said they planned to go up the zigzag. Although it was shorter than the other road that climbed the hill, it had dangerously sharp bends and very few cars attempted it in the dark. They weren't frightened – and neither was I until the driver stopped the car halfway up, close to a popular lookout point that had great views of the surrounding countryside.

My heart was in my mouth. I had always been warned about

situations like this: never accept lifts from strangers. Not one to do things by halves, I had got into a car with four strange men. Two of them got out and two stayed. After less than five minutes the first two returned to the car and the other two disappeared into the woods. With a huge sigh of relief, I realised they were disappearing into the woods to relieve themselves. We continued the journey to my home at the top of the hill without incident.

Ten o'clock had long since been and gone when I got back. Dad was furious, mum was anxious, and gran felt that I had let her down, but they were all mighty glad to see me home safe and sound.

A couple of days later I was walking through the village when a car pulled up; two of the good Samaritans had come to check that I was alright and that I hadn't got into too much trouble with dad. What gentlemen!

Out of the blue, dad suddenly announced that he was leaving the RAF. It had been agreed that he could take early retirement on medical grounds and his pension was safe. We were on the move again, this time to London. Home of Carnaby Street and Kings Road. I couldn't have asked for anywhere better. Swinging London here I come! By mid-February we had moved from our bungalow in Box Hill to Manor Park in East London and an unprepossessing three-bedroom terraced house on a nondescript street near Stratford. I was pleased with the move, noting in my diary that the house was 'gorgeous', my room was 'fab' and there were some 'really fanciable' boys living in our road.

Having moved school yet again, my education and level of commitment were certainly suffering. Instead of returning to school after the Easter break, I told the headmistress I had decided to leave. She tried to talk me out of my decision and assured me that if I just applied myself I would pass my examinations easily. She told dad that he should be encouraging me to go to university, not to leave school. Unfortunately it suited him to have me at home looking after mum.

Not having formal qualifications or a degree was something I regretted for most of my life until, at an advanced stage in my career, I rectified the situation by taking countless courses, attending summer schools at Oxford University, and completing a media degree in America and a qualification as a professional theatre arts teacher.

The situation at home might have been funny if it weren't so tragic. It was disruptive, not just for me but for my young brothers, although we all learned to live with the constant yo-yoing of dad leaving and then coming back and then mum leaving and coming back. The two rarely stayed at home together. As there were constant rows, the boys and I were glad when they split up, however briefly.

The pop scene was changing and most of the discos and youth clubs had made the switch from live bands to less expensive taped chart music. Stratford Town Hall still put on live music and my friends and I would go there on Saturday nights to dance and meet boys. We were also camp followers, and sometimes girlfriends, of some of the local groups, and we always made sure we looked our best in new outfits with miniskirts and boots. We all channelled Twiggy or the first supermodel, Jean Shrimpton, with our hair newly ironed and pale makeup with dark kohl panda eyes and minimal lipstick.

Although I was popular with the boys, I was always considered a little stand-offish. 'Be proud of being a snob,' mum would tell me. But I still maintained my obsession with The Beatles and I was desperate to make contact.

On Paul McCartney's birthday (18 June), I dressed smartly in a new white woollen suit dad had bought me and had my hair fashioned into a neat topknot with a pale blue ribbon – just like the model Patti Boyd (who went on to marry George Harrison) in a photograph I'd seen. In my handbag I carried a miniature bottle of vodka that I thought Paul and I could share to celebrate his birthday.

I took the Tube 'up West' to what I thought was the headquarters of the Beatles fan club. I was bitterly disappointed – the address I had been given turned out to be a dingy little house in a part of London I can't identify even now, but for some reason I think it was Acton, not exactly a glamorous location. The only thing of note that happened that day was that, as I was striding out happily on my way to my supposed meeting with Paul, a dirty old man approached me, invited me for a drink and offered to pay me £10 to go home with him. I was upset and frightened but by then I was lost so needed him to show me the way to the nearest Tube station.

John Lennon had published a spoof diary with trivial, repetitive entries ('Got up. Went to bed. Got up') but my own diary reveals that everyday life really was repetitive and banal, for me at least: 'Got up. Went to work. Had a row with mum. Went out. Came home late. Had a row with dad.'

My work life was erratic. I rarely kept a job for more than a few weeks – office work bored me and retail was not my thing, although at various times I worked in shoe shops, in a friend's dress shop, and even briefly in a kitchen installer's showroom.

London was swinging; instead of going to work, I would go up to the West End with girlfriends. We would spend hours walking up and down Carnaby Street, drinking minute cups of frothy coffee in Wimpy Bars and meeting pop stars.

The pop world converged on Carnaby Street and the combination of fashion and music and the spirit of 'Cool Britannia' meant we would meet and become friends instantly because of shared interests. In the 1960s, Carnaby Street was a Mecca for us, and even today it teems with young people and foreign tourists dedicated to the spirit of Swinging London.

CHAPTER 3

SCHOOL'S OUT FOREVER

The three-bedroom mid-terrace house in Manor Park, E12, wasn't as close as I'd hoped to the centre of swinging London. In fact, as the crow flies, it is about 15 miles, on London Underground it is a dozen stops, and by taxi the fare was close to £5. As a Saturday girl working on a jewellery stand in the local market I earned £1.

Usually the journey to the West End was undertaken by public transport unless we got a lift from some boy with a car or travelled home in style by cab after a night out with friends. I'd always been a bit of a rebel, and now I had the cause and the kids to hang out with, the ones your parents are sure are having a bad influence on you. They were. There was only one friend from Surrey I kept in close contact with. Sarah came to stay practically every weekend. Sometimes she stayed all week too.

We'd moved to London when dad's service with the RAF came to an end, and he soon found a well-paid managerial position in the medical records department at St Thomas's Hospital. He'd achieved his ambition to be a £1,000-a-year man – plus he had his RAF pension.

A severance payment from the RAF meant that we could go on a spending spree to buy new furniture for our new, unfurnished home. We'd always lived in RAF quarters so had no real furniture of our own, although we had several storage crates shipped back from Singapore containing a new stereo radiogram – which would take pride of place in the front room – and all our household possessions, including fine china dinner sets, cutlery, bedding and ornaments.

Opening packing cases after nearly two years was like delving into an Aladdin's cave, with all of us finding clothing, books, records, photographs and other personal possessions we thought we had long since lost. Dad spent generously on the best furniture for the new house: a lovely red velour three-piece suite for the front room – our Sunday best parlour – and new bedroom suites for us all.

After the house was furnished, dad had a great idea. He would take mum and me, plus Sarah – our ever-present visitor – and treat us all to brand new outfits from Marks & Spencer. Mum chose a pale blue summer suit, with a narrow skirt and medium length, which really suited her. I selected a white A-line skirt and boxy jacket. Sarah went for a pretty pink two-piece with a little bow on the front.

We were all delighted with our choices, especially when dad splashed out to buy us matching shoes and handbags and then treated us all to lunch at a local restaurant. It was a happy, fun day and dad was in his element. He was playing the hero and we all made a fuss of him – especially Sarah.

A tall, slim blonde with rosebud lips and neat features, Sarah was a year older than me. In fact, she was a year and one day older than me. She had turned 16 the day before I turned 15 the previous October. She had left school and was attending some kind of college secretarial course.

I never did find out when my father had first started his affair with her. But they both later confessed that it had started long before we moved from Box Hill. The day that mum discovered the two of them together in bed in our house goes down in my personal history as one of the worst days of my life, alongside the double suicide attempt in Singapore.

Poor mum. She went ballistic and the fallout lasted for many years afterwards. We all dreaded anything on TV with a character called Sarah, because we knew that painful memories would be dredged up and a huge row bound to erupt.

The betrayal and anger she felt at the time must have been devastating. She adored my father. He was her world. She had never had – and never did have – another man in her whole life. He had been her first serious boyfriend and was certainly the only man with whom she ever had any intimacy.

It was a Sunday morning. Sarah had slept as usual on the bed settee in the front room. Mum got up earlier than usual and walked into the front room with a cup of tea for Sarah. Dad was in bed with her.

From upstairs, where I had been fast asleep in my bed, I heard an agonised shriek, followed by a crash and the sounds of screaming and yelling. Not a totally uncommon occurrence in our house but this time it sounded serious. I ran downstairs.

Mum had thrown the cup, saucer and tea all over Sarah. She was slapping and punching dad and yelling and swearing at him. Sarah, in her nightie, was trying to hide behind the settee. Mum directed a stream of obscenities at her and told her to get out of the house.

Dad was trying to negotiate a ceasefire and I went with Sarah up to my bedroom, where she began to pack. According to her, it was all a bit of a misunderstanding: mum had misread the situation and overreacted.

What had really happened, they tried to convince us, was that dad had got up early and had checked on Sarah because she hadn't been feeling too well the night before. He hadn't actually been *in bed* with her and certainly hadn't been there all night. All innocent, she kept protesting, 'Your dad was *on* the bed – not *in* the bed – and he was feeling my forehead to see if I had a temperature, not touching me in an affectionate way. There was nothing going on.'

As for me, I was too naive – or too dumb – to know any better. Since she had been coming to visit us in London, Sarah had declared that she had met up with a nice boy, John. I was never actually introduced to him but she would go off to meet him. It would have been too incredible for me to work out that John was in fact my dad and that they were both out at the same time. Of course, with hindsight it all became blindingly obvious, but at the time I didn't suspect a thing.

As the whole story came out I felt angry at having been duped by the pair of them. Worse, I had been the one Sarah had worried with, and ultimately shared the relief with, when she had thought she was pregnant. The sense of injustice and outrage was made all the worse by the fact that mum refused to believe that I had known nothing. In fits of temper she would frequently turn her rage on me and more than once threw her wedding ring across the room at me.

Sarah did not come near mum or me again. She and dad continued to meet and for a while it looked as if he might walk out on us to go and live with her. Later I heard that she had moved to the Isle of Wight after giving him an ultimatum. He either left home or she would find a new life. When he died 30 years later I found a photo of her in his belongings.

He chose to stay, but of course the pain and resentment on both sides made mum and dad's relationship strained; bickering, rows and emotional upsets were common. The fact that there were times of relative peace when they managed to be happy in each other's company is testament to the abiding love they had for each other.

Through all these months we had no real home life and the family was disintegrating. The boys ran wild after getting into trouble at school and I stopped going to school on a regular basis.

Mum was often too unwell to be left alone. Dad was the breadwinner and needed to go to work, so more often than not I had to stay home and look after mum. Her fascination with pills continued and she often took large overdoses that rendered her unconscious for days at a time. The Rolling Stones song 'Mother's Little Helper' was most apposite.

It was my job to check on her every few hours, see that she was breathing, that her airways weren't blocked and turn her over so that she didn't develop bed sores or bruising. The epileptic fits continued and she might suffer several in a short period of time followed by weeks or even months of relative calm. Most of the time she stayed in bed.

Another crisis was looming. Dad was drinking too much, too often, he was in financial trouble and he had problems at work. As best I could, I ran the house and tried to look after the boys. My brothers were now all young teenagers. They either had no parental control or too much. Being left to their own devices meant they often got into scrapes, and when things went wrong dad was always too ready to punish them. The next time they went out, they would rebel against his strict discipline and get into trouble again – it was a vicious circle. However, on one occasion they were brought home in triumph by the police. The boys had found a lady's handbag containing hundreds of pounds; they handed it in at the local police station and were given a cash reward by the grateful owner.

My new stamping ground was the Notting Hill area of London. I had made friends with a group of young people who lived in a communal house that was owned by one of the boy's parents, a bohemian couple who lived in the basement. The father was a musician at the Royal Opera House and would go to work late in the afternoon dressed in his evening suit. His mother was an artist who encouraged a creative crowd around her eccentric son, who suffered from mental illness and often disappeared for 'rest cures'. He wrote music and painted and I imagined myself his muse – though if I anticipated inspiring any great works of art I was disappointed when he wrote me a song called 'She's Alright But She's A Moody Girl' and drew a Picasso-esque portrait with three eyes.

The mother used to let me stay at their house, but once she took me home and tried to persuade dad to let me go back to school. She could see that I was drifting and needed an anchor, which wasn't going to be provided at home where the welfare of us children was not high on the agenda. It was every man for himself – sink or swim.

Things were going wrong for all of us. Erratic school attendance had already meant that I had failed to study for my exams. Although the head teacher tried to persuade me otherwise, I left school without taking any O levels.

My interests lay elsewhere. Without any parental guidance or control at home, when I could escape from family obligations I ran with a wild crowd. At 15, we were smoking cigarettes, going out with boys and playing with Ouija boards. We would set up a board made from bits of paper and an alphabet and we'd watch as some force spelled out messages. The makeshift séances would go on for days, with a changing cast of characters as we took it in turns to maintain contact with the glass.

A lifelong interest in the psychic realm probably started there. During the marathon sessions a succession of personalities from the spirit world would queue up to pass on their messages. Sometimes they were personal, sometimes they were obscure, and at times they gave advice on our current lives or made predictions about the future.

Of course, adolescent girls can generate an enormous amount of psychic energy with their emerging sexuality and highly charged emotions. But soon the sexuality and emotion would be channelled into the real thing – the quest to lose our virginity. With the right person, of course. But along the way you have to kiss an awful lot of frogs. My best friend Tina and I had a thing about pop stars, preferably famous ones but foreign ones were exciting too. Mum was still very unwell, so, when we could persuade her to go, she would stay with her parents in Scotland – and then the mice would certainly play.

My fascination with The Beatles had not diminished and I neglected schoolwork in favour of dreaming up elaborate schemes to meet the Fab Four. One of these involved being sealed in a packing case addressed to 'The Beatles, The Bahamas, West Indies'. Complete madness!

School was an East London comprehensive where they were quite modern and allowed us to have 'record sessions' – a forerunner of a disco – in the gym at lunchtime. Only girls ever attended the sessions, which gave us the perfect opportunity to plan the escape and hide the packing case. Goodness knows who had ordered and collected the large wooden box. That wasn't my problem. I had volunteered to be sealed up and transported to the Caribbean over a summer weekend.

Due consideration had been given to my comfort and safety. We checked that the box had natural air holes and put in some supplies for the journey, including a blanket on the floor so I could sleep. During last period on Friday I sneaked into the gym, concealed myself in the packing case and awaited the girls who were to seal the top down and arrange for collection by the mail services.

When I heard voices in the gym and the lid being removed I was very excited that the adventure was about to begin. Next stop, the Bahamas. I envisioned The Beatles being surprised but thrilled that one of their fans had gone to such trouble. No doubt I'd be rewarded with a great holiday together with the boys – and I would be back on Monday in time to tell my friends all about it at school.

'Get out of there, at once!' I recognised the voice of one of the younger female teachers. 'What do you think you're playing at?'

The game was up. We were to report to her first thing on Monday morning to explain ourselves. Bang went my plans for a weekend in the sunshine – probably just as well, as I hadn't packed a bikini and was still wearing my school uniform. Life was not fair.

An insatiable desire for excitement and an inability to refuse a dare meant that I was increasingly getting into trouble at school. These days it would probably be called attention seeking and someone in authority might bother to enquire about family circumstances. Back then, no one ever did. Mind you, I wasn't there often.

Playing truant had become a favourite pastime, and with no one at home during the day to notice – or with mum there but not noticing – I often didn't bother going to school. On those days, like generations of schoolchildren before and since, my friends and I would hang around the local shops. A desire for makeup, clothes and records we couldn't afford led to numerous counts of petty shop-lifting.

I was never very good at it. My nervousness drew attention to the kids who were brave or stupid enough to actually steal the goods. I couldn't even be trusted to act as a lookout or a decoy. It was probably inevitable that we would get caught. Teenage girls targeting fashion departments when they should obviously have been in school – it was a dead giveaway.

However, one of the girls was a real expert, a habitual shoplifter, bold as brass. She had rich parents who bought her anything she wanted, so she just took items for the kicks. I'll never forget the fateful day I became an accomplice and joined her in her spree. She stole several items of clothing from one of the large stores while I kept the shop assistant occupied asking irrelevant questions.

We made our way outside without stopping at the tills. A few yards from the store, as we were breathing a sigh of relief at having completed our mission, our way was barred by a middle-aged woman.

At first I thought she was going to ask for directions. Instead she said, 'Would you please accompany me back into the shop as I have reason to believe you have goods which you have not paid for.' My legs turned to jelly, breathing became difficult and I started to sweat. It was such a shock that I didn't even consider running or denying the charge. It seemed like every eye was on us as we were accompanied back into the shop and marched to the manager's office.

He made it clear straight away that he intended to call the police and our parents. I have no idea how long the police took to arrive. All I know is it felt like a lifetime. I was sick with fear and shame. After taking a statement the police transferred us to a local police station. The short ride in the police car held no excitement, only the knowledge that I had now earned my stripes as a real juvenile delinquent.

At the station, a woman officer led me into a cell and locked the door. I nearly fainted with fear. The concrete cell was almost bare, with just a small iron bunk in the corner and a grey blanket. The place stank of urine, cigarette smoke and booze. The walls were covered in graffiti – mostly of the 'Kilroy woz 'ere' variety – and I swear I could see bloodstains where people had dragged their fingernails down the wall, but that was probably my overactive imagination. For the whole time I was locked up in that dreadful cell, I cried and prayed fervently to God to get me out of there. My friend, who was in the next door cell, sang – loudly.

Dad arrived after two or three hours; I had lost track of time. Little Miss Rich Girl's parents couldn't be contacted – they had gone out for the evening. The police agreed that dad should sign us both out. He didn't look at me or say a word while we were in the police station, but as we stood together on the pavement outside, he turned to me and with a look of such disappointment in his eyes, said: 'Not you Ellen. I never would have believed it of you.'

To this day, the memory of that confrontation is without doubt the most painful and shameful of my life. In that moment, I promised myself – and later my dad – that I would never do anything criminal again. I certainly learned my lesson.

Dad made a good impression on the policeman and the probation officer. The reports that they produced convinced the judge in the juvenile court to give me probation: two years. The other girl, who faced more charges than me, was threatened with a custodial sentence but in the end she too was given probation.

Our parents decided that we were a bad influence on each

other and tried to separate us, but it did not last long. In fact, our joint experience forged an even stronger bond between us. Long before we lost our virginity to boys, she and I indulged in mild sexual activity together, but the real goal of our pursuit was members of the opposite sex.

We would make regular excursions to London. The lure of Carnaby Street was still great and in what became known as the Swinging Sixties we would meet all kinds of weird and wonderful characters just wandering along the streets. Invites were offered to parties, to music sessions, and we would hang out in the fashion shops, record stores and coffee bars.

It was there we met our beloved pop stars, both real and wannabes. In those days, every young guy with a trendy haircut and fashionable clothes imagined they were about to be discovered. The groups who really were involved in the music scene were always looking for nubile young ladies to impress by taking them to clubs, recording studios and concerts.

Back home in East London there were several chart-topping groups who lived and played in our local area and we would follow them as they toured the dance halls and pub venues. We were friends with The Tremeloes, The Small Faces, and 'Rod the Mod' – Rod Stewart. An American girl called Anna introduced us to the Texan pop star Shawn Phillips and through him Donovan and some of his friends. Shawn was then living in Connaught Square in London's West End; pop star Donovan also sometimes lived there when he wasn't touring. It was at that flat that I smoked my first joint, although I like to claim that, like Bill Clinton, I never inhaled. Truth was I preferred Benson & Hedges in their iconic gold pack.

Top of the Pops was on a Thursday evening and there was much excitement as a crowd of us gathered together in Shawn's rented flat in Cadogan Square to watch Donovan's first recorded appearance, singing 'Universal Soldier'. We lazed on large silk cushions and tried our best to be cool. We were in with the in-crowd.

Donovan himself wore an Indian outfit of tunic and baggy trousers – the same as he had been wearing on screen. After the TV show had aired we shared a taxi to another friend's house. As we waited on the street, a crowd of fans spotted him and started asking for his autograph. I would have liked to ask for an autograph myself to show my school friends back in Manor Park, but it was not the done thing. I was a friend – not a fan!

Before taking my final exams, I dropped out of school and started drifting from job to job. It appealed to my sense of rebellion to start work in an office in the morning, go out to meet friends at lunchtime, and not bother to go back in the afternoon. The petty rules and regulations of office life were too restricting for a free spirit like me and I refused to conform to any form of discipline.

It proved difficult to find a job that suited me. I had a very short-lived career in retail – less than a week before I decided I wasn't cut out for selling. One job that lasted for an extended period, probably at least six weeks, was working the early shift in a small hotel.

My latest passion was a group of Swedish pop stars who were based at the hotel while touring Britain. The manageress of the hotel offered me and my friend a tailor-made solution to the problem of how we could hang out with the boys and get paid for it.

Our shift started at 7am and after serving breakfast we would join the housekeeping staff servicing rooms and finish by about 2pm. Right about the time that Thomas and Frederick, our boyfriends, would be waking up.

We were then free to spend the day travelling with them to

recording studios and record shop appearances before going on to that night's gig in one of the many village halls, pubs and county hotels that still had live music in those days.

Work was not a priority, so, just as I had arbitrarily given up going to school, I now rarely went to work. Genuine recurring throat problems were a good excuse to miss work, but a stay in hospital to have my tonsils removed led to a new, exciting job.

In hospital I met a girl called Carole who worked on the housekeeping staff of the Dorchester Hotel in Park Lane, and through her recommendation I was given a job on the switchboard – having just had my tonsils removed, my voice had an attractive lower register. I enjoyed my time at the Dorchester; there was an excitement in being part of a great, iconic hotel. Being on the switchboard in the days before fully automated telephone equipment, we were able to talk directly to the hotel guests, albeit if only when they asked for their calls to be connected.

Friends loved hearing about my telephone conversations with hotel guests, including royalty, the Sultan of Brunei and Hollywood film stars Tony Curtis, Charlton Heston and Ursula Andress. In my fantasy, I was a real uptown girl, far from Stratford and the East End. I was upwardly mobile. Where to next?

God was looking down and laughing.

Most of my friends had already surrendered their virginity, but, despite the fun I had had with Thomas and Frederick, I was to hold onto mine for a while longer. Another pop star was to claim the prize. Hal was a handsome, dark-haired mop head from the Midlands who played in a band that had a few minor hits. Hal and the other band members were living in London with their manager, a Jewish lawyer called Dan, while they made their bid for stardom.

As loyal fans, we would spend hours writing letters to the various pirate radio stations, many of them based on ships outside the 3-mile limit so they didn't need a British broadcasting licence. Before BBC Radio 1, these stations were the mainstay of popular culture, and if they played a record it could get into the charts.

Hal was my first serious boyfriend and lover, and his betrayal led to me finding it difficult to trust men. I determined that I wouldn't be treated so badly in future relationships. The courtship – or seduction – started as a fun adventure. With no responsibilities or proper jobs, we made the best of being young and single. The group had a mini and we would bomb around London sightseeing, visiting friends and making mischief.

Like The Beatles, Hal's band had done a stint in the German clubs. He was hoping to emulate The Beatles' success and it was a good publicity angle that he had hung out with the Fab Four when they were still The Silver Beetles in Hamburg. The story was also good for pulling birds.

Hal's flat was close to Petticoat Lane in East London and was a second home to me and various other visiting girlfriends. I liked to play house, so I did the housework as no one else did. On one occasion, Dan, the lawyer, went crazy when he discovered that I had misunderstood the instructions for washing up in a kosher home and the need for items to be washed separately in different-coloured bowls.

Hal would come home late at night and I'd be waiting for him. I had worked out a system at home whereby I would appear for part of the evening then disappear out of the bedroom window at around 10pm to go to Hal's.

We slept together but did not make love; I was still under 16 and he made a big deal out of 'respecting me'. Of course, really he was just waiting for the right moment. He knew that if he forced the issue, I would probably flee, being young and easily scared off.

Fending off amorous advances was nothing new, but being ignored was. After some nights of being 'respected', I started asking him to do me the favour of deflowering me.

'Virgins are his speciality,' a friend of his told me afterwards.

His seduction techniques were well practised, but only an innocent 15-year-old would have fallen for his line about being the only man with the sensitivity and expertise to take a girl's virginity in the most painless and respectful manner. In fact, perhaps he *was* good – I hardly felt a thing, though he did make an elaborate show of turning back the sheets to reveal a single spot of blood on the white sheet.

When I walked out of the flat the next morning, I felt as if I had grown a few inches. I thought everyone would be able to tell that I was now a real woman. It felt scary and exciting – and something of an anticlimax.

Hal's career took off and he suddenly got very busy. More and more often he found excuses for not seeing me. 'Will You Still Love Me Tomorrow?' had a hollow ring to it.

If I had been childish enough to think that losing your virginity to someone meant they felt seriously about you, I was soon disabused of that idea. Besides, he suddenly remembered his fiancée back home. It was funny how her name had never come up before. Now, he had an attack of conscience, and said it would probably be better if we didn't see each other for a while.

The last time we said goodbye, on a railway platform as he headed back home to the Midlands, he told me tenderly, 'Remember, though, I'll always love you. And if you ever need me you know where I am.' A farewell kiss and he disappeared into the carriage and out of my life forever.

Too late, I realised that here was something where I couldn't turn back the clock or change the past. 'What will I tell my husband on my wedding night?' I wailed to my friend Tina, convinced that I wouldn't now be having sex again until I got married.

'Tell him your hymen broke riding horses,' she offered helpfully. We weren't really big on horse riding in London E12, but she meant well.

However, it wasn't long before my sexual activity was more regular and more advanced. I could lose my virginity only once – after that there was nothing left to protect and I had several sexual partners in the months that followed. Free love and the pill went together with our 1960s female emancipation, and although I was never a card-carrying member of the bra-burning brigade, I did decide to claim for myself the supposed freedoms of liberation.

Aided and abetted by the youth revolution, I completely abandoned myself to the delights of sex, drugs and rock 'n' roll. And being around music and groups so much of the time, it seemed only natural that I would try my hand at lyric writing as an extension of my daily journal keeping.

Hal had always taken a great interest in the love poems I wrote to him, and I also sent him songs I'd written. 'No Dice' (quoted below) was one I wrote for him and also 'Let's Be Friends', 'He Lies' and 'You've Done It Again'. He should have been writing songs for me. 'Poor Little Fool' would have been appropriate.

'No dice'
I sit here wondering what to do,
You see I really feel quite blue,
I smile as people walk on by,
But inside I just want to cry.

SCHOOL'S OUT FOREVER

You've already put me down twice,
But this time you called 'No dice.'
You said we were finished, you had to be true,
Your girl back home was waiting for you.
I guess you thought that then I'd see,
You never really did anything for me,
But baby I wanted to help you,
And you must know that I still do.

You're going but if you ever need anyone to comfort you,
Baby, you know just what to do,
Call 'Dice' and I'll be there, anywhere,
Just call 'Dice', baby.

CHAPTER 4

STREETS OF LONDON

Around this time I took up with another boyfriend – Jim Wallace. He wasn't a pop star but he looked like one. In fact, he was a dead ringer for George Harrison, who I had a crush on at the time.

Jim was to become an old faithful, and we had an on-and-off relationship for many years. I would call and he'd come running. Unlike Hal, Jim was a gentleman: good, supportive and strong.

The fact that he too had a long-standing fiancée mattered little to me. My intentions were never serious, and in many ways he was more a friend than a lover (although it usually ended up in a huge row when he tried to explain that to Cathy, his fiancée).

In times of trouble, I would call Jim to come and collect me or accompany me on various outings. It might be a job interview, a visit to a relative or a trip out of town to meet another boy. If Cathy was there when I rang, she would go ballistic and he'd walk out, leaving her with his mum.

Jim would go to extraordinary lengths for me. He was

football crazy and over the moon when he got tickets for the 1966 World Cup final – Germany versus England – but the fixture clashed with a trip I was making from London to Scotland and he came to wave me off instead.

Before my coach left Victoria at 4pm, we spent the afternoon watching the World Cup on a TV in the window of Radio Rentals. For years afterwards, whenever I turned up with Jim, his mates would say, 'So it was you who made him miss the most important football match ever.' He never let me forget it, but it just went to show how chivalrous he could be. Jim restored my faith in the opposite sex – although, like many women, I still chased the mean ones and gave the nice guys the run-around.

Travelling to Glasgow on that date had not been my idea. In fact, I didn't want to go at all. London was much too exciting for me to leave it for a city I'd only ever visited on infrequent trips to see dad's relatives. Mum's parents had moved out of Glasgow shortly after I was born, and if I had ever considered myself Scottish – which I didn't – home would have been the small village of Dollar.

Now dad was proposing that we should all decamp from London to a housing estate on the outskirts of Glasgow where the council had offered him a property. Much as I resented the move, I had no choice. Under the terms of my shop-lifting probation I had to live with my parents unless they gave permission for me to live elsewhere. The parents of two of my friends had said I could live with them in London, one aunt offered me a bed in her home, and the mother of a male friend said I could stay with them. Dad was having none of it. He threatened to return me to court if I refused to go with the family. I even tried running away a couple of times but he tracked me down.

So, on Saturday 30 July 1966, with a heavy heart, I boarded

the coach for Glasgow. My novelty value as an English young lady led to me making lots of friends in the area and there were plenty of relatives to help us settle in. The boys fared less well, being that much younger and still at school. Their English accents made them a target for name calling, bullying and worse. Very quickly, all three of them developed Glaswegian accents.

As my seventeenth birthday approached, I joined a modelling agency and got various promotional jobs at exhibitions and events. Many of these were held at Kelvin Hall, which hosted the Scottish Ideal Home Exhibition as well as large-scale musicals, pop concerts and sporting events.

Work became one long party, with me a centre of attention as I graced exhibitor stands in miniskirts or other revealing outfits. The hours were long but the pay was good and I enjoyed the company of the other girls who modelled for the agency.

Male visitors often propositioned us, and although we would go for drinks or a meal, it was all transient – organisers, customers and exhibitors changed from week to week. That suited me fine. It never occurred to me that someone might come along with the old cliché 'I'm gonna make you a star', but there did seem to be a distinct possibility of moving on to other ventures or other venues. However, my life was about to change.

The initial approach came from an unexpected quarter. I had thought it might happen when the pop group Dave Dee, Dozy, Beaky, Mick & Titch played a sell-out concert and the lead singer and I spent some time together. Nothing really intimate, just a bit of hand holding and kissing in the dressing room between shows.

'That old guy's there again, watching you,' said my friend and fellow dancer, Isabel. We were dressed in white with a red heart sewn onto our miniskirts and we were go-go dancing to pop music at the front of a stand promoting the Milk Marketing

Board. When the music finished we made our way to the back of the stand and I started to make myself a hot chocolate, one of the perks of the job, with lashings of frothy hot milk.

'Can I talk to you?' I heard a man say. He had stepped through the flimsy curtain that blocked off the staff area.

'The public aren't allowed in here,' I told him somewhat sharply.

'What time do you finish?' he asked.

'Not that it's any of your business,' I said, still frosty, 'but the exhibition closes at 10 tonight.'

He was expensively dressed, well spoken and obviously used to getting his own way. 'I'll pick you up outside,' he said. 'Ten o'clock. Look for the Rolls-Royce.'

He handed me his business card and was gone. A Rolls-Royce, now that was my kind of lift. It was probably a joke, but the card looked genuine enough: 'Mr Tommy Shields, Managing Director, Radio Scotland'. The station was one of the more successful pirate radio stations – it was before the Marine Broadcasting Offences Act of 1967 outlawed them all – and broadcast from a boat in the North Sea off the west coast of Scotland.

True to his word, Tommy, a gentleman probably in his early sixties, was waiting for me when I got off work. The chauffeur opened the door as I approached the only Rolls-Royce outside Kelvin Hall and I joined Tommy in the back. He instructed the chauffeur to drive to the Central Hotel. My brain was working overtime. At what point could I make a safe escape while still getting a ride in a Rolls-Royce?

We made small talk on the journey to the hotel and Tommy admitted that he had a proposition he wanted to put to me. As we pulled up, the chauffeur helped me from the car and I was somewhat relieved to hear his boss tell him to wait – he wouldn't be long. Tommy led the way into the Central Hotel and I meekly followed.

'Good evening, Mr Shields,' said the doorman. They obviously knew him here.

He headed straight for the lounge and chose a table in one of the alcoves. The waiter approached and Tommy ordered tea and sandwiches. I was enjoying this. As long as we were in a public area, nothing untoward was going to happen. There would be no embarrassment as he discovered that I wasn't interested in his proposition, only in his car.

Tommy proved to be a most amusing and interesting companion and a perfect gentleman with a wealth of stories to tell. 'Now down to business,' he said when we were settled. 'How would you like to do a show on my radio station? There are going to be changes to our schedule and your English accent will be quite unlike anything else we've got on air at present. Have you ever done any broadcasting?'

This was a dream come true. 'Of course, I'd love to do a show,' I told him, though I had to admit that I had no experience, except for *listening* to the radio for hours on end. Pirate radio, including the ever popular Radio Luxembourg, was the only real outlet for popular music in those days and I, along with everyone else of my generation, listened to radio much more than we watched television.

We talked some more and Tommy invited me to visit the offices of Radio Scotland, which were based in Hillhead in Glasgow's West End. He got up to leave, called the waiter over and paid the bill.

'I'll order a taxi to take you home,' he said, disappearing towards the concierge's desk. When the taxi arrived, he gave the driver the address, paid him and instructed, 'Make sure the young lady gets home safe and sound.'

I found out later that Tommy Shields was a well-known businessman in Glasgow, formerly a STV (Scottish Television) man, and reputedly a tyrannical boss, but he could be kind and generous too. He had many interests and Radio Scotland was just one of them – it was a labour of love for him.

Running a radio station from a leaky boat, *The Comet*, a former Irish light ship based three miles off the Scottish coast in Troon Bay, that was always about to stray into illegal waters, was an expensive and worrying venture and his priorities did not always tally with those of the station staff, especially those at sea.

I arrived just as an order was being enforced not to allow women aboard the ship as it was causing too many problems; Tommy's plan was for me to do a weekend request programme from the safety of the studio. Also, the weather had deteriorated and the boat was letting in water; when the on-board disc jockeys weren't broadcasting, they were bailing it out.

One jockey, the ebullient Stuart Henry, who went on to Radio 1 and later Radio Luxembourg, had to be rescued from the ship when he became violently seasick. Stuart was a joker and on more than one occasion when I was travelling on the Glasgow subway he appeared (wearing a large fur coat and floppy hat), scooped me up and put me on or off the train on the opposite track to my intended direction of travel , all the time laughing like a drain.

But at that time Stuart and the team at Radio Scotland weren't laughing much. The government was threatening criminal proceedings against illegal pirates and the owners of the boat were refusing to allow tenders out with food supplies until repair bills were paid.

Tommy addressed the audience in his weekly 'fireside chat': 'We won't give up. My heart goes out to the lads on board ... the terrible conditions they are suffering ... they're like my own sons.'

As well as taking part in a regular request spot at the weekend, I soon had a full-time receptionist job at the station during the week. None of us ever wanted to go home. We were having too much fun making programmes, compiling playlists from the new releases, manning the radio station and organising concerts, sporting events and public relations activities to promote Radio Scotland to the public and advertisers.

The office in Cranworth Street was a Mecca for visiting and local pop stars and the returning disc jockeys, who were on board for three weeks then back on land for one. Some of the station newscasters of the time included Bob Spencer, Richard Park Paul Young, Tony Meehan and Jack MacLaughlin

On changeover day the crew would come crashing into the office and whisk us all off for lunch or partying. There was never a dull moment. Glasgow had its own fashionable in-crowd and the radio station was at the heart of it.

There was a thriving club scene and up-to-the-minute fashion boutiques. The mantra was 'tune in, turn on, drop out'. Love, peace and flower power. These fundamental concepts rallied the youth to their peaceful revolution, where we did little but talk and contemplate our navels. Cannabis was the drug of choice for many of my generation and I embraced the hippy lifestyle with gusto.

As a gesture of solidarity with the anti-Vietnam war marchers in San Francisco, we organised our own love-in. Wearing our uniforms of flowing skirts, flowered tops, beads, bangles and Afghan coats, we staged a sit-in at the Botanical Gardens. Ringing bells, chanting and smoking dope, we soon attracted the kind of publicity we wanted for our cause.

A ragtag crowd of about 30 young protesters, drop-outs and university students was escorted out of the gardens by the park-keepers, while the police kept a watchful eye on proceedings from the police box at the entrance. They didn't intervene in our peaceful protest and the event was good-natured for the most part. It made the news bulletins in the regional papers the next day.

Dad didn't have too much to say about my teenage rebellion – unlike the previous occasion when I had graced the front page of the newspapers. Then, I had bunked off school to welcome The Beatles back from America at London Airport and had appeared alongside other girls screaming with delight. He had imposed his usual punishment: I was grounded after school and for the weekend. Expecting a repeat of that, I was surprised when he seemed to find my new lifestyle amusing. Perhaps the difference was that I was no longer a schoolgirl. Since we had arrived in Glasgow, the regime had become much more liberal.

Much of the time I went my own way, often staying with girlfriends. Mum had family support and didn't need me so much. As long as I made regular appearances at home, dad didn't question my movements.

He and mum had been welcomed back into the bosom of dad's large Scottish family, most of whom lived in Glasgow, and their social life revolved around visiting different members of the family each weekend. On the occasions when our house was the rendezvous, I would endeavour to be away for the night. Various aunts, uncles and cousins would gather late on Saturday afternoon. There would be a whip-round and a couple of the men delegated to go and collect the drink. There would be singing, with each family member performing their party piece, and everyone was expected to take a turn entertaining the company. The singing included well-loved old country numbers as well as the inevitable 'When Irish Eyes are Smiling' and popular classics like 'Danny Boy' and 'My Mother's Eyes'.

Like many Glasgow families, mine was a mixture of Catholics and Protestants. Inter-marrying had taken place on both sides of the family: my paternal grandfather was a Protestant married to a Catholic, and my maternal grandfather a Catholic married to a Protestant. At some point in the night's revels, someone was bound to start a chorus of an Irish rebels' song, followed by 'The Sash My Father Wore'. When I was growing up, I never knew which song was synonymous with which religion.

My probation order was still in force so I couldn't go too far, but I developed a good relationship with the young female officer who I had to report to on a monthly basis. Whenever I had problems or was unsure about a course of action, I discussed matters with her. At the end of my two-year term, she wrote me a touching letter and said she would be sorry not to see me anymore, but she wished me all the best for my future life. I think I was one of her few success stories, as I never again offended or breached the terms of my order.

It was to be my first and last brush with the law. I had made a vow to my dad, myself and God that I was on the straight and narrow from that day on, though my 'crime' could probably be classed as stupid teenage rebellion rather than an indication of any serious criminal tendencies. Ten years later, the probation details were wiped from my file. Even though it had all been such a long time ago, the relief I felt knowing that I no longer had a criminal record was immense.

Back at the radio station the joint was jumping. In a joint venture with other radio companies, we launched a series of protests, petitions and fundraising events to fight the Marine Broadcasting Offences Bill. All to no avail. At a special party, a Clan Ball, at the Lyceum Ballroom in Glasgow, the assembled crowd listened as Radio Scotland was officially taken off the air at midnight on Monday 14 July 1967 when the new law came into force.

For a few days we bravely soldiered on, hoping that something would happen to change the situation. It didn't. However, I did become part of the movement to keep the station's name alive and jumped at the chance to join the staff on the Radio Scotland magazine, *242 Showbeat*. The thinking was that the magazine would continue, as would various sponsored events and promotional activities.

As for me, I'd discovered a new passion: journalism. All my life I had been an avid reader and writer. I kept a daily diary from the age of about 12 and essays were always my favourite subject at school. Now I discovered that I could be paid for doing something I loved. In the office of *242 Showbeat* in Baltic Chambers, Glasgow, I started to learn my craft. On the bus to and from work I would avidly read every book the library could produce, from *Teach Yourself Journalism* to *The Craft of the Writer*.

Baltic Chambers on Glasgow's Wellington Street is an imposing example of Victorian grandeur. The red sandstone building was part of the old Baltic shipping exchange building and its carved details of boats celebrate Glasgow's links with the sea and its cultural and merchant past. A cavernous edifice with grand staircases, high ceilings and huge marble-floored offices, it had once been a centre of commerce in the bustling port, handling the tobacco and spices that came from the Americas and made the city second in wealth only to London.

242 Showbeat moved there when the pirate radio station was taken off the air, its staff sacked and its own offices shut down. The editorial team was compact to say the least. Just three of us were charged with getting out the fortnightly publication, while a businessman with the title of 'managing director' made infrequent visits when he wasn't busy at his other job – selling lawnmowers to Scandinavians.

As well as myself, Girl Friday cum editorial assistant cum trainee journalist, there were two professional journalists. Both made the daily journey over from Edinburgh then returned on an early afternoon train to sign on for their late shifts as subeditors on the *Scottish Daily Mail*.

Gavin Petrie was the moving spirit behind the title. He was a highly capable journalist with enthusiasm, imagination and bags of energy. Gavin was the editor. The other executive was a thin-faced, wily old newspaperman called David. Between the two of them they handled all the production, wrote, subbed and laid out the broadsheet colour magazine, and made the journey to the printer to see the publication through its final stages. They also sold adverts and tried desperately to keep the publication afloat, negotiating with the printers and other suppliers as we robbed Peter to pay Paul. It became regular practice to persuade advertisers to pay in advance so that we could pay the printers, who refused to start printing before they received their money.

More than once I was despatched to the local telephone office to plead that the lines should not be cut off before the managing director returned from abroad and countersigned the outstanding cheques.

Each edition was a triumph of endurance, ingenuity and often plain cheek, approaching people to do things for us above and beyond the call of duty. Editorially, the magazine was a colourful mix of pop music, fashion and gossip. The comings and goings of local pop groups such as Studio Six, the Beatstalkers, the Pathfinders and the Poets (some members of whom later went on to become very successful under the name White Trash), were always of interest. Also featured were the various visiting pop personalities and touring musical productions.

Gavin, with his extensive journalistic and production experience, gave the magazine a modern, fresh, exciting layout. Firing on all cylinders creatively, he would come up with new feature ideas and catchy headlines in a frenzy of activity right up to the last second when he needed to catch the train to Edinburgh.

Briefcase under his arm bulging with layouts, interviews and news stories, he would fly out of the door, one arm in his leather jacket, yelling instructions over his shoulder. He was a human whirlwind. He was also an accomplished musician and artist – he played guitar in a pop group and had many of his drawings and cartoons featured in magazines, books and newspapers. He was an enthusiastic teacher and good delegator. More and more he allowed me to become a fully fledged member of the editorial team. Encouraging me to write pieces, he would first take me on interviews with him and then gradually trust me to go alone.

Through his eyes I began to learn to see the potential in every story and to think creatively when I was confronted with any good news situation. I learned to keep my ear to the ground and cultivate contacts who could keep us supplied with the unending supply of material that every publication needs.

Back in the office, I picked up the basics of selling and editorial layout as well as subbing pages and marking up copy for the printers, while negotiating printing fees and ordering pictures and artwork from outside agencies. I always was a fast learner, a skill that held me in good stead all through my professional life.

The offices at Baltic Chambers were a hive of activity and quickly became a place where the in-crowd hung out. Pop people, photographers and disc jockeys all enjoyed the hospitality of our coffee machine and the chance to meet up. In return, they would help with ideas and columns for the magazine.

We were still proclaiming ourselves the flagship publication of the now defunct Radio Scotland, but, as time went on, memories of the illegal broadcasts faded. Fans were now being catered for by the new legal pop music station, BBC Radio 1, and many of its best disc jockeys were old pirates – Tony Blackburn, Emperor Rosko and our own Stuart Henry among them.

Gradually the identity of *242 Showbeat* was being eroded. Without a radio station, it was increasingly difficult to retain commitment and loyalty. News came through that the ship that had been the broadcasting base for Radio Scotland had sunk off the west coast. *242 Showbeat* followed soon after. Gavin decided to use this as a chance to make a career move to London. That's also where I was headed.

Life at home became a battlefield after I declared that I was going back to London. Dad knew he had no control over me now and he alternated between ignoring me and shouting at me.

He would turn particularly nasty after he had had a few drinks and would accuse me of betraying them and caring more about my own selfish desires than about the good of the family. Threats of violence were commonplace, but although I was frightened, he never hit me. I guess he knew that that would be just the excuse I was looking for.

When the threats didn't work, he would try to blackmail me: 'What about your mum? It will break her heart if you go. She needs you – you're her only daughter.'

Her own mum had died while we were in Scotland and this had upset her badly. As a regular weekend outing, mum and I often made the two-hour coach trip to Dollar, 50 miles from Glasgow, to visit granddad and take flowers to gran's grave. Mum and I grew close as we shared our grief. Since returning to the country of her birth, mum's own health had shown some improvement. At least she was no longer so frightened and her epileptic fits were less frequent and less severe.

One day, when we were having a cup of tea together, enjoying the companionship of mother and daughter, I asked her how she honestly felt about me going back to London.

'I want you to go,' she said. Then she started crying. 'Don't let your dad hold you back. We all depend too much on you. You deserve your own life. You go with my blessing. But you know I will miss you.'

Her own mother had set aside her reservations and had encouraged mum to leave home and follow her husband to a new life, first in England, then abroad. My mum followed her example and gave me her blessing. Now my mind was totally made up.

In preparation, I started to organise accommodation and work in London. Also I decided to pursue my ambition to break into modelling. One of the photographers I had become friendly with through media connections offered to do a set of photographs for a portfolio.

Those were the days of the miniskirt, and Mary Quant had made PVC very fashionable. One photograph featured me in a short, black PVC coat, unzipped to show a hint of breast. I was particularly proud of the pose and carried a copy of the photograph everywhere I went for a time. Unfortunately, one day I left my handbag lying open and dad caught a glimpse. He demanded to see it. The suggestive pose gave him another excuse to try to stop me leaving home.

He declared that I was in 'moral danger', but I had already successfully completed my two-year probation order so there was no one to listen to his protests. I was already 18 and he couldn't stop me leaving.

On a Sunday night in March, I boarded the coach from Buchanan Street. At the last minute dad relented and he and mum accompanied me to the station to see me off. For 10 hours of the journey, I sobbed my heart out. Leaving the two of them was the hardest thing I had ever done and right up to the last minute I thought my nerve might fail me. But I had to go. I had to do it for me.

Many years later my brother James, who was 13 when I left, told me that he had been convinced I would go back for him, or at least change my mind about going. He too had cried for hours. Thank God I didn't know that at the time, or my resolve really would have failed.

On subsequent trips home it was always the same. I had to steel myself not to give in and stay in their dysfunctional world. I'm not sure where the determination came from, but that single-mindedness – some would say self-centredness – ensured that I could live my own life, although I was consumed by guilt and a constant worry about what was going on back home.

Unlike some runaways, I always stayed in touch – I still cry at The Beatles' song 'She's Leaving Home'. I wrote and telephoned regularly and made frequent visits home. It would be untrue to say that they got on fine without me – they would have benefited from my being there to take care of them – but they did make a life for themselves and grew ever closer to their Scottish relatives. This lasted for a couple of years, then mum and dad decided that they too were ready to make the return journey to London.

It didn't faze me too much when mum and dad turned up on my doorstep and declared that they were fed up with Scotland, but the doorstep happened to be of a flat where I was now living with Gavin Petrie. In my letters I had always claimed that I lived with a girlfriend, although they did know that I had been going out with Gavin since he and I arrived in London two years before. It was purely coincidental that the start date of his new job on one of the capital's biggest pop music papers should be the same as when I was due to join the London branch of a shipping firm.

Through an agency in Glasgow, I had secured the position after an interview at the Scottish headquarters. I had no intention of staying in the job but it gave me a starting point. I had also managed to find myself somewhere safe and respectable to stay so that mum and dad wouldn't have to worry. I was to live in a hostel for young ladies.

Bourne & Hollingsworth, a large London department store in Oxford Street, provided accommodation for its female staff. A friend of a friend had recommended me and so I moved into a shared room in the hostel in a fine building next door to the Royal Academy of Dramatic Art in Gower Street.

By one of those bizarre coincidences that happen in life, Gavin and I had arrived in London on the same day. Gavin had been waved off from his home town of Edinburgh by his mother and his fiancée, a hairdresser called Jean. Eight years older than me at 26, Gavin was having a hard time deciding to marry and settle down. As he told me at the time, his going to London had not pleased his mother or Jean, but they accepted that it was probably a good career move.

Jean had no intention of leaving her salon, so the arrangement was that Gavin would go back home in a couple of years having made a name for himself down south. It didn't work out that way. Although he and I had never been emotionally involved, he was attracted by my wild, unconventional behaviour. If Jean was a 'nice girl', I was the party girl – and a lot more fun.

We arranged to meet up on our first day in London, and after helping me move into my halls of residence he set off for his first day as a writer on *Disc and Music Echo*. We met up in a pub on Tottenham Court Road to compare notes on the first day of our new lives. Gavin already had invitations lined up for the rest of the week at various record company functions. The *Disc* editorial team were social animals and wanted to introduce him to the contacts he would need for his work. We soon established a routine. I would call him at lunchtime and he would give me the rundown of all the events on offer. It was not unusual for us to make an appearance at three or four music, film or promotional parties or premieres.

All the big record companies hosted events at least once a week and, in those days of tax-deductible entertaining, they were often lavish. Boat trips down the river would be used to launch a record, cocktail parties were held to meet the bands, and dinners at expensive restaurants were hosted to introduce visiting record company executives or foreign journalists. It was a rare day indeed when Gavin would meet me at a pre-arranged spot without an embossed card requesting the pleasure of his company – 'plus one', of course.

Gavin and I became a couple from that first day, although for the first month or so, like the cliché says, we were 'just good friends'. Both newly arrived in London, we met new friends and threw ourselves enthusiastically into the London scene, where we were lucky to be right in the thick of things through Gavin's work connections. Gavin had a flat on the Piccadilly underground line at Manor House, and at weekends I would go and stay.

My first job in London proved rather boring and I moved on to work for a firm of Jewish fashion manufacturers off Tottenham Court Road, round the corner from where I lived. Three brothers ran the firm, a small company specialising in high-quality ladies' wool and silk suits. My job was a kind of house model cum secretary.

The middle-aged brothers all had their own areas of responsibility. The oldest brother was dark and brooding, a bit serious, and he managed the financial side of the business. The youngest, a whizz-kid, dealt with sales. And in the middle, taking care of the office and warehouse, was the most attractive of the three, a charmer with steel-grey hair and an immaculate dress sense. Harry took a great interest in the clothes he asked me to model for clients. He also took a great interest in me.

I was just 18 years old and wore the shortest minis imaginable. My hair was still long and straight but now had a rich auburn colour. After work he often took me to posh restaurants for dinner – places such as Borscht 'n' Tears, a Russian restaurant where the atmosphere was lively and the food exotic – and then on to a supper club on Piccadilly where they had a small dance floor.

Harry was much older than me and I was flattered by his attention, although I always kept him at arm's length. After dinner, he would drive me home to the Bourne & Hollingsworth hostel and we would engage in our customary struggle – he would try to kiss me and I would try to get away without causing offence. Curfew at the hostel was midnight, and if I timed it right we would arrive as the witching hour was approaching and I could make my excuses and leave.

Over dinner one evening, Harry had a proposition: the mistress charter. He would find me a flat and pay the rent – plus gifts, of course. In return, he would call twice a week and be indulged with sexual favours. He had worked out his plan – probably he had used it before – but there was one stipulation. I had to dump Gavin. No boyfriends were allowed at the flat, although I would be free to live my own life for the five days a week when he wasn't there. And I wouldn't be expected to work. Harry was married, of course, but he seemed more worried about his brothers' reaction if they ever found out, and so I would need to leave my job.

It was quite an exciting prospect, my first offer to be a 'kept woman'. Strangely enough, I wasn't surprised or shocked, just convinced that it was not something that appealed to me at the time.

Harry promised to be generous with money and clothes; indeed, he often told me to keep outfits I had modelled in the showroom and he would pay for them. I loved striding through London's West End dressed in designer outfits – usually coat/dress combinations in startling jewel colours or colourful patterned ensembles.

But as much as the thought of being a paid mistress intrigued me, I was having far too much fun as the girlfriend of a pop music journalist. Gavin never knew about the proposed arrangement but he grew increasingly less tolerant of my excuses about work situations that resulted in me going to dinner with the boss.

When the opportunity came for Gavin to move into a flat in central London with two other Scottish journalists, he jumped at the chance. The Westminster home of a Lord and Lady was available for rent while the aristocratic couple were abroad. A small, purpose-built apartment block less than half a mile from the House of Commons and the same distance from New Scotland Yard, Strutton Court was to become a legendary address for wild parties and outrageous behaviour. Three journalists with various girlfriends, friends and lodgers were to turn the elegant, beautifully furnished flat into a den of iniquity with almost nightly revels.

Chief reveller was a crime reporter for the *Daily Express*, Glaswegian James Dalrymple, a brilliant journalist and an incorrigible drunk at that time; though the rest of us weren't far behind in the drinking stakes. There was also a reporter from Edinburgh, a former colleague of Gavin, who worked for the *Daily Express*. Though quieter than James, he also liked his drink and knew how to enjoy himself.

Gavin was the perfect foil for the two. He was fascinated by the rough, tough James, a hard-fighting man if he could stay standing long enough to deliver a punch. As east coast men, Gavin and his other flatmate shared many interests and mutual friends and considered themselves a cut above Scots from the west coast.

James would always say he was a one-woman man, which roughly meant that he would generally have only one woman in his bed at a time. As one girlfriend would depart, often after a few days, James would be on the phone ordering up another one. Usually they did the shopping, and it helped if they had a burning desire to do some serious housework too. There was a rota in the flat for washing up, cleaning, shopping and cooking, and the three men were most punctilious about doing their fair share of the chores – or, more accurately, getting the women in their life to do them.

James regularly lost his keys and, when he arrived home after the pubs shut, he would smash the kitchen window to gain entry if no one answered the door immediately. Unfortunately, on more than one occasion he was so drunk that he also smashed the window that held the extractor fan. It cost about 10 times more to replace the window and fan rather than a plain window. Still, he would usually pay up without too much fuss once he was sober.

On one famous occasion James's outrageous behaviour almost caused his flatmates to burn to death. He had gone to bed drunk and fell asleep smoking a cigarette. At some point in the night, he woke up in discomfort from either the heat or the smoke and staggered down to the flat of a friend. This wasn't unusual – visitors often took up the beds in the flat and James would crash out on the friend's settee.

We were awoken by the fire brigade knocking on the door. Someone had reported a fire in our flat. Sure enough, James's mattress was emitting smoke and fumes. He was nowhere to be seen. The fireman threw the mattress over the balcony into the courtyard below. But where was James? Next morning he appeared as if nothing had happened, demanding to know why there was a burned mattress outside. Although he was often wild when drunk, James was an award-winning writer and he encouraged me to pursue my journalistic career.

The fashion house boss had paid for me to attend a day-release course at a typing and shorthand college and I also attended classes in the evening. James Dalrymple would set me homework that involved writing reports on the daily news items and give me dictation so I could improve my shorthand speed. Like the true professional he was, he never tired of encouraging a young recruit and inspiring a passion for the highest ideals of journalism and the crafts of writing and reporting. He was one of the best journalists and teachers I ever met.

My other career interest – modelling – was greatly aided by the neighbour whose couch James had slept on during the night of the fire. A famous casting director, she pointed me in the direction of London modelling agencies and even hired me for various television and cinema advertisements.

One that had a huge audience was an ad for Guinness. I had to walk past a bar where people were enjoying their Guinness and flick my hair over my shoulder as I passed. We rehearsed for a couple of days in an old church in Marylebone High Street and then, under the watchful eyes of several top Guinness executives, filmed the advert for hour after hour. The pints of Guinness had to be presented perfectly, with exactly the right proportion of white head and black body, and the male drinkers had to drink the right amount before I walked past. Finally, late on a Friday afternoon, the filming was finished and I realised why the job paid so well. The hours were long and exhausting.

For years afterwards, whenever the ad was shown on TV or at the cinema, I would excitedly point out to whoever was with me: 'There I am. Look. See me flicking my hair? That's me, that's me.'

Not quite the 15 minutes of fame promised by Andy Warhol, more like 15 seconds, but family and friends were impressed. (I did have an Andy Warhol moment when I met him at a nightclub. He stood in the doorway, languidly shaking hands and having a photograph taken with each person who arrived. That was another 15 seconds of fame.)

Doing the daily rounds of modelling agencies with a selection of photographs was tedious; it was made worse by often having to wait in line for hours without even being seen by anyone.

One agent with whom I had signed up had a cramped, dreary waiting room with a small hatch through which you could glimpse the everyday business of the agency unfolding. Bookers would hand out slips of paper through the hatch to despatch models to various castings. On a bad day you could sit all day and not be sent out. On a good day you might be sent miles away to a potential job, only to discover when you arrived that they had already selected the required models. The work quota was high and earnings low. Waiting for a big break or a glamorous job in an exotic location soon lost its attraction for me.

Meanwhile, at the flat, a dramatic situation was developing. A young woman had moved in; a practical and pretty schoolteacher who was another Scottish friend of a friend.

None of us knew at the time that the reason for her sudden departure from Scotland was that she was pregnant. It seems strange now, when more than half of babies are born to unmarried mothers, but back in the late 1960s there was still a stigma. Determined that her parents wouldn't find out, she had applied for a transfer to London to do some relief teaching. As her condition became more apparent, we all became protective of her. We looked forward to having a baby in the flat, although we hadn't worked out the practicalities or how the young lady would cope with not telling her parents that she had become a mum.

The day of the birth arrived and off she went to hospital. The proud father, who was still on the scene, came home to tell us that his girlfriend had given birth to a healthy baby boy. We all joined in the celebrations. However, visiting the new mum in hospital, it became clear that something wasn't right. The new parents avoided naming the baby and answering questions about long-term issues.

Finally, they spelled out the situation. The baby was to be adopted, but to comply with the legal requirements he had to be cared for at home for six weeks before he could go to his adoptive parents. How we ever got through those six weeks, I'll never know. Perhaps we naively thought that after six weeks of living with the baby the decision would be reversed. It wasn't, and on the day when the baby was collected by the authorities we were all in tears.

The girl returned home to Scotland, her parents none the wiser. But before she left, her boyfriend decided to make it up to her for having put her through her ordeal. His proposal of marriage was accepted and the flatmates had yet another excuse to party. Some months later, Gavin, James and I travelled to Scotland for a typical Highland wedding. The secret of the baby was never mentioned; that chapter was closed and the newlyweds settled back into the bosom of their proud families, vowing to live happily ever after. They didn't. Divorce was just a matter of time – and two more children – away.

God was certainly laughing on that occasion.

CHAPTER 5

LOVE AND MARRIAGE

L iving together was still considered daring and racy in the late 1960s, but Gavin decided it was time for us to get a place of our own. This we did just across the other side of Victoria Street, not far from Strutton Court. Our own little flat in a custom-built block looked out over Caxton Hall, the famous London registry office where many politicians and celebrities married.

It was less than a year before we were booking our own wedding there. Gavin and I had posed as a married couple to get the tenancy on our new flat and I always wore a wedding ring. Hotel bookings were always made as Mr and Mrs – they might refuse you a double room otherwise.

Now editor of *Disc*, Gavin's career continued to flourish and our social life was still a constant round of parties, premieres and receptions. We had also joined another social set: the cops and robbers who made up the clientele of the Grafton Arms in Strutton Ground in the shadow of New Scotland Yard.

The pub was famous as the former stomping ground of the Goons and had been owned and named after their manager, Jimmy Grafton. Many of the early *Goon Show* radio programmes were recorded in the attic of the Grafton Arms. Harry Secombe, Spike Milligan and Michael Bentine still visited the pub, though I never saw Peter Sellers there.

As regulars at the pub and friends of Fred, the current manager, the members of the in-crowd were encouraged to stay for 'afters'. After-hours drinking was a regular ritual that involved being invited by the landlord to stay as his personal guest. No money for drinks was supposed to change hands, and, in the spirit of cooperation between landlord and the police, serving officers were often among the 'invited guests'.

One evening, around midnight, Fred opened the door in response to frantic knocking, expecting to find late arrivals. Instead, he was confronted by uniformed policemen looking to catch after-hours drinkers. Fortunately, we were all schooled in the rules of the game and, when asked if we had paid for our drinks, insisted, 'No. We're guests of the landlord' – all of us except one crusty old gent called Leo who always kept himself to himself. When asked what he was drinking, he replied, 'That's very kind of you, officer. I'll have a Guinness please.' No charges were ever brought.

Having become particular friends with one of the Scotland Yard detectives, I accepted his invitation to the Swallow Club in the West End. The detective was a contact of James Dalrymple, who was still working as a crime reporter on the *Daily Express*. I managed to convince Gavin and myself that I was visiting the club in the line of duty as a trainee crime buster. As it happens, I got a better story than I could have dreamed of.

The club was a smart, sophisticated cabaret club. Dressed up to the nines and enjoying the attention of my own personal detective, I was halfway through a sumptuous dinner when he was called to the phone: a murder on his patch. Within minutes, a squad car arrived at the front door of the club and off we set for the scene of the crime. Feeling like a femme fatale straight out of a Raymond Chandler novel, I sat in evening dress in the back of the squad car outside the home where a murder had been committed.

It was 'a domestic', an open-and-shut case that needed no great detective skills, according to my escort. We were back at the club and finishing our dinner in little more than an hour. Just another night in the city.

I phoned James and gave him the story, and the next day I compared the report he had written with my original first-person piece. He paid me well for tip-offs – knowing the right people meant I was often on the inside track of breaking news.

One story that I passed on to him and that made the front page of the *Daily Express* nearly got me into serious trouble. Being between jobs, I had started temping for an agency and had been working at a government department for some weeks when I got access to a big news story.

According to one of my colleagues, a local builder called Frank Thorogood was likely to be charged with the murder some years earlier of Brian Jones of The Rolling Stones. I passed the story to James. Even today, the death of Brian Jones in a swimming pool at his Surrey home remains a mystery. Thorogood was never charged but the rumour mill still turns out accusations periodically.

James thought I had given him an even bigger scoop the day I called him to report that John Lennon had been murdered. In his excitement he failed to hear me mention that I had read it on an *Evening Standard* billboard.

Over the years, there have been many times when my loyalty

has been divided over what to report in the press. Unless an individual was talking off the record for a very specific or personal reason and they made that clear, my inclination and professional judgement have always come down on the side of journalism. Although many things have happened over the years to change the way newspapers are viewed – and much of their recent bad press is their own fault – I was proud to call myself a journalist. I took the view that it was my job to discover and report what was going on in the world.

Life in the pop music fast lane continued. We attended almost every pop concert and festival going and saw performances by practically every big group of the time. We were also among a privileged audience invited to a rare non-appearance by John Lennon and Yoko Ono – they writhed about inside a sack for almost an hour while we watched film of them naked, singing songs from their new album, *Two Virgins*.

Legendary performances by stars such as The Who, David Bowie and Chuck Berry, appearances by The Osmonds, The Jackson Five and The Carpenters, and musical high jinks in the strange shape of Tiny Tim were weekly occurrences.

When The Osmonds visited *Disc*'s offices, girls watching the Lord Mayor's Show got a shock on looking up and seeing their favourite pop group happily waving to them and the Lord Mayor. The girls were screaming, crying and passing up autographs for the band to sign. The Bay City Rollers was another group that featured large in our work and social lives at that time; as Edinburgh boys, Gavin had known the guys and their manager, Tom Paton, back in their home town.

I still treasure my memories of evenings spent sitting in a theatre green room as part of David Bowie's inner circle, gazing at him, fascinated by his eyes – one blue and one brown. He was always welcoming and hospitable, and we visited him backstage after various London shows. In his later incarnations as Ziggy Stardust and The Man Who Fell to Earth, he personified for me a towering theatrical celestial being. His presence was other-worldly, while his down-to-earth, easy-going nature was a credit to his ordinariness. He was – and still is – a bright, shining star. I had a huge crush on Bowie and still do. Gavin agreed I could leave home and run off with him if David ever suggested it. He never did. What's the supermodel Iman got that I haven't got? Don't answer that!

One raucous night in the Grafton Arms, a young Frenchman claiming to be a ship's captain said that he had the power to marry people and Gavin and I agreed that he should give us his blessing. Many people in the pub were surprised to learn that we weren't already legally man and wife, and the idea gained momentum. On 4 April 1970, when I had just turned 20 and Gavin was about to celebrate his twenty-eighth birthday, we married for real.

Caxton Hall was a wonderful place to be married. Although a registry office, it had a certain kudos being a place where many celebrities and politicians got married; it was impressive outside and ornately decorative inside. And, being literally on our doorstep, we had no need of wedding cars.

It was our big day and we decided how it was to be conducted; in many aspects the wedding was thoroughly modern, with tradition and fashion subtly blended. Gavin designed the wedding invitations himself, our families – aside from parents – were not invited, and the official wedding photographer was a press photographer engaged to take candid rather than formal shots.

Our old friend James Dalrymple was Gavin's best man and a

friend from my Glasgow days, Janis, was my matron of honour. The wedding party comprised of only some dozen people, although we did have a reception for a hundred or so guests at the Grafton Arms.

Gavin, somewhat the worse for wear, attempted to carry me over the threshold on our wedding night, but sadly there wasn't room for us both to get through the narrow doorway of the sleeping compartment on the midnight train from King's Cross to Edinburgh.

We were to spend our honeymoon in Gavin's parent's home on the outskirts of Edinburgh. As we emerged from a taxi at the neat maisonette in a quiet, respectable street, my case flew open depositing frilly underwear all over the street. We hardly needed a 'Just married' sign in this land of winceyette pyjamas – the negligees were a dead giveaway.

Chilly as it was up there even at that time of year, I persevered with floating around in chiffon, even if we did need to huddle close to the open fire to keep warm. Gavin's mum had baked us a wedding cake with a little bride and groom on the top and thoughtfully left out glasses and a bottle of champagne. Feasting on wedding cake and champagne, I decided that married life had a lot to commend it.

We were entertained by Gavin's Scottish friends as the visiting honeymooners and during the trip we made a trip to visit a property that had been left to Gavin's mother and aunt by his grandmother when she died. The whitewashed stone-built cottage was in a small village halfway between Glasgow and Edinburgh. It was badly in need of decoration and modernisation but we loved its rustic charm. As a wedding present, Gavin's mother bequeathed the cottage to Gavin when she passed on, but the aunt lived well into her nineties, by which time Gavin and I were long since divorced.

Still, the cottage became a favourite place for holidays and Gavin even talked of moving back to Scotland when he tired of life in London. He had big plans for the cottage. However, it's a true saying: if you want to make God laugh, tell him your plans. Within six months of getting married, we were on the move – but to Kent, not Scotland.

London friends Margie and Colin had bought a house in the commuter town of Beckenham. On a warm, sunny weekend, Gavin and I made the journey from Victoria to Beckenham – 20 minutes door to door, as people always tell you when they want to persuade you that moving out of town is a good idea.

Lunch in the garden, a stroll to the local pub down a tree-lined road and waking up to the sound of birdsong convinced us that we too needed to take the commuter special and improve our quality of life. Within weeks we had our foot firmly on the first rung of the property ladder and were living next door to our friends in a brand new two-storey housing association maisonette with a turreted ceiling, spiral staircase and all mod cons.

It was a perfect place for two newlyweds and we threw ourselves with enthusiasm into decorating and furnishing our first marital home. The decor was modern and minimalist in pine and polished wood with functional hessian wall coverings and bright orange carpets, all straight out of *Ideal Home*. Gavin was accomplished at do-it-yourself, a skill he had learned from his father, and I loved the art of combining fabrics and colours to give a bright, fashionable and individual feel to the house.

Starting a family was never really on our agenda. Gavin had been an only child and was quite self-sufficient. My reasons for not wanting children were more complex, but I persuaded myself that I was a thoroughly modern career woman who, thanks to the contraceptive pill, had no need to be tied down with children at an early age.

Our parents often pointed out that they would like to be grandparents. They didn't put too much pressure on us, just subtle hints and occasional references to the fact that they weren't getting any younger. We didn't succumb to their emotional blackmail. There was plenty of time for babies later when we were established financially and secure in our careers. God was listening again to those plans – and laughing.

Neither Gavin nor I were ever to know the joys of parenthood. I didn't know how much I would come to regret our decision to wait, but we had no doubts at the time. With the arrogance of youth, we took the view that we were in charge of our own destiny. Everything was working out beautifully.

Those were happy times. We were in love and enjoying ourselves. Building a home and a life together was satisfying and exciting. Being part of a small, young community meant that we had a readymade supply of friends and our social life was full and varied.

Most weekends one of the young couples in the small close of some 30 houses would throw a party and there were plenty of dinners and lunch invitations. Warming to my role as young wife, I bought stacks of cookery books and developed a few tried and tested menus with which I could, if not impress, at least satisfy visiting friends and neighbours.

Gavin's job meant that we were still regulars at pop festivals such as the Isle of Wight, though they were generally less comfortable than I would have liked. Wet, cold and exhausting, in the middle of a muddy field, I prayed that Jimi Hendrix would wrap up his seemingly never-ending solo (he played for over three hours). To the spellbound audience, some of whom still talk of his performance that day as an epiphany, he was God. To me it was, 'Oh, God, get me get of here.'

Although Gavin and I, along with the rest of the music

journalists, would stay in nearby hotels, it was part of the job to be on-site for hours as the less well known bands played, often into the early hours of the morning. Record company hospitality revolved around marquees serving continuous free food and drink, so there was always somewhere warm and dry to escape to when the going got tough.

Superstars went even further in their search for luxury. Mick Jagger and his first wife Bianca had three caravans on-site: one for sleeping, one for wardrobe and makeup and one for socialising. Bianca would strut into the press enclosure at the front of the quarter million-strong crowd looking stunning. No wonder – she had a travelling circus of hairdressers, makeup artists and wardrobe assistants. How the other half live!

The rest of us, even those with the coveted 'Press – access all areas' pass, were often knee-deep in mud and cold, tired and battle weary. Of course, the drink and drugs consumed might also have contributed to our debilitated state. Release, the drugs charity, always had trained helpers on duty for the poor unfortunates who ended up spaced out, fucked up or on bad trips.

Smoking pot, and perhaps dropping some recreational speed, was the most that I and the crowd I mixed with got involved in. Alcohol tended to be our drug of choice. Champagne was usually on tap in the hospitality tent and we drank freely as we interviewed superstars and partied with the big name performers. Some of them became friends – or at least as close as journalists and those they write about ever get.

I was a late starter in the drinking stakes, but once I got the taste for alcohol there was no stopping me. Until I was 19, I was the butt of many jokes because of being teetotal. However, when I had been away from home long enough to forget why I didn't drink – I drank. On one occasion, staggering down our quiet country road in Beckenham after midnight with Margie from next door, we stopped to light our cigarettes from a works traffic lantern. As we struggled to open the catch, a police car pulled up. The kindly coppers offered us a lift home, where we invited them in for a drink. They declined alcohol as they were on duty, but they accepted a coffee and then left.

It was all quite innocent. And full marks to the police for delivering us home safe and sound. However, we agreed it was probably best not to tell our husbands, who were both away, about our late-night guests. We didn't count on a dramatic development.

The next day at work, Margie rang me in a panic. A local policeman had been arrested on suspicion of murdering his wife. He was one of our good Samaritans. We lived in fear of a knock at the door until the investigation was complete; he was charged, and we weren't implicated in any way. Of course, we really hadn't been involved, but the fact that we had sat drinking coffee with a wife murderer made us look very carefully at who we invited into our homes from then on.

The wild behaviour continued. On one occasion, while Gavin slept, I wandered next door late at night. A young trendy couple, our neighbours were friends of David Bowie, who had been brought up in the Bromley area a few miles from our new home. I had met Bowie for the first time with them long before he became famous; he was still performing his mime act at the time.

On this particular evening they had a hairdresser friend staying overnight. Somehow it seemed a good idea for me to have a change of image from my current dark blonde. 'Chop the lot off,' I told the girl. And she did just that. We all agreed it looked great, but my hair needed a stronger colour to carry off the new shorter cut.

'Make sure it's noticeable,' I urged her as she mixed the red henna in a metal bowl. 'Leave it on for an hour at least.'

While the hair colour developed we sat around on cushions,

drinking, smoking, talking and listening to music. At dawn I crept back home, unlocked the front door, tiptoed up the stairs and climbed into bed beside Gavin. The next morning, when he woke up, he let out a shout when he saw my short red hair. He had gone to bed the evening before, leaving me watching TV. The next morning, a transformation. And to the best of his knowledge I hadn't strayed from the house.

Boredom often set in when I was left alone, late at night. Children's paints left behind by a young niece provided the inspiration for one late-night scheme. In multicoloured paint, I wrote over the newly decorated white walls 'I Love You'. Gavin didn't love me when he saw it but I couldn't really see what all the fuss was about.

He and I had a huge row and I accused him of being a fuddy-duddy with no sense of humour or romance. I knew that accusing him of lacking romance would hurt. As a Scottish, Protestant, only child, Gavin had never really learned how to express his feelings. Not that he didn't try. He composed a love song that he proudly played to me on the guitar. As I recall, it went: 'I'm waiting for the sun to go down, I'm waiting for the stars to shine, I'm waiting for the right time to tell you I love you.' It's not easy for me to remember the words, as he played the song to me only once. It seems I smiled in the wrong place, he thought I was laughing at him, and he refused to ever play the song again.

Getting him to say 'I love you' was like drawing teeth. 'I show it,' he would say. 'When I'm out and there's a thunderstorm, I rush home in case you're frightened. When I hear a new record I get excited about, I can't wait to share it with you. When I cook a meal I know you'll enjoy – all these things show I love you. A hundred times a day in different ways, I show my love for you.'

Why couldn't he just say those three little words? He was

right, of course, he had always loved me. I knew that. What I didn't know then was that I was the one incapable of showing love. Saying 'I love you' was easy.

Returning from a trip to the South of France for a music media festival, my husband presented me with a bottle of Chanel No. 19. He delighted in telling me how much trouble the saleswoman in the French *perfumerie* had gone to make sure that he bought the correct Chanel number for his beloved wife. 'Describe her to me,' said the saleswoman. 'Is she blonde or brunette, tall or petite, curvy or slender? Is she fun or sophisticated?' Gavin shared with me the description that had led to him being allowed to purchase No. 19. 'She's slim and beautiful with long dark blonde hair and I love her.'

A whiff of Chanel No. 19 still transports me back some 40 years. My husband was telling me he loved me, but I couldn't hear it. Not yet married two years, I had already started looking for other male conquests to make me feel loved.

Women and drink can be a dangerous combination, especially where men are concerned. The deep fears and insecurities that already drove me made it almost inevitable that I would be unfaithful. Desperate to prove myself worthy, I got the only validation I could through men. The love 'em and leave 'em attitude I had adopted to guard against being hurt served to keep me enslaved for years.

The fact that I was a married woman didn't totally escape my notice, but even though my encounters weren't all sexual, they were usually amorous. I loved to flirt and be the centre of attention. Showing off was second nature to me. Other women's husbands, boyfriends or partners were never safe when I was around and, like many women who claim to prefer the company of men, it is probably more accurate to say that I didn't know how to be loyal to women friends. Or to a husband.

LOVE AND MARRIAGE

Shortly after getting married I landed a job on the 'agony aunt' problem page of *Woman's Own*. Although only a selection was printed in the magazine, we answered every one of the 1,000 letters that arrived every week and I specialised in young people's problems. One day the medical adviser, a dynamic health campaigner called Claire Rayner, was visiting the offices and made me the target of her advice. 'If you want to be a writer, go out and do it. Don't get stuck here in a safe job playing at journalism.'

I took her advice to heart and by the end of the month I had handed in my notice and left to make a name for myself instead of labouring in someone else's shadow. Years later, when she and I appeared on a TV show, Claire was touched and delighted when I told her about the part she had played in my subsequent career.

My next port of call was a specialist publication called *Australian Outlook* that reached its target audience through the good offices of Australia House and the Australian banks and state offices in London. I never got to visit Australia but through the pages of the magazine I practised and refined my writing, subediting and newspaper production skills. As part of a tiny editorial team, I had plenty of responsibility, for 'putting the paper to bed' at the printers.

Newspaper ink was now running in my blood. I had found my true vocation. A journalist married to a journalist.

Gavin and I made regular trips to visit his parents, Jimmy and Bella, on the outskirts of Edinburgh. Mum tended house and baked; dad looked after the garden and his prize roses. Their quiet, ordered life was as far away as you can get from my raucous family set-up.

Although polite, Jimmy was a man of few words. Gavin's

mum liked to embarrass him by telling the story that they had been married for over five years before her husband told his friends in the pub. When one of his friends remarked that he had bumped into Bella in town and he might invite her to the pictures, Jimmy reluctantly told him, 'I'm married to the lassie and we've got a wee boy.' He always claimed that the subject had just never come up.

During one of their infrequent trips to London, we were walking through Soho after seeing *Jesus Christ Superstar* when Jimmy disappeared into a doorway. Reappearing, he told us he had been worried about the safety of a 'poor wee lassie' who had left her front door ajar, so he had thoughtfully closed it for her. A handwritten note, prominently displayed on the door, read 'Model 1st Floor'. Jimmy still did not understand the situation and remonstrated with us. 'You never know who might be wandering in there,' he told us with genuine concern. He failed to realise that he had effectively put a young lady out of business for the night.

Gavin's mother, Isabella, known to all as Bella, was a dignified and charming lady, conservatively dressed and softly spoken, with small neat features and ready smile. Her hair had already turned a silvery grey by the time I met her, but a formal portrait of her younger self playing at a piano recital showed a beautiful girl in pearls with dark, wavy hair and graceful hands. She always reminded me of the schoolgirls in the classic Dame Maggie Smith film *The Prime of Miss Jean Brodie*.

Decades after her son Gavin and I were divorced, Bella and I still continued to meet up for afternoon tea in posh Edinburgh hotels. Right up to her death in a care home in the 1990s, when Derek Jameson and I were presenting our nightly Radio 2 show from Glasgow, I would go to visit her and we always exchanged cards and flowers on birthdays and Christmas.

Only shortly before she died did she reveal that she had never told Gavin, now long since remarried, or her husband Jimmy that we had maintained contact.

After Gavin and I announced our separation, Bella wrote me a brief, sad letter admitting that she and his father were devastated. There had never been a divorce in their families.

'I cannot help but blame myself,' she wrote, 'for as much as I loved my only son, Gavin, I was never able to reach out to him emotionally or even tell him I loved him. I am sure it must have been very hard for you to have a husband who could not express his emotions.'

It certainly explained a lot about Gavin. I still have the last birthday card he sent me before our permanent split; while I craved romance, he chose a card that said 'To A Good Sport' and had a picture of a footballer on the front. He claimed it was a joke. I wasn't laughing. The marriage was over.

Before my doubts and fears about the marriage took root, Gavin and I did achieve a level of marital satisfaction and we both took pride in making a home together. While we were newly married and still in our happy honeymoon phase, we had times of domestic bliss. Curled up together on the settee, watching television, I found a degree of contentment. I had all I had ever wanted: a modern home, enough money to furnish it and a husband who I never doubted loved me and I knew to be loyal and dependable. He was good for me, a stabilising influence.

With hindsight, I can see clearly the part I played in failing to make the marriage work; I find it less easy to see where he failed. Coming from my dysfunctional family background with severely flawed role models for parents and marriage partners, I had little emotional maturity or concept of compromise that would allow me to build a solid foundation for a long-lasting relationship.

Conflict was the order of the day in my family, with all emotions riding a rollercoaster of extremes. When there was a truce in the ongoing war between my parents, there were sweet periods of love and harmony, but they rarely lasted long. My solution to disagreement was to pack a bag and leave home. In my view, the grass was always greener on the other side.

Gavin was very different. He had probably never heard his parents arguing. Jimmy laid down the law and Bella complied, like a good wife. He was an emotional lightweight who buried his head in the sand, walked away from an argument and found peace away from a nagging, unhappy wife by tending his vegetable patch or knocking in a few nails. Gavin was well-liked and a very sociable character. As an only child, he had overcome any feelings of loneliness by developing the ability to make and keep friends, and our home was a gathering place for his old school friends, work colleagues and fellow musicians.

He was also supportive of me professionally and encouraged me to pursue my ambitions in journalism. He offered his expertise by editing and helping me research features I was commissioned to write on a freelance basis for various magazines, newspapers and publications.

As Gavin and I began our third year of marriage, I committed myself to building up freelance opportunities. I had already been commissioned by *News of the World* for several features and on one occasion they sent me to Cornwall – an eight-hour journey on public transport – for a half-hour interview about 'pyramid selling', a practice that was illegal.

The job of journalists in those days of high expenses and large editorial staffs was all about face-to-face interviewing. Phone interviews were considered a very poor substitute for actually meeting and getting to know a person. Certainly, it is much easier to establish rapport and get people to talk freely when you are sitting opposite them, often sharing a meal or at least a cup of tea.

Having finished my interview with a farm worker who had

been fleeced by the pyramid selling scheme, I couldn't get a bus out of town till the next day. So, from Cornwall, I took a taxi to visit James Dalrymple and his wife Maggie, who were now living and working in Plymouth. It cost about £30 – more than a week's wages.

We spent a companionable evening in their local pub and I travelled home on the milk train overnight to London, scaring myself and jumping out of my seat at the slightest noise or creak as I sat alone in a first-class carriage reading Edgar Allan Poe horror stories. I loved tales of the 'world beyond'.

As well as working hard on establishing a freelance career, my new 'must-have experience' was to get 'The Knowledge' from the Guru Maharaja Ji. We all knew how The Beatles' lives had been transformed by an Indian holy man, but the one I chose to prostrate myself before was later investigated as 'a fraud'. He was undoubtedly a self-promoter who persuaded followers to hand over their life savings to his religious order while he enjoyed a life of fabulous wealth in the United States. There, he was chauffeured around in a gold Rolls-Royce wearing priceless jewellery and was venerated by his poor, trusting disciples to whom he had promised spiritual enlightenment.

Some of my friends, seeking a spiritual path, had become followers through an ashram in north London. I became a 'seeker'. We sat for hours in temples listening to 'satsang'; attendance was a prerequisite for receiving a coveted invitation to the ashram, where, for the chosen few, the Guru would make a personal appearance – in spirit at least – and bestow enlightenment. I particularly looked forward to the promised 'sacred nectar' that I would taste in my throat as the divine entered me and I gained 'The Knowledge'.

My best friend Ann, with whom I had worked on a magazine, seemed to be most impressed by the ability to 'conjure up' a taxi in central London at will. She left her husband, sold all her possessions and gave the proceeds to the Guru's spiritual foundation. Last I heard, she had gone off on a quest to India. I sincerely hope she found peace and enlightenment. I certainly tried hard enough to achieve it. Every day for three weeks I attended the ashram, which was near Alexandra Palace, a long journey from my home in Beckenham, Kent, and was in place on my prayer mat straight after breakfast. We also had to bring gifts of fruit or flowers and present them by bowing to the garishly coloured and garlanded photograph of the Guru. With the other novices, I was required to sit for up to 10 hours in a bare room with nothing to distract our attention, in silence, praying and waiting for the Mahatma, who would pass on 'The Knowledge'. The Guru himself was now a little too highly elevated and world famous to undertake trips to local ashrams in terraced houses in north London.

After three weeks, I overslept one day and in my absence the Mahatma appeared and passed the gift of 'The Knowledge' to all my fellow disciples, who instantly became enlightened. One of them told me, in the spirit of love and compassion, that I had been preventing the energy from coming through as I was suspected of not adhering to the strict discipline of no alcohol, no smoking, no eating meat and no sex. I'm not sure which part I had failed to uphold – truth is, it may have been all of them. It was a sad day for me as I really did need a spiritual crutch and I continued to search for one for many years.

However, one enduring legacy of that experience was that I learned to meditate, an invaluable practice that I have continued for all my adult life. I meditate every day, and over the years I have taken courses in transcendental meditation and have studied advanced meditation techniques. It certainly quietens my mind and allows me to get some clarity on life, even in the midst of excessive turmoil. I may not always appear cool, calm and collected, but I do cherish an inner tranquility and a strong belief in a deeper inspirational source from which I draw peace and strength.

In the strange, seemingly random way that things happen in life, some years later I was roller skating along Hollywood Beach in Florida when I ran into a group of people who invited me to visit them in a brightly painted blue house I had never noticed before at the northern end of the promenade. They excitedly explained that they were on a spiritual quest and awaiting 'The Knowledge' from the Guru Maharaja Ji. I didn't accept their invitation, even though by then my life was free of smoking, drinking and eating red meat – and I could even have complied with the no sex rule.

Through the years, my quest for spiritual enlightenment has been fulfilled, sometimes in the most magical and life-changing ways. I now accept that I am a spiritual being living a human existence. I truly believe that no experience is ever wasted; they all lead eventually to the path we are destined to follow.

I am pleased to call myself a spiritual Gnostic – the opposite of agnostic. The ancient religion of Gnosticism proclaims the believers' 'knowledge' that there is a higher level of existence. They never doubt or question the existence of supreme beings and higher spiritual experience.

One of my next ports of call for the spiritual enlightenment that I already believed to exist was a wonderful meditation and healing centre. This was run by one of the most spiritual people I have ever had the privilege to know, my friend and mentor Lee Everett-Alkin, a medium, healer and former wife of both 1960s pop star Billy Fury and zany comedian Kenny Everett.

At Lee's sanctuary, 'House of Spirit' in Artesian Road, west London, I found my spiritual home. Lee and I have been friends for over 30 years now, and even though the miles and years often keep us apart, there is a deep and unending connection with this lady in my heart.

We first met when I was sent by a newspaper to interview Lee. She was still married to Kenny Everett and their lives were inextricably linked, even though the two lived in separate houses in the same street in Notting Hill Gate. After the death of Billy Fury, Lee had married Kenny, knowing that he was gay. She tolerated his boyfriends and was a mother figure and his best friend almost up to his death from AIDS in the 1980s, although the two fell out regularly.

Lee was already living with the man who was to become her third husband, John Alkin, a tall, handsome blonde-haired actor who had parts in the television series *Z Cars* and various films. The odd arrangement was known to all of Lee, Kenny and John's friends, but it was many years before any member of the inner circle would break their silence and admit that the Everett marriage was a sham. That was a testament to Lee, who was always fiercely protective of Kenny and John. John understood Lee's strange fascination with Kenny, who was always getting himself into scraps with gay lovers. In fact, when the real story came out it was through one of Kenny's ex-boyfriends.

Even though I was a journalist, I chose to concentrate on the story I had been sent to cover: Lee's involvement in the 'world beyond'. I always believed that when the time was right, I would be first in line to get a scoop on the Everett marriage and have exclusive interviews. When the story did break, in the early 1980s, I was despatched by the *News of the World* to confront Lee and John on their boat, which was moored in the Thames. They graciously posed for a photograph to illustrate the story 'Kenny's Wife Flees with Lover' after the story broke.

Kenny would not agree to an exclusive interview; the

consequences of the story could have had a hugely adverse effect on his BBC television career and his publicists had not yet worked out how to deal with it.

On television and in private, Kenny was a hellraiser, a party animal who loved excess and set out to shock and cause chaos. One Halloween, I was invited by Lee to a party at the countryside home of a fabulously wealthy songwriter. We had to drive miles down country roads in pitch-blackness and it was a wonder we ever found the house, mansion-sized as it was.

In keeping with tradition, I and most of the other female guests were dressed as witches. With neon blue hair, a short leather miniskirt, plenty of cleavage and fishnet stockings with suspenders, I expected to attract plenty of attention. However, the main attraction of the evening was the outrageous costume worn by Kenny. He had been made up by the makeup department at BBC Television Centre, where he was filming one of his hugely successful series at the time. His character for the evening was a road crash victim. His ripped clothes, face and hair were blood-soaked and he was covered in cuts and bruises with fake glass sticking crazily out of bright red gashes. The effect was terrifyingly real. The partygoers, most of whom were used to Kenny's flamboyant behaviour, loved the joke and reacted enthusiastically. Then they went on with the party.

Kenny craved more attention, and so a few of us agreed to make our way down the dark lane to the local pub. The reactions of the drinkers there raised the roof and, satisfied that he had achieved the degree of horror he had anticipated, Kenny led the gruesome crew back up the lane. But he had one more trick up his sleeve. Despite all our protestations that we were likely to be arrested, he insisted on lying down in the middle of the road, forcing any passing car to slam on their brakes and making them think they were witnessing a genuine road accident. The story would have made all the front pages, but as the only journalist there I was sworn to secrecy. The party photographs still survive and it is obvious that we were all having an extremely raucous time. There was one other famous face among the party guests: entrepreneur Richard Branson had come dressed as a red devil. He chased every girl in the party, threatening them with his long red tail and claiming to be looking for virgins. I don't know if he found any that night, but he certainly had plenty of success with his Virgin company over the coming years. His airline colours always remind me of that bright red costume he wore to the Halloween party. He always did have an eye for the best branding concepts – and for great photo opportunities.

That party is a perfect illustration of the paradox that was Lee. She was deeply spiritual and committed to her healing work at 'House of Spirit' and the meditation circles that she conducted, but she was also a fun-loving Yorkshire girl who enjoyed a laugh, a drink and a good time.

Professional and personal lives were kept pretty separate and she refused to allow 'House of Spirit' to be polluted by smoking, excessive drinking or too much party spirit. In fact, the smell that most often pervaded the pretty four-storey town house was that of home-cooked soup and shepherd's pie.

Lee was a passionate cook. Having started out by bulk cooking and freezing ready-meals for her husband Kenny, she then began making them commercially and now owns a factory producing her own range under the name 'ChilliQueen'. That is as well as running a highly acclaimed educational establishment, Obsidian College, which teaches and trains therapists, doctors and healers in the spiritual arts.

Sitting in a meditation circle was an education in itself for me, and it was through an informal intervention on the part of

Lee that I eventually gave up drinking and achieved long-term sobriety. Lee had watched many friends in show business go through the stages of addiction and many of them got well. She encouraged me to do the same.

It was after a weekend visit to their riverside house in Berkshire, when she and John took Derek and me out on their boat on the Thames, that I finally realised how out of control my drinking had become. When we got home, Derek told me that I had rowed with Lee. I wouldn't believe it. I had always looked up to her and would never think of arguing with her. Lee was gracious and tried to spare my feelings, but she admitted that there had been a falling out and it might be time for me to get help. It hurt and upset me to think that I had let her down – and within 48 hours of that incident, I had given up drinking for good.

The deep bond that Lee and I shared wasn't just friendship; part of Lee's spiritual expertise, acknowledged worldwide through her work with Obsidian College, lies in her ability to regress people to former lives.

As a believer in reincarnation, I had been regressed many times by Lee. By experiencing different former lives and working through some of my problems and issues in those lives, I believe I was eventually able to tackle the problems that were destroying my life at the time. Through regression I was restored, healed and helped to recovery. I also believe Lee's conviction that she and I have travelled many lives together. I believe I lived through many reincarnations with Lee and was one of the close-knit circle of her friends and acolytes in this life who had been nuns together in past times.

One of the most amazing and unforgettable experiences played out at a regular weekly meditation circle at the House of Spirit. A blind man turned up at the house, saying that a voice had guided him there and had told him that Lee would heal his soul. In a past life, Lee had been a nun during the Spanish Inquisition, and when she placed her hands on him she clearly saw that he had been the soldier who had tortured her. He began sobbing and said that he wanted to ask for forgiveness – that was the healing he had come for.

My fascination and connection with the psychic world continued and I was privileged to work with the wonderful medium Doris Stokes. Already in her sixties before she made her huge media breakthrough, Doris was an old-school spiritualist. As a result of a newspaper article, she gained a worldwide following and sold millions of books about her *Voices in My Ear* (the title of her autobiography), appeared on television shows and performed in front of record-breaking audiences on stages all over Britain and Australia.

Our friendship began when Derek and I met Doris at a press reception and she invited us to the launch of one of her books. Sometime later, we went to see her but builders were making a terrible noise and she said she wouldn't be able to concentrate for a sitting. I didn't really mind, but then Doris suddenly asked me if my mother's name was Amy, as she thought she was with us in the flat. She also talked about my father being in the RAF and mentioned various family names. When we got home, I discussed the visit with Derek and we decided that either Doris was genuine or she had been checking up on me, which seemed extremely unlikely.

I had tried to contact mum before, so this made me very happy. Many mediums are a bit vague, but Doris always gave those extra details that made it all so positive. Now that I knew mum was alright and was still looking out for me, I felt that a chapter of my life had ended.

When I first met Doris, she had said, 'You could be a good

medium. I'll have you on the platform working within a year!' And she was partly right: on her national theatre tour, I acted as her chairman, introducing her from the platform and coordinating communication between members of the audience and Doris.

There was one time in Newcastle when she asked me to sort the letters she always received wherever she was appearing. I had to divide them into those that needed a reply, those for an appointment, and so on. After a while, I said to her, 'This job must break your heart sometimes. Some of those letters are almost too tragic to read.'

Doris immediately responded, 'Oh, you're talking about the little black girl with plaits and beads in her hair.' I was – but Doris hadn't seen any of the letters. She told me that the girl, who had been murdered, was actually sitting next to me. The letter was from the girl's mother, who wanted to see Doris. From the huge bundle of letters that she hadn't read, Doris had picked up on this tragic story. That was all the evidence I needed.

Travelling with Doris was like being on a rock tour. Her management company always supplied limousines for her to make a grand entrance into cities where she was performing and she would stay at the best hotels, attended by her entourage of publicists, managers, journalists, friends and hangers-on.

Hotel staff would queue up at the door of her suite hoping for a reading, a private word or reassurance from Doris that 'your loved one is close by'. She never rested and was always doing sittings.

Doris helped people see that their loved ones were okay, so there was no reason to mourn. Just as she had for me, she gave people back their lives.

CHAPTER 6

I DON'T WANT TO TALK ABOUT IT

'All human life is here': that was the strapline of *News of the World*. As an investigative reporter for the biggest selling newspaper in the world (it had a circulation of 6 million), I certainly got to see life. In those days, *News of the World* specialised in major investigations that often lasted many months, and once I had become a regular on its editorial teams, I was involved in more and more of its undercover work.

At the time, Corin Redgrave, a member of one of Britain's leading acting dynasties and brother of Vanessa and Lynn Redgrave, led the Workers Revolutionary Party, a left-wing reactionary force composed mostly of middle-class would-be class warriors. This meant that he attracted the attention of *News of the World* executives – 'reds under the bed' was a recurring theme in the days before the Berlin Wall came down and the Cold War ended.

After the expulsion of some Russian spies posing as diplomats in 1972 and the legendary headlines 'Reds sail in the sunset' and

'Booked any good reds lately?', I was taken on as part of the undercover team who were to infiltrate the Workers Revolutionary Party.

Like many fanatical groups, they were anxious to recruit new members to their cause and gaining access to their meetings was relatively easy. In a room in a south London pub, I got talking to some members who were only too happy to discuss the organisation and its beliefs and aims.

Armed with copies of a socialist newspaper and *Anarchy Today*, I infiltrated the inner circle and was soon accepted as a potential recruit. Initiation seemed to involve reading long tracts from boring communist manifestos and drinking beer while regurgitating Marxist propaganda.

For several weeks I had been attending meetings and socialising, all the time keeping a taxi with its meter running outside the pub in case of trouble. A breakthrough came when I was invited to a weekend camp to be held in a farmer's field somewhere in Derbyshire. The details of the location were to be kept secret, but Corin Redgrave had bought a property in Parwich, Derbyshire, called White Meadows Villa, which became known as 'The Red House' and training camps were held there. There, I was assured, I would hear inside reports of planned subversive activities from the man himself, Corin.

My source, a young, intense, scruffily dressed male student, got quite excited as he outlined the kind of inflammatory material we were due to be presented with at the camp. Roles would be allotted to allow us to infiltrate ourselves into the wider society in time for the coming revolution. Having always believed that the first ones to be shot in the revolution would be the soft-handed intellectuals, I worried about my pampered pals who had obviously never done a day's work.

Working undercover is exciting, unpredictable, and scares the life out of you at times. You have to be prepared for anything, able to think on your feet and conscious at all times of the role you are playing. Acting skills are required.

Having travelled up to Derbyshire by train, first class and with a four-course dining car silver service meal, at the station I joined up with some of the others on their way to the camp. Stupidly, it hadn't occurred to me that there would be comrades on the train from London. Arousing suspicion at this early stage in the proceedings could be dangerous and counter-productive. I hoped that they hadn't seen me on the train and that it had been crowded enough to make it feasible that we had all been in the same carriage without noticing each other.

I had dressed casually, and warmly, for the upcoming outdoor adventure, and as a compromise had retained my best three-quarter-length cashmere coat. Gold packets of Benson & Hedges cigarettes and an expensive Cartier lighter might have attracted unnecessary attention, so I had switched brands to something less conspicuous and had bought a couple of throwaway lighters.

We were met at the station by a Che Guevara lookalike in a transit van. On the journey to the camp, he regaled us foot soldiers with tales of derring-do from other theatres of war. Warming to his theme, and obviously out to impress his audience of rookies, he started to tell us about his biggest triumph. He claimed to have beaten up two journalists who had attempted to infiltrate the camp the previous day, and one of them apparently was still in hospital with a broken arm.

Fear gripped me. I was on my way to a field in the middle of nowhere with no transport and no means of communicating with the outside world (no mobile phones in those days). For all our London meetings, I had had my trusty cab driver standing by. Now, when my personal safety may well be at risk, I was defenceless.

What to do? Should I feign illness and ask to be allowed home? Was the story of the attack on journalists true? If so, what paper were they from? Had my cover been blown? I had to brazen it out. Denouncing newspaper scum with the rest, I tried to find out just what was the truth of the story.

Security was tight on the camp and we were informed that we would need to be escorted between different zones. I decided to try to steer clear of the guy who had been our driver and to get the lie of the land. Disengaging myself from my travelling companions, I breathed a sigh of relief when I saw one of the inner circle who had befriended me in London. He introduced me around and then took me to an army camouflage tent where Corin – who died in 2010 – was giving a lecture. Good looking and intelligent, he outlined some of the party's plans for the future. The main theme of his rallying call seemed to be raising funds and public awareness.

Then came what I'd been waiting for: revolutionary talk. The Workers Revolutionary Party would not rule out violence. Overthrowing the bourgeois government of the day was high on the agenda. But not yet, not now, and not by them.

I had got what I'd come for. It would be foolish to push my luck. So, using a ploy that had worked on other occasions when I had needed to get myself out of a dodgy situation, I told the member of my south London cell that I needed to get home, quick. Unexpected women's trouble. He didn't ask questions but immediately offered to drive me back to the station. With relief I boarded the last train for London – mission completed.

My newfound friends would not be seeing me again, but when they read the exposé of their activities in the following week's *News of the World* they would know why. Although the more outrageous aspects of their propaganda made a front-page story, my impression was that the Workers Revolutionary Party was no threat to the security of the country or to the British people. Though they might have been be very dangerous to journalists.

Another undercover investigation that went belly up involved cruelty at a children's home on the outskirts of London. My job was to infiltrate the staff and check out claims of ill treatment made by a former resident. After weeks of meticulous planning and interviews, I was accepted on the domestic staff at the home. One of our reporters was already working there and I was needed to corroborate his findings.

On day one of my live-in job, our cover was blown. I got an emergency call from the *News of the World* office telling me to get out, sharpish. 'My mother's been taken ill,' I told my immediate supervisor. 'I'll have to go home straight away.' This is what is known as 'making my excuses and leaving'!

Retrieving my belongings, I scarpered down the path and walked to a public phone box where I phoned a cab to take me back to the paper's Bouverie Street office for debriefing.

It may come as a surprise – in light of subsequent events that led to the closing of the paper over the phone-hacking affair in 2011 – but there was a high level of morality involved in *News of the World* investigations. All stories and claims had to be substantiated, recorded and documented to the highest standards, for legal as well as journalistic reasons.

I was never directly involved in any of the paper's sex exposés. It was considered unacceptable for me, a married woman, to be put in a compromising situation, though I might play a part in setting up scenes or acting as backup if someone under investigation called to check the authenticity of a person's story.

When an investigation of any kind was under way, special

phone lines were set up in the office and they had to be manned appropriately by reporters who were aware of the context and ongoing nature of the investigation. Also, in the days before mobile phones, the reporters had to have instant access to executives who could make decisions on when to pursue a story and when to pull out.

The lead executive in charge of most investigations during my time at *News of the World* was Nick Lloyd, later Sir Nicholas Lloyd. He went on to become editor of *News of the World* and *Daily Express*, positions that my second husband Derek would also hold. Nick had a fine sense of how an investigation was progressing and he always supported his reporters, especially when they were working in the field. Unlike one news desk executive I knew of, who told an on-the-job reporter who had been threatened with dogs, 'Go back and knock again. I'm not scared of their dogs.' No, he was safely back in London.

Nick Lloyd was an inspiring and considerate boss, who always knew when a great deal of effort had been put into a job. And he was generous with expenses – 'Claim a couple of nights on the hotel expenses and give yourself a day off,' he would say. Nick now runs a very prestigious public relations company and is married to another former newspaper editor, Eve Pollard.

Nick tells one story about me from those days that I dispute. He claims that at a newspaper party I dressed in a black cat suit and prowled around on all fours. He refuses to accept that this is a figment of his imagination. Still, as the cynics say, 'Don't let the facts interfere with a good story.'

My time as part of the investigative team was happy and fulfilling, and it was a privilege to work with some really experienced journalists who lived by the principle that the newspaper had a duty to expose only those who were up to no good.

I DON'T WANT TO TALK ABOUT IT

As a young married woman, I spent far too much time with colleagues in the local Fleet Street pubs, making contacts and talking shop instead of heading home to hubby in the suburbs. However, we were both achieving career success, and towards the end of 1972 Gavin and I started looking at larger properties. Our housing association maisonette was ideal for our needs and our budget, but our offer on a large semi-detached house close to the railway station in Beckenham was accepted.

The main attraction was that the corner garden was huge – there was even a private lake at the bottom of the garden. The lake enchanted me and I pictured myself in the role of Lady of the House – and the Lake. That lake bestowed bragging rights, whoever you were out to impress. Gavin was more interested in the well established vegetable plot, the opportunity for huge improvement work in the house, and the fact that the conservatory housed a trailing grape-bearing vine that would be perfect for making wine. I envisaged myself serving wine direct from our own vineyard, complete with personalised label: Château Petrie.

All the formalities for the mortgage had been completed, but before the ink was dry on the contract I took fright and decided that I wanted out. I didn't have the courage to tell Gavin but I tortured myself with the thought that I didn't want to live in the house or be married. My bags were packed metaphorically and I was ready to run away.

Or, more accurately, ride away. By then I had persuaded Gavin to buy me a small 125cc motorbike. It would be a convenient and economical way for me to get around. Unfortunately, I never passed my test and on its last outing before he banned me from riding it, I caused a major incident at the local launderette and terrorised people innocently waiting for their washing. I had overloaded the motorbike, and, as I revved up the engine, the bike bucked up into the air as I inadvertently hit the accelerator. It mounted the pavement, heading straight for the plate glass window of the laundromat. I will never forget the look on the customers' faces. Sensing a disaster about to happen, I jumped off and kicked the bike over, tipping my clean washing all over the pavement. I called Gavin from the nearest phone box to come and rescue me. He rode the slightly damaged bike home and confiscated my crash helmet.

That experience turned out to be an omen for my car driving efforts. After about 200 lessons with a very patient lady instructor at the British School of Motoring, it took 13 – yes, 13 – attempts to pass my driving test. You could say that I am not a natural driver, and I certainly had none of the innate sense of balance needed for riding a motorbike.

I had taken the bike on a major journey only once. It wasn't meant to be long distance, just a leisurely drive from Kent to the leafy suburbs of Surrey for a show business interview. I arrived six hours after leaving and was very fortunate that the kind interviewee – a very charming actor from one of the daytime television dramas – allowed me to leave my motorbike at his home overnight. He drove me in a very racy little sports car to the station and I caught a train home. Gavin collected the bike the next day.

You could say that being married to me was a challenge, and Gavin tried his best to provide the love and support his erratic, impractical wife needed. But it's hard when you are dealing with flawed people. Emotionally I was all over the place – up one minute, down the next. With my upbringing, it was hardly surprising, although I take full responsibility for my own behaviour and choices.

I can't remember now what great event in the couple of

intervening months should have changed my mind about the move. I started to fuss and fret and to behave badly. Time after time I would open my mouth, determined to tell Gavin I didn't want to go, only to change the subject and say nothing. Somehow I knew that the frustration I was already feeling in the marriage would make the task of creating a long-term home for the two of us impossible.

Truth was, I wanted out of the marriage but didn't know how to say so. Gavin himself had said before we married, 'I doubt if you'll stay longer than 10 years, but at least I'll never be bored.' But we had been together for only five years, and married less than three. There were still lots of good times in the marriage. We enjoyed each other's company and Gavin was an excellent husband: a good provider, enthusiastic about decorating and constantly improving the home and garden. He cooked and did a hundred things every day designed to make me happy and comfortable.

Now we were set to move into a large, somewhat neglected property that would require masses of time, dedication and resources to make it the luxury, modern home we envisaged. I was growing up and changing all the time, and do-it-yourself was not on my agenda of exciting things to do with my life. One night, days before we were due to exchange contracts, I asked Gavin to reconsider. I told him that I wasn't sure about the house. He was shocked and angry and confused. How could I say that I wanted out?

In a state of confusion and guilt, I agreed to go ahead with the house purchase and accepted that it was probably nerves. At that stage, I consciously started to suppress my feelings. It was too scary to be honest, so I decided to go along with what was most acceptable to Gavin – and to other people.

When we arrived at the property with our furniture van, the

outgoing owners had not yet left. Their removal van had been delayed. Instead of moving into our new home at about 10 o'clock in the morning, we had to cool our heels outside till gone four in the afternoon. When we finally took possession we made an inspection; now that all their belongings had gone we could see the house was a shambles.

Every room was filthy. Every cupboard was dirty. It took two skips to get rid of all the rubbish they had left behind. I sat on the bare stairs and cried my eyes out. Mum and dad came, and together with Gavin they set about making the place habitable. If we could have moved out again there and then I would have done so.

Over the next three years, Gavin worked night and day to make the house into our dream home. I had no heart for it. He settled on autumnal green and brown shades for the main living area – colours I would never have chosen. The bathroom was painted chocolate brown. His earth-based colour schemes were the complete opposite of the decor that appealed to me. He undertook major wardrobe and cupboard-building tasks that took months of his time and attention. I let him get on with it. This was his project; the house never felt like mine. If only I had known then that I was a spring/summer person and needed light and sunshine to thrive. I am an air sign and need to be up in the clouds. I am a romantic; Gavin was a realist.

Gavin was off to Cannes for a music trade festival. To wish him goodbye, I made an oriental meal and served it on a low table as we sat on the floor cross-legged. But instead of the occasion being romantic and intimate, he complained about being uncomfortable and turned up the dimmed lights so he could see what he was eating. We were totally at cross purposes. I decided to have a girly week while he was away and invite some friends to stay. We had a week-long party and I felt less stressed by the end of it. That week planted the seed that the life of a single girl was much more fun than being married.

As luck would have it, I was called for an interview for a feature writer's position at the weekly newspaper *Reveille*; I had applied to some time before. At the second interview, they said I had been shortlisted and they would let me know whether they would be offering me a permanent job. The wait was frustrating but I knew that if I landed the job, I really would be on my way career-wise. *Reveille* was owned by Mirror Group Newspapers and I was determined to work hard, impress and hopefully be transferred onto one of the national or Sunday papers in the group.

Until I got confirmation, and because we now had a large mortgage to service, I had to take on dead-end temping jobs in our local town and not just rely on freelance newspaper work. I thought I would die of boredom working in banks and insurance companies. I needed excitement – and a writing job.

As editor of *Disc* music magazine, Gavin was invited to present silver discs to artists for record sales and also to attend receptions to promote the magazine. I had always been part of that world and accompanied him, but now I was mostly based at home, juggling freelance work with temping it was not practical for me to travel up to London for a reception that might last only an hour. When Gavin came off the train at Beckenham station, he often went straight to the local pub, while I stayed at home, getting more and more dissatisfied. I had my heart set on a return to London and a job at *Reveille*.

On the day that the features editor of *Reveille* called to tell me I had got the job, Nick Lloyd, who was then a features executive at *News of the World*, also called to request my services. I couldn't do both, so I accepted the job at *Reveille* and asked Nick to keep me in mind for freelance work. We moved into our new home at the same time as I got my new job, so joining the staff at *Reveille* gave me the opportunity to pursue my career instead of home building.

'You're sitting on my chair,' said the icy voice behind me. I couldn't see who was speaking but the tone of authority brooked no argument.

'Sorry,' I stammered, turning around in the swivel chair to face the voice. 'I'm new. I was told to sit here.'

Margaret Pride, a ferocious middle-aged feature writer, was not placated. 'Well, it's my chair and my desk. Find somewhere else,' she said without a smile.

Embarrassed and somewhat taken aback by such downright unfriendliness, I prepared to gather my belongings and move. From across the office came Hilary Bonner, the show business journalist who had been told to look after the new girl. 'Don't worry about her,' she said, nodding in the direction of Margaret's back. 'Hates anyone young and pretty. Thinks they'll get all the best stories.'

Hilary was a large-boned, no-nonsense kind of person with a long mane of blonde hair. A horsey type. Literally. When not writing about the world of television, Hilary's passion was horse-riding. She lived in the country and I heard some years later that she married a very rich landowner, although that may have been untrue because she was the long-time girlfriend of *Coronation Street* actress Amanda Barrie – Fleet Street was in the dark about their relationship for years (although Barrie has since written about her sexuality in her autobiography, *It's Not a Rehearsal*).

My job would be writing features for the television pages along with Hilary, but on my first day she found me a new desk – carefully avoiding the one reserved for author Stuart

Farrer, the official office 'white witch' – and handed me a pile of readers' letters. 'Look busy with these and when the pub opens we'll go over for a lager,' she told me. And just after 11 o'clock she beckoned me to follow her out of the side door of the building.

She ordered the drinks and, standing at the bar, proceeded to give me the rundown on the various members of the editorial team, telling me about those who were cooperative and those who should be given a wide berth. I had already made one or two observations and she filled me in on the office politics.

We passed a companionable hour gossiping and then strolled back to the office. 'I'll collect you for lunch at about quarter to one,' said Hilary. 'We'll go and check out some of the contacts you'll need to get to know.'

The offices of London Weekend Television were opposite our headquarters in Stamford Street, close by London's Waterloo Station. On my first official 'meet and greet' outing, Hilary and I made our way to the bar on the second floor of LWT's building overlooking the Thames. She seemed to know everyone in the bar and she introduced me to producers, directors, press officers and assorted actors and actresses.

The press officers of companies such as LWT were our lifeblood as they could provide details of upcoming stories and series arrange interviews and organise private showings of the new TV offerings. Television writers had one of the best jobs in a newspaper, being invited on location for all the new series and being regularly wined and dined and invited to receptions to meet the casts and production teams.

Being so close to our offices, LWT was a home from home and it was not uncommon to be in their building several times a week – or even a day during particularly busy times for television schedule announcements and high-profile productions.

After enjoying the hospitality of the press officers, as well as the bar, Hilary and I made our way back to the *Reveille* offices, calling into the office pub on our way. It was about half past three before we were back at our desks.

'Read the *TV Times* and familiarise yourself with some of the programmes,' Hilary instructed. Reading was just about as much as I could do. I was feeling pleasantly sleepy and not really fit for work.

A couple of cups of coffee later, it was fast approaching home time.

'Pub's open,' Hilary called over cheerfully. 'We usually go for a couple of drinks after work.' She gestured to some of the others on the features desk. 'Are you game?'

Taking the view that a refusal often offends, I made a quick phone call to Gavin at his place of work and told him to expect me later.

A couple of drinks turned into a couple more, and as I got to meet more and more of my new work colleagues, I decided I was going to enjoy the job. It was almost 9 o'clock when I decided to abandon all thoughts of public transport and called a minicab to take me the 20 miles home. Arriving sometime after 10 o'clock, I told myself that the £20 taxi fare was a necessary expense on this first day in the job. It was a special occasion.

Day one at *Reveille* was a very good indication of the way the rest of the working week would develop. And it wasn't long before I discovered that the TV companies would often provide the taxis home and generous expenses would pay for the rest.

Several times a week I arrived home by taxi many hours after finishing work. Very often Gavin was doing the same. He was now in new offices in Victoria, where he was an executive on the woman's magazine *She*. He later went on to be a very successful television and radio comedy scriptwriter (collaborating with Jan Etherington) and associate producer on shows such as *Second Thoughts* (which enjoyed a re-run in 2013). It starred Lynda Bellingham and James Bolam and featured a 'first wife' played by Belinda Lang, who many people assumed was meant to be me. It was followed by the less successful *Duck Patrol* with Richard Wilson, and later *Next of Kin*.

Home life was non-existent during the week. At weekends Gavin would get down to some serious do-it-yourself. Showing willing, I would try to help but practical work has never been my forte. Often I was reduced to stripping wallpaper or sweeping up leaves – or keeping well out of the way of the manual work and escaping to the monk's seat overlooking the lake to read a book or write up an interview.

It was no surprise that my drinking really took off when I joined the staff of *Reveille*. In the four or five years since I had started drinking, socialising had revolved around parties and alcohol. Now work too revolved around drinking. Practically all my work was conducted in pubs, clubs or restaurants, where we journalists plied our trade and used the tried and trusted method of drinking to lubricate the wheels of revelation and disclosure.

The first show business star I was sent to interview at *Reveille* was the comedian and legendary performer Bob Monkhouse. In my eagerness to do well, I spent hours researching his life and career and writing out my carefully worded questions. I needn't have worried – Bob was a dream interviewee. As we drank tea served in bone china cups by his wife Jackie in their elegant St John's Wood drawing room, Bob entertained me with enough great stories and anecdotes to fill my notebook. I concluded that even for an audience of one – and the 1 million readers of *Reveille* – Bob was an unstoppable showman.

By my second month at *Reveille*, my diary was filled with

visits to television studios all over the country. Monday: Birmingham – overnight stay at Chateau Impney to celebrate a milestone episode of the popular soap opera *Crossroads*. Tuesday: Granada, Manchester. Wednesday: Thames Television at Elstree to interview an actor on the ATV television series *General Hospital*. Thursday: in office writing up interviews. Friday: ATV House, Great Cumberland Place, London. The constant round of television company visits plus trips abroad for television specials and hospitality junkets was to govern my work life for the next seven years.

As well as show business stories, I wrote about fascinating ordinary people such as 'The Wonder of Woolies', a serial offender who broke into Woolworths stores and rearranged the merchandise. He had not spent a Christmas Day out of prison for 30 years, though most of his sentences were short. We ran a fun feature taking him to meet Father Christmas, see the tree at Trafalgar Square and visit Harrods. Woolworths would not let us inside their store for a photograph. Come Christmas Day, I invited him to dinner with my family. I still have the necklace he gave me as a present. 'I didn't nick it, missus, honest,' he was at pains to point out.

Then there was the impressive sounding United Temples of the Church of Satan, where they invited me to become the first female member of their coven. Apparently they had 500 members worldwide, but only three attended meetings in their lock-up garage in Enfield, north London. When we asked the leader to be photographed without his hood, he was adamant: 'Can't do that. My mum would kill me.'

In a small Scottish seaside town, I interviewed a lady who had been accused of murdering her policeman husband but got off scot-free. Arriving at her home unannounced, I peered through the window and was met by the sight of the lady in question dancing around her suburban living room dressed in a bright red prom skirt and low-cut blouse, all alone. Spotting me at the window, she agreed to let me in to talk to her. Given the opportunity, a surprising number of people do want to tell their stories to the press, even when we turn up out of the blue.

This pretty, dark-haired, lively mother of two had been charged with killing her husband. Claiming self-defence, she admitted bashing in his skull with a hammer and dragging his body downstairs to hide it overnight in the garden shed. The next morning she got her children up, gave them breakfast and sent them off to school as usual. Later that day she phoned a family member and the police and confessed to her crime. She was found not guilty.

It was a dream job, one of the most exciting in the world. You never knew from day to day where you would go or who you would meet, but, as is so often the way, I and my fellow journalists still found much to complain about – especially the unpredictability of a life where you could never plan social events or dinner parties and work always needed to take priority.

It would be easy to blame the erratic work pattern and the need to have an overnight bag ready in the office for last-minute trips for my inability to commit to my marriage, though it would just be an excuse. But I loved the job and the constant travelling, staying in five-star hotels on expenses, being at the heart of news events, and mingling with celebrities, actors, producers, directors and publicists.

It was a fascinating, glamorous, wonderful life, and fulfilled all the cravings I had experienced for an extraordinary existence.

For any journalist, there is nothing to beat the buzz that you get from picking up a newspaper and seeing your name there on the by-line, especially on a big exclusive or major story. It's what we do the job for – that and to entertain and educate and to ensure that the general public is kept informed about what happens in the world.

In a celebrated libel case against the BBC in 1984, my second husband Derek explained why he had risked his life savings – and lost them – to fight a case against the satirical programme *Week Ending* on Radio 4. He defended his decision by saying, 'I brought this case to prove that decency, honour and integrity still exist in Fleet Street.'

For me, the pursuit of truth in any story was always the ultimate principle, even though it may not always seem that journalists are striving for such honourable ideals. As a show business writer on a weekly entertainment magazine, I did not often face matters that tested my conscience, but my commitment was always to the newspaperman's avowed intention to do the right thing and expose wrongdoing. Even taking into account the worst excesses of newspaper malpractice and phone hacking, I still like to believe that the journalists were searching for the truth and not just in a battle with their rivals for circulation.

It is inevitable that conflicts of interest arise when show business journalists become friends and confidants of the people they are writing about. Compromise is necessary to preserve the relationship and continue to do the job. I had one firm rule: if you tell me this is off the record I won't report it, but I would rather you didn't make me party to any secrets that you do not want revealed.

My loyalty to a friend and commitment to my employer were sorely taxed on one memorable occasion when I had obtained an exclusive interview and red-hot world exclusive, which had been disclosed to me freely by the person concerned.

He is dead now, and as you can't libel the dead, I can reveal the name of the film actor involved. Welshman Victor Spinetti, friend of Richard Burton and Elizabeth Taylor and star of The Beatles' films *Hard Day's Night* and *Help!* (and many other hugely successful box office hits), 'came out' to me and confessed that he was homosexual.

In an intimate, heart-searching interview conducted over many hours, Victor talked about his dilemma in being 'the only gay boy' in his Welsh village, the relationships and affairs he had had and his struggle to keep the secret from his film fans. Victor and I were alone in the room, chatting and drinking champagne, and he assured me that he was ready for the world to know his secret.

I told him I would confirm the details with him the following day. Back in the office, I wrote the story and presented it to my executives. They congratulated me on obtaining a totally exclusive story with fascinating quotes, a wealth of background information and photographs to back it all up, and began to prepare a front page 'splash'.

At lunchtime I returned to Victor's apartment and he agreed to sign and initial each page after reading the story. It was most unusual – though I understand it's more common these days – for the subject of a story to be allowed to read and approve it before publication. However, this was a very important story dealing with highly sensitive personal issues and we wanted to make sure that we had taken all the legal precautions to save ourselves from any adverse consequences – or even injunctions that would have prevented us running the exclusive.

Victor signed the pages and a letter agreeing to publication. In the best Fleet Street tradition, the presses were ready to roll when he rang me in tears and asked to have the story withdrawn. Both his agent and a close friend had convinced him that it could do irreparable harm to his career, as homosexuality was not so accepted or openly discussed in those days.

Reveille's senior editorial executives would have been well within their rights, morally and legally, to refuse to kill the story and to tell Victor to sue. However, after much discussion, they agreed to drop it and to find a substitute front-page story.

I was disappointed, of course, but I would probably not knowingly choose to be held responsible for an individual throwing away their reputation or livelihood. Fact is the revelation would probably not have come as a great surprise to many people inside or even outside the entertainment industry. But, as they say, that's show business. You win some, you lose some.

At a party for the *Daily Express's* William Hickey diary page at the Clermont Club in London's West End, I was introduced to Vicki Hodge, daughter of Baronet Sir John Rowland Hodge. Vicki was well known to newspaper executives and readers as a blonde model who had had a well publicised part in a film called *Confessions of a Sex Maniac* and a colourful past that included holidaying on the Caribbean island of Mustique. Princess Margaret had a house there and the younger royals often escaped to the island to let their hair down and enjoy themselves away from the prying eyes of the press.

Prince Andrew, before his marriage, had a reputation as a party animal and Vicki had caused a sensation by revealing details of a beach party on Mustique where Prince Andrew had frolicked in the surf with beautiful models – including Vicki. The photographs were splashed across the pages of the Sunday papers and Vicki was famously quoted as declaring that 'no one had claimed the crown jewels'.

Vicki and I got into conversation at the Hickey party but on this occasion she had much more serious matters on her mind. Another guest at the infamous beach party had been her lover

John Bindon, a friend of Princess Margaret and, it was said, a member of the London criminal underworld. He was also an actor who played alongside Mick Jagger in *Performance*.

Insiders claimed that Bindon was a court jester to Princess Margaret and the story – which might well have been apocryphal – was that she particularly enjoyed his party piece of balancing jugs of beer on his private parts. Whether true or not, it earned Bindon a reputation as a wild man and royal entertainer. However, those days of royal parties and high jinks had been eclipsed by more serious issues. John Bindon had been charged with the murder of a gangster called John Darke. He was later acquitted on a plea of self-defence, but at the time of the party he was on remand in Brixton prison.

Vicki talked openly about his current situation and even spiced up the story with details about her daily visits to him in prison. She claimed that on early morning visits, John demanded she dress provocatively and the guards kept a discreet distance as she and John indulged in sexual antics under the table. Vicki knew full well that I was a journalist, but she never asked me not to disclose any of the confidences she had revealed so gleefully in our conversation.

I knew that I had a great front-page story and asked if I could have her phone number to follow up with an interview. She happily obliged. Vicki was a publicity seeker and her story of Prince Andrew's 'crown jewels' regularly made the papers – usually when she had something to promote. Now she needed publicity for her beloved John, and perhaps she felt she could help him by softening the gangster image being portrayed in the press with stories of his more 'romantic' side.

Whatever the reason, she gave her permission and the newspaper lawyers went through the story word by word with a fine-tooth comb. This was mainly to ensure that we were complying with libel laws and sub judice regulations, given that Bindon was on remand but hadn't yet been tried.

Vicki was a darling of the tabloid press, partly because her father was a baronet and so she was considered a posh little rich girl slumming it with the criminal classes. But despite the many previous stories about her and her exploits, the *Mirror* lawyer was concerned about the potential damage to her reputation, as well as about leaving the paper open to allegations of libel. However, he wasn't worried that we were claiming she was the girlfriend of a criminal charged with attempted murder.

Determined to protect my exclusive story, I answered all his concerns as fully as I could. He read and re-read the copy I had given him, and I assured him that I had checked my facts and obtained permission to print the story. As I sat across from him at his desk in the legal department, I tried to anticipate what might be causing him such concern. Deep in legal deliberation, he seemed completely unaware that the cigarette in his mouth had burned down and was about to deposit ash all over his dark suit.

Finally, he removed the cigarette from his mouth, looked at me steadily, and said in a grave tone, 'We are in danger of severely impugning this young lady's reputation. She is a *married* woman.' I had to go back to Vicki and get an assurance that she did not object to having her marital status revealed, even though she had used her scandalous reputation to her advantage for years.

My relationship with Vicki up to the time of publication was friendly and she did not voice any worries to me about the appearance of the story. That changed on the day the story was splashed across the front page of *Reveille*.

This change of heart often happens when people actually see what they have said written down in black and white – and it seems likely that Mr Bindon in his prison cell did not take kindly to revelations about his girlfriend arriving knickerless at the prison gates for visits. However, it seems unlikely that the story did his hard man reputation any harm and Vicki's titillating stories are still being sold as 'kiss and tells' to national newspapers over 30 years later. John Bindon died in 1993, aged 50, from a medical condition, not the more sinister end that some might have predicted for him.

CHAPTER 7

THAT'LL BE
THE DAY

There must have been writers at *Reveille* who went to the library and had a sandwich at lunchtime – but they weren't part of my social circle.

Every day there would be the potential for a visit to a television studio or location or to the offices of an agent or publicist. And having done the rounds, there were always the local pubs and restaurants where we met up with colleagues and swapped shop talk.

By now *Reveille* had moved into an office next door to the main *Daily Mirror* building in Holborn, which gave us the chance to fraternise with the rest of the Mirror Group's journalists and opportunities for extra work on a freelance basis.

Gavin was enjoying his new role on a general interest woman's magazine and he also took on lots of extra freelance commissions. From his pop days, he had retained a close relationship with the singer and actor David Essex. David, like many other British pop stars, was huge in countries such as

Japan. Gavin had produced a book about David that I had helped to write, so when a Japanese publishing company decided to do a David Essex special, they approached Gavin. While Gavin tackled the musical side, my job was to do the personal, female stuff. We had several meetings with David at his home in Essex to put the material together.

David was about to star in the pop film *That'll Be the Day* and the follow-up *Stardust*. In *That'll Be the Day* he played a character called Jim MacLain, an aspiring pop star – he was surely conceived as a David Essex double. In *Stardust*, the aspiring star had made it. Ringo Starr played Mike and Keith Moon also starred as J D Clover.

My screen debut came when Gavin and I were given bit parts as friends of the pop star who were whisked to safety by a security man when a pop concert got out of control. Filming took place in Manchester and hordes of David Essex fans were invited to a live concert that would be filmed as part of the movie. The fans played their part well, as a screaming, uncontrolled, hysterical mob.

I appear on screen for a few brief seconds in the film, being lifted over a fence by the security man. Another moment of extremely fleeting fame. My Andy Warhol full allocation of 15 minutes would not come till sometime later.

Filming took several days and we were guests of the film company at their location hotel. The Who drummer, Keith Moon, who played the drummer in the film, was also staying at our hotel. We knew Moonie well and had been to parties at his house in Berkshire. On one occasion, police were called three times because the music was too loud and disturbing the neighbours – who lived five miles away.

Sober, Moonie was one of the loveliest guys you could meet. Drunk, he was a madman. After filming finished on day one, we gathered in the hotel bar to celebrate. By midnight things were getting seriously out of hand. Moonie was looking for trouble and I was a willing accomplice. For some reason, which seemed a good one at the time, we had taken the party into the lift. Sitting on the lift floor, constantly refilling our glasses from a bottle of champagne, fellow hotel guests had to step over us to get into the lift and press buttons to their floors.

Perhaps one of them was rude, because the next time the lift was empty, Moonie decided that no one else was going to get into the lift. At each floor we would press the 'close doors' button before anyone could get in. Some irate guests complained to the hotel staff.

The loud ringing of a telephone disturbed our hard-won peace and gave us quite a shock. It was the emergency phone in the lift. 'Would you please vacate the lift?' said an authoritative voice on the end of the line. 'Other guests wish to use it.'

Moonie was livid. How dare they talk to him like that? He pulled the phone from its cradle, complete with the wires, and put it in his pocket. Mayhem reigned. He still refused to let anyone join us in the lift, unless they were prepared to get down on the floor, have a drink and join in the party spirit. The hotel staff were not amused. Without warning – now that there was no phone with which to communicate – they stopped the lift. By now there were four or five of us party animals inside.

Lights started flashing as the emergency system was activated, but it was only the fact that we had run out of champagne that persuaded us to surrender the next time the lift doors opened at a floor. Stepping nonchalantly from the lift at reception, Keith Moon walked over to the harassed night manager and told him, 'You'll need this.' From his pocket, he brought out the lift's emergency phone.

Early in the morning, after more drinks in Keith's room, we again emerged looking for what we laughingly called 'fun'.

Roaming the corridors in search of excitement, we found pairs of shoes that had been placed outside bedroom doors for cleaning by the night porter.

Keith thought it was wrong to ask a member of the hotel staff to do such a menial job so he came up with a way to render it unnecessary. He gathered armfuls of shoes and threw them down the open lift shaft.

Total madness, but we were well and truly drunk by now. Knowing that we all had an early call the next day, we eventually agreed to call it a night. Back in my own room, I fell into bed, shattered. I was soon awoken by the fire alarm. A false alarm. As if we didn't know, Keith's idea of a joke. Time and again in the few hours till morning, Moonie managed to set off the fire alarms.

The hotel management vowed that none of us would ever be allowed to stay in any of their hotels again.

On another occasion during a party – I seem to remember that Keith Moon was there too – the American singer Harry Nilsson and I retired to one of the bedrooms in a Knightsbridge luxury apartment to smoke dope, snort coke and fool around. Sadly, Gavin put paid to my plans to meet Harry the next day at Heathrow airport and join him on a Caribbean holiday. Husbands can be such spoilsports.

BBC disc jockey Tony Blackburn and I enjoyed a night of madness – but no hanky-panky – in an out-of-town hotel. It was five o'clock in the morning and he was due on air for the early show. Waiters were laying tables for breakfast and Tony and I were still drinking triples.

CHAPTER 8

HELP ME MAKE IT THROUGH THE NIGHT

My husband Gavin had developed a circle of friends at one of the 'local' pubs on the high street in Beckenham, less than five minutes' walk from our home.

I was not part of that scene: I've always had a huge resistance to anything 'local'. Shops, bus routes, even local papers bore me rigid.

At weekends, no matter how much he had had to drink the previous evening, Gavin was in the habit of getting up bright and early. He would enthusiastically pursue his do-it-yourself work, banging, hammering and painting from about seven in the morning till lunchtime, when he would return to the local for a few pints. Nightclub hours were always more my thing and it was often nearly noon before I'd surface. I was still on cups of tea and the daily papers when he was ready to knock off for lunch.

Before the introduction of all-day drinking, the pubs closed from around 2 or 2.30pm till about 5.30 and it wasn't unusual for him to bring people back for an afternoon drinking session. It was a Sunday afternoon when he arrived with an Australian couple he had befriended and I took an instant dislike to the girl. She was a few years older than me, well built and a hearty, outdoor type. She was drinking pints along with the men.

At some point in the afternoon, she and I got into a noisy disagreement about something or other. It was probably nothing of great importance but with opinions fuelled by alcohol we were determined to get our point of view across. What I do remember is that she called me childish. I was incensed. Stomping upstairs in a temper, I slammed the bathroom door and locked it. Then I opened the bathroom cabinet and took out a large bottle of Paracetamol. I poured a quantity into my hand and slugged them down with a glass of booze I had thoughtfully brought along.

As I recall, I went back downstairs to argue some more and then went upstairs again and lay down on the bed to await death. Sometime later Gavin found me and the empty bottle of pills. I must have been completely unconscious because I have no recollection of the ride in an ambulance to the local hospital.

The rubber tube they stuck down my throat to enable them to pump my stomach made me choke. A rather brusque nurse held my head as I tried to struggle. She made it patently obvious that she had better things to do than look after drunks who took overdoses of pills.

No one knew how many I had taken. They kept asking me but I was pretty much out of it. Trying to keep me conscious was obviously part of the procedure even though all I wanted to do was sleep. As the hours passed and the contents of my stomach had been emptied, I was becoming aware of my surroundings. By then I was ashamed of myself and kept apologising to the nurses for having put them to all that trouble.

My throat was sore from the rubber tube and my head hurt from the alcohol and Paracetamol. However, it seemed I was just going to have to suffer. Headache pills were definitely off the menu.

The next morning I awoke in the hospital bed wearing a hospital gown. Who had undressed me? I didn't know. Worse, I had no cigarettes and no money to buy any. Gavin had gone home at some point during the night. I asked for a phone to be brought to my bed.

'Get up here immediately,' I demanded when he sleepily answered the phone. 'I want to come home and you need to bring me my cigarettes.'

He later admitted that he hadn't rushed to collect me. The drama of the previous evening had left him feeling angry and upset.

In any event, the hospital refused to let me go until I had seen a psychiatrist. When asked why I had tried to kill myself, I clearly remembered what had happened and triumphantly told the doctor about the Australian girl who had called me childish.

'Well, you certainly showed her,' he said. The irony was not lost on me.

Gavin arrived during the interview and the psychiatrist asked him some questions about my behaviour patterns and upbringing. It seemed that my first serious suicide attempt had been a 'cry for help'. Attention seeking. To my astonishment, the psychiatrist suggested that Gavin should take me home and put me over his knee. Punishment for being a 'bad girl' would complete the process of my acting out, thereby showing me that my behaviour was unacceptable and then we could get on with our lives again – a clean slate.

Perhaps he should have taken the psychiatrist's advice; it might have prevented me needing to 'cry for help' at least half a dozen times more. It would have been more useful, though, if the psychiatrist had simply suggested that I give up drinking.

It would be more than a dozen years before I would reach that solution.

Gavin showed his anger towards me by publicly humiliating me. He refused to get a taxi to take us the five miles home and, having failed to bring a change of clothes for me, he made me travel home on the bus in the floor-length house dress I had been wearing the previous day.

Relations between us were strained but neither of us had the knowledge or insight to deal with the way I increasingly over-reacted because of my emotional immaturity – and because of my heavy drinking. We put the incident behind us and Gavin agreed not to tell my parents. However, it wasn't long before they found out. A few months later I went through exactly the same thing again, only this time mum and dad were visiting and I locked myself in the bathroom while taking the pills. Perhaps I was more drunk than on the previous occasion, because this time I collapsed on the bathroom floor. Talk about history repeating itself.

Dad and Gavin smashed the bathroom door, and, having failed to revive me, called the ambulance. Another stomach pump, another interview with the psychiatrist, and more apologies all round. A pattern had been established. The second time around, the shame was not so great, the shock was not so profound – but my throat was even worse than the first time.

Still, no one mentioned that drink might be the cause of my problems, even though I never tried to kill myself when I was sober. Another 'cry for help' went unheard.

Fortunately, most of these drink-induced dramas were confined to the weekend and I managed to keep working and learned to keep the suicide attempts secret.

However, I was suffering from a physical illness and the symptoms were causing me more and more distress. Now started the period that came to be known as 'Ellen Petrie is ill'. One of my jobs at *Reveille* was to write a named weekly pop gossip column. As I became more and more debilitated and took more and more time off work, other journalists would be seconded to write the column – at first still with my name at the top and later under their own names with a small line at the bottom stating 'Ellen Petrie is ill'.

Later, with hindsight, self-knowledge and proper medical attention for my condition, I would say of that period that I 'enjoyed bad health for years'. My weight had dropped dramatically, sleep patterns were erratic and I was particularly sensitive to temperature changes. With all the classic symptoms of a thyroid malfunction, it seems incredible that it took the doctors at my local surgery nearly two years to diagnose my condition.

Wearing a matching scarf with every outfit had become part of my personal style. Even I thought I was doing it as a fashion statement. However, there was another reason. Scarves hid the very prominent Adam's apple that I had developed. Arriving at the doctor's surgery one morning with my usual long list of diverse symptoms, I was seen by a visiting locum. For the first time, this doctor asked me to remove my scarf.

'How long have you had the goitre?' she asked on seeing the large lump on my throat.

'Best part of a year,' I told her.

Before lunchtime she had admitted me to Bromley Hospital and I was being examined by an ear, nose and throat specialist. An overactive thyroid was immediately diagnosed and as well as starting a course of drug treatment to correct the imbalance, which was very severe by now, it was also decided that an operation was needed on my throat.

Without delay I was scheduled for surgery.

On the day that he performed my operation, the consultant was appointed Surgeon Royal to the Queen. A nurse told me the announcement had been in that day's *Times*.

Lying on the hospital trolley outside the theatre, I was already drifting after having been given a pre-med. 'Count backwards from 10,' he instructed while inserting a needle into the back of my hand. 'Congratulations on being appointed Surgeon to the Queen,' I struggled to say, but I never finished the sentence.

When I came round in the recovery room some hours later, I opened my mouth to ask the nurse if he had realised what I was trying to say. No sound came. I was speechless and would be for some days. My only means of communication was through written notes. My throat had been cut from ear to ear and was now clipped together with sterile staples. Still groggy from the anaesthetic, I began to fear that if I jerked my neck back suddenly my head might roll off. For days I kept my chin firmly down.

The good news was that although the goitre had been extremely large – the surgeon described it as like having a half pound block of butter lodged in my throat – the lump was benign. But even after the goitre was removed, I was kept in hospital while they attempted to regulate the production of thyroid in my system.

Thyroid problems, while not life-threatening, are serious because the thyroid gland affects every part of the body. Over the years, as well as the thyroidectomy I underwent, I would have a whole range of treatments, including drug therapy and advanced procedures such as taking radioactive iodine. For five days after that I was not allowed to visit any public places in case I contaminated other people. Still, the thyroid continued to be overactive.

Left: Mirror, mirror, who is the fairest of them all? Me, aged two, pondering my future.

Above: The way we were. Me, aged 10, with (left to right) brother William, dad Gerry, mum Mamie and brothers James and Gerard.

Right: 'The sixties were beginning to swing and nothing was going to stop me from joining in. Youth was on the march.'

Above: Reporter at large. Ellen on the features desk of *Reveille* in 1973.

Below left: At the Sydmonton Festival for the first run-through performance of *Phantom of the Opera*.

Below right: Stepping out at a film première in London in the1970s.

Above: Party animals in London in the 1980s.

Below left: Leaving the London Palladium after the Royal Variety Performance in 1986.

Below right: Dancing cheek-to-cheek. Ellen and Derek's engagement party in Tenerife in 1988.

(Photo: © Steve Lewis/The Sun /Newssyndication.com)

Top: Our engagement made front-page news in *The Sun*.

Below left: Celebrating the publication of Derek's autobiography.

Below right: 'Oh yea! Oh yea!' Ellen and Derek's wedding day at Arundel Cathedral, Sussex, in 1988.

(Photo: © Mirrorpix)

Top: With Rupert Murdoch at the launch of Sky TV in London, 1989.

Below left: Oh yes I did! Playing the Spirit of Greenwood in the *Babes in the Wood* panto at the Theatre Royal, Brighton, in 1992.

Below right: 'At home' in a luxury apartment in Glasgow's West End while broadcasting the BBC's *The Jamesons* show from Scotland in 1995.

Top: Ellen shows a leg... on radio. Co-presenting *The Jamesons* BBC Radio 2 show in 1990.

Below left: The Jamesons 'at home' at their house, 'Angel's Rest', in Brighton, 1998.

Below right: Life in the fast lane in the USA. Me on a borrowed Harley-Davidson in Ohio.

Left: 'The show *Sobe Wonderland*, that I co-authored, directed and performed in, was an over-the-top musical fantasy – pure Miami.'

Right: 'Playing Nessa in *Fit To Be Tied* in Miami allowed me to act outrageously and dress glamorously.'

Left: Ellen and Derek glammed-up for a *This Is Your Life* party.

Right: Immortalised by the ship's photographer on a New Year cruise.

HELP ME MAKE IT THROUGH THE NIGHT

Some people say that it can be affected by stress, and I have met sufferers whose thyroid activity changed after a traumatic event such as bereavement. Despite all the medical treatment I received, no one was ever able to attribute my thyroid activity to any particular cause, although it is true to say that over the years it has often been particularly active at times of emotional disturbance.

At the time of the initial problem, being sick was highly likely to have been another attempt on the part of my body to tell me that all was not well. My marriage to Gavin was increasingly unsatisfying and my throat problems seem to have been a way of forcing myself to swallow emotions and of refusing to allow myself to voice what I really thought.

Bless him; he did try to be a good husband to me. When I was in hospital he visited every day and brought me gifts of sweets, magazines and flowers. When visiting hours were over, he would rush home to work on a surprise that he was preparing for my homecoming.

The surprise was a whitewashed patio and barbecue corner that he had built in the garden. All his own work, he had excavated the site, concreted it over and even made his own fancy cut-out brick wall by hand, as well as laying crazy paving. By the time he came to collect me from hospital – by taxi this time – the patio was finished and he had even bought a new set of garden furniture.

Full marks to him for enterprise and effort. I did appreciate all his endeavours, but somehow it wasn't enough. It wasn't long before the house and the patio would be sold.

Gavin showed his love in actions, but I craved words. It seemed that neither of us could say what we meant. My poor throat had to be cut before I could admit that I wanted to scream. The marriage was coming to an end.

There was the odd one-night stand that I am embarrassed to admit to but that I never considered as endangering the marriage – they were really just for a bit of excitement. Apart from that, I had had one long-running on /off affair.

It had started before my marriage and the man involved was also married. During difficult times in our primary relationships, the affair went through periods of great intensity, while at other times it was quiet. At the end of 1975, as I got back to full health and strength after a year of hospitalisation, the affair was full on.

There were long periods when we had no contact, but after a few months, or even a couple of years, I would make the call. We carried on a sexual relationship, usually when I was already on an assignment somewhere. On visits to television studios up and down the country, I would meet up with my secret lover. Fortunately, his job involved a lot of travelling so he too had ready-made excuses for being away from home.

Whenever I felt that Gavin wasn't paying me enough attention, I would turn to my old faithful, who could always be relied upon to make me feel desirable.

Even now it would cause much distress if I were to reveal his identity. He is married with children and, last time I heard, he was doing fine, and it's now more than 30 years since the affair came to its glorious end.

But back in 1975, the game was on. Being together properly, officially, suddenly became a possibility. Over long, lingering, amorous encounters and too many late-night drinks, we agreed to leave our respective partners. Like star-crossed lovers, we plotted and planned our escapes, thrilling to the excitement of doing something so daring, so wild.

The truth was that I was more than ready to leave home and the illicit affair was just another piece of the jigsaw. I would probably have been too scared to run away alone, so, without any thought of all the hurt we would cause, I instigated the next move.

First, I would leave and find us somewhere to stay. Then he would leave and move in. After which we would live happily ever after. Madness reigned. God may not have been laughing – more likely he was determined that on this occasion my plans would be well and truly spoiled.

It was not the first time I had packed my bags to leave the marital home, but I suspect that neither Gavin nor I knew that this really would be the last time.

Gavin and I would never live together again as man and wife. Not that that stopped us sharing a bed on occasion when I went down to visit the cats, to collect belongings or after a long and melancholic lunch or dinner.

My behaviour was so erratic that perhaps my impending departure was a relief to him. He never really knew from day to day where I was or what I was doing. On one occasion, when Gavin was due to be away overnight, I called my old boyfriend in the middle of the night and told him to come over. Unfortunately, by the time he arrived, I had passed out, drunk – and my husband was home. Emotionally I was a mess. I didn't know what I wanted. It was impossible for me to be faithful but I did expect it of my partner.

Although it was some months after the official separation, the marriage well and truly finished the night when I admitted there was someone else. Gavin wasn't going to stand for that. I tried one last dramatic venture: I ran up the stairs of a multi-storey car park and, as I saw Gavin walk away and refuse to turn round, I threw my shoes from the top of the building. Then I had to race down the stairs to retrieve them. Gavin was nowhere to be seen. This time there was no going back.

Three days before St Valentine's Day in 1976, I left my husband Gavin. We had stayed up all night discussing the situation. There were tears, recriminations, protestations of love, suggestions of trying again, but ultimately the decision was made that I would leave in the morning.

I like to say that I walked away, but he did carry my bags to the station. It was agreed that we would not tell our families until we had time to acclimatise to the break-up of the marriage. For that reason, I moved into a small hotel in Victoria where I was to stay for some months. Gavin stayed in the marital home.

We met for lunch, dinner and drinks in Fleet Street frequently, ostensibly to talk about what to do next but really because we genuinely were friends and after an eight-year relationship each of us was a little lost without the other.

Perhaps inevitably, the long-running affair for which I had finally left home also came to an end around that time. Apart from a brief few days when I had first left home in March, he had not taken the irreversible step of leaving his wife for me. The affair fizzled out when it no longer provided the excitement I craved.

He never admitted it, but it is my understanding that Gavin also had someone else – a relationship that started before our marriage ended. Who could have blamed him? There was a woman's name that used to surface regularly, though I don't know about the extent of their relationship. I am glad to say that he did go on to have a long running and successful work and marriage partnership with his television series co-writer, Jan Etherington.

Once, I went to the house and found makeup in the bathroom and a pair of women's shoes in the bedroom. I threw them out through the kitchen window, but unfortunately it happened to be closed at the time. Gavin was furious and in no uncertain terms made it clear that my having chosen to leave the marital home meant that he was entitled to invite other women there. He wasn't going to live like a monk, though I would have liked him to do just that.

We both continued to work, me at *Reveille* and Gavin at *She*. If he had to go away on business, I would move back into the house and take care of things while he was gone. It was difficult to make serious decisions about moving on and somewhere deep inside I probably thought that after I had enjoyed my freedom and got over my mini mid-marriage crisis, I would go home again to my husband.

However, both of us seemed to find that ending the marriage came as a relief. Although we were in no hurry to get a divorce, we conceded that we were unlikely to get back together again. It would have been ideal for me if I could have put him on ice to await the time when I had grown up enough to continue our relationship and sustain a marriage.

For some years, Gavin was still my 'go to' man when I needed something done at my own new home or I had a problem. I also often phoned him in the middle of the night professing my undying love. But the time was fast approaching when we would have to make the final decision to make a clean break. Divorce, sell the house, split the proceeds and move on with our lives. I couldn't justify hanging on to him any longer.

Gavin, and my first marriage, were consigned to history.

Around that time a very dear friend and sometime lover took me to Paris for dinner – we were already having lunch in London when he produced the tickets and whisked me off to the airport for an afternoon flight to Paris. The spontaneity and romance of such a grand gesture were always guaranteed to turn my head. The Paris trip was a success, but that was not always the case when I followed my heart rather than my head.

Despite the many risks I have taken professionally and personally, things have rarely turned nasty – I seem to have been divinely protected. But in one hotel in Birmingham, the situation got way out of control.

At a television reception I met a good-looking actor whom I fancied straight away. We made eye contact and wordlessly we agreed to take the attraction further. All night we circled each other, flirting and building up the sexual anticipation. Eventually, as the party was winding down, he asked my room number and said he would come up for a drink. We both knew that rather more than a drink was being offered.

We left the reception separately and he followed me to my room. I opened the door when he knocked. He barged his way in, grabbed me roughly, pushed me back against the door and held his hand across my throat, making it hard for me to breathe. My heart was racing with fear but I thought that maybe he was acting out some elaborate sexual fantasy. That might have been true, but he wasn't asking my permission to engage in it.

He was aggressively pushing my skirt up and attempting to undo his trousers at the same time. Determined not to make him angrier or more aroused than he was, I tried to reason with him and suggested we would be more comfortable on the bed. He let go of me. As I walked towards the large double bed, all I could think about was what I could do to prevent him having sex with me.

There is always controversy about the point at which women are within their rights to say no. The law states that it is right up to the moment of penetration. Yes, I had invited him to my room and we both knew the game plan. However, I had not asked for his rough, drunken treatment of me and I did not want to have sexual relations with him.

Under no illusion about what would happen if I attempted

to fight, I decided that flight was my best option. I ran to the bathroom and locked the door behind me. When he realised what was happening, my unwelcome guest started hammering on the bathroom door. I didn't care. If another guest heard the commotion and called hotel security, that would give me the escape route I needed. I checked whether there was a phone in the bathroom – there wasn't.

Sitting on the toilet seat, I decided to wait it out – till morning if necessary. Time passed and all was quiet in the bedroom. When I heard the outer door open and close, I judged that it was safe to leave the refuge of the bathroom. I was wrong. Either I was stupid or he was clever, but when I opened the door he was waiting for me. This time he grabbed me, shoved me onto the bed, yanked my underwear down and climbed on top of me.

I was genuinely terrified and in tears. He thought it was funny. His features distorted with rage and contempt, he forced my head down into the pillow with his hand around my throat. Looking me in the eye, he snarled at me over and over again, 'What did you expect? Are you getting what you wanted?'

Ask any woman why she doesn't report a vicious, unprovoked attack like the one I sustained and she will probably tell you, 'I was ashamed. I thought I'd asked for it.' Like many women, I never told anyone. Although I had few outward scars, the attack had sickened and scared me. You never forget a terrifying experience that scars your psyche and leaves your self-esteem in shreds.

The name of the man in question continued to appear on my radar for some years afterwards as he was still acting, but fortunately I never had the misfortune to see him again in real life. However, having experienced the way he treated me, I believe it extremely unlikely that it was a one-off. It is highly probable that I was not the only woman he overpowered and raped.

He may or may not be aware of what he did, but there are plenty of men who still think that such behaviour is excusable, especially if they – or the woman – are drunk at the time. I am in awe of and deeply grateful to those women who do speak out and put themselves through the intrusive and inevitably humiliating process of reporting rape and pursuing the perpetrator all the way to court. I was not so brave – nor could I claim that I would be today – but hopefully the incident did ensure that I modified my own behaviour and taught me to be less naive about putting myself in danger. Hopefully, wisdom comes with age. I can also take comfort from my firmly held belief that I did not deserve what happened to me. A woman should always have the right to decide who she will or won't have sex with, and men need to accept that 'no' means 'no'.

CHAPTER 9

GIRLS JUST WANNA HAVE FUN

Two of the most colourful characters to pass through Hobbes Hotel in Victoria, which is where I lived when I first left my husband Gavin, were the Australian sisters Katie and Gemma. Exports from Bondi Beach, they were determined to have a summer to remember in swinging London.

After a near-fatal car crash late at night back home in Sydney, Gemma had decided she needed the holiday to recuperate. Younger sister Katie was along for the ride.

They had come over on a boat that took nearly six weeks and they would regale drinkers in the bar of the hotel with stories of their exploits on board. Wild parties among the younger passengers attracted so much attention and disapproval that the sisters, considered ringleaders, had even been officially warned about their raucous behaviour.

Gemma and Katie were both beautiful, dark-haired, dark-eyed girls who knew how to use their healthy, tanned good looks and fit young bodies to get their own way. Fresh from bed at around noon, they would appear in the bar dressed in silk dressing gowns requesting freshly squeezed orange juice to top up their first glass of champagne of the day.

As day gave way to night, they would demand tequila complete with the mythical live worm that they thought was needed to give the drink its kick, along with lemon and salt to complete the ritual. They would give us Poms lessons in how to drink tequila. First you lick the salt from between the thumb and index finger, then you suck the lemon and gulp the tequila straight from the bottle, being careful not to swallow the worm – which they insisted really was in the drink, though in fact was a marketing gimmick.

These girls really didn't care about anything or anyone; they swore like troopers, smoked like chimneys, drank like fish and saw the funny side of every situation.

In tow they had a young Australian boy who was permanently glued to a surf board. He carried it everywhere – even in the bar it would be standing by his stool. From him I learned about 'Big Wednesday' – the desire to find the 'big one', the biggest wave, the best buzz, the greatest ride on the surf. Gareth was intense, with a slightly demonic look about him. He had done Australia and now he was looking for kicks in Europe. A young boy with a mission, Gareth knew exactly what he wanted. He drew up a list of all the surf beaches he intended to check out – Cornwall, Germany, France – and he was gone. Off to pursue his dream. I hope he found his ultimate kick, although I don't know what he would have done with the rest of his life.

I envied him. The rest of us also seemed to be looking for that ultimate high but without knowing where to look. Restless, hyperactive, looking for the buzz, chasing the action, but would I even know it when I found it? And would it kill me? I was going to find out.

Moving on from the hotel, I took the lease on a newly refurbished luxury basement flat in Putney, near the River Thames. With me as I moved in on that spring day just after Easter was a three-ring circus from the hotel: Katie, temporarily minus sister Gemma, who had followed Gareth to the continent; Candice, a Jewish princess who had outstayed her welcome at the hotel; and a strange young woman known only by her initials, KC, who claimed to be a musician but turned out to be a very emotionally unstable human being.

On day one in the flat we decided to throw a house-warming party. Unfortunately, the newly installed electricity system had not bargained on four girls who managed to have every electrical appliance in the house on at the same time. The combined demands of kettles, toasters, food processor, hairdryers, irons, heated rollers, curling tongs and foot spas meant that the electrics blew a fuse.

No one knew how to fix it and we couldn't raise the landlord, so the party went ahead by candlelight. At least it saved us from alienating our neighbours when we had hardly even moved in – the party didn't even have loud music as we couldn't use the record player.

Our invited guests sat around in the candlelit living room drinking and smoking and snacking on peanuts and crisps. The laid-back atmosphere was soporific and produced a feel-good factor that saw us all drifting off to bed and sleep early.

'It's going to work out just fine,' I kept telling myself as I settled down to sleep in my new flat, my new life and, with any luck, a new me.

How silly that I didn't know, wherever I travelled, I always took along my insecurity, anxiety and self-doubt. My flatmates were carefree young, single girls; I was some years older, at 27, and still a married woman, albeit one on the run from a husband

and suburbia and determined to prove that I was as cool and funny as the best of them. Anything they could do, I could do, and better.

Before the year was out, I would have tried suicide again, increased my dependence on drugs, developed an eating disorder, and descended into the twilight world of prostitution, pimps and sexual violence. I was not on the game myself, my role was that of an interested bystander, but I did get invited to some of their parties and helped make arrangements for the other girls. Being a working Fleet Street journalist meant that I led a double life, which was deliciously illicit, exciting and scary, and I was always on the look-out for a good story. I always thought one day I would write '*Diary of a Call Girl*' based on their exploits.

One evening there was an impromptu jam session in progress at a flat I was visiting near Victoria Station. Accompanying two guys on guitars was the haunting, hypnotic voice of an attractive but ravaged blonde. She was introduced as Marianne. Drifting off on a cloud of dope, her deep expressive voice seemed familiar – so too did the pouting lips and husky laugh. She sang for us songs that would feature on her future albums *Dreamin' My Dreams* and *Broken English*.

The mystery was soon solved: Marianne Faithfull, the 1960s icon who had been the girlfriend of Mick Jagger and a pop star in her own right, and whose exotic background included being the daughter of a foreign baroness.

Marianne was a notorious heroin addict – tabloid newspapers would track her down from time to time and report the excesses and losses of her drug-fuelled lifestyle – but she was currently in a relatively clean phase. She was about to get married to Ben Brierly of the punk band The Vibrators and was trying yet again to get her life back into some kind of order.

After that first meeting at the drug dealer's, it became a regular event to run into Marianne. She was putting together a new band and as we sat smoking dope, she would entertain us with some of the new songs she was working on.

That summer she married Ben and they moved into a flat in Holland Park in west London. Combining a house warming with the wedding reception, Marianne invited some of us to help them celebrate.

Mint juleps were on the menu, and, when I arrived, Marianne was standing at the oven stirring a large pot of bubbling green stuff. She had been given a recipe on a trip to America but couldn't quite remember it. I helped by filling glasses with sprigs of mint and pouring in the warm liquid. No one seemed quite sure how they should taste so there were no complaints, especially as we had been overgenerous with the alcohol.

Seeing Marianne so content and domesticated, it was easy to believe that she was on the road to recovery and that the heroin habit that had plagued her life might have lost its hold on her. Sadly, it wasn't to be. She went on to use heroin for a number of years and it wasn't until the mid-1980s that she kicked the habit for good. And in 2011 she made a recording come-back, releasing her 18th studio album followed by a European tour and performances at The Barbican and Queen Elizabeth Hall in London.

★ ★ ★

London opened its doors to scores of rich Arabs in the mid-1970s. Strict religious adherence back home meant that they needed to be in a foreign country before letting their hair down. Record oil prices gave them money to burn and their appetites for wine, women and song ensured they had a steady stream of companions willing to show them – and be shown – a good time.

Clubs such as Playboy attracted a clientele of playboy Arabs and many girls who would never have considered themselves prostitutes but enjoyed the lifestyle afforded by these exotic foreigners. Good-time girls might best describe them – I suspect the situation was similar to the one that existed between many British girls and Americans during the Second World War.

First to be seduced by the chorus of Middle Eastern visitors was flat-mate Candice, herself an exotic character. This Jewish princess never got up before noon. Then she would spend some four or five hours getting dressed and ready to go out. Wrapped up in colourful floor-sweeping dresses and coats, her almost waist-length black hair brushed till it shone, Candice would step into her 4-inch heels. She was tiny, and the shoes gave her the appearance of a doll balanced on a wide, jewel-coloured dress.

Mid-afternoon was when Candice ventured forth on a carefully planned and well rehearsed strategy to pick up rich gentlemen friends. Harrods' perfume hall was her pitch. She would walk around, trying out the most expensive perfumes and loitering till a potential customer approached and asked if she would like him to buy something special for her.

She had other regular clients that she met on certain days; it would probably have come as something of a shock to them to realise that the exotic beauty entertained other admirers. Having made contact in the perfume hall, Candice then indulged in a protracted and tantalising game of courtship that was as subtly orchestrated as her favourite, expertly blended fragrances. Candice could have run a school for courtesans.

A typical afternoon's work would revolve around the serious business of present buying as she led her prospects from the perfume counter to the dress department, stopping en route at the jewellery section. Afternoon tea on the terrace of the fourth-floor Georgian restaurant would follow while she flirted and seduced and held herself at arm's length. The delights to come were kept tantalisingly out of reach until the last possible moment.

Often it would be weeks – once even many months – before Candice would be faced with making the ultimate sacrifice, usually in the opulent surroundings of some luxury hotel room. As many of the Arabs were only visiting, she would delay and procrastinate until they were due to leave and then promise that the deal would be completed on their next visit to London.

A master of intrigue and drama, Candice would come up with wild and wonderful stories as to why she had to leave before anything intimate happened. She was a class act and it wasn't unusual for her to end up with her conquests desperate to offer anything to have their evil way with her. Proposals, engagements and marathon late-night phone calls were par for the course.

It may seem strange that these gentlemen were so prepared to play the waiting game, but the strict rules of courtship in their own countries meant that they were used to this long drawn-out process. Chances are that they were also paying visits to more accommodating and perhaps less experienced ladies of the night.

Candice's charades certainly paid rich dividends. Having met her potential clients in Harrods, she affected the demeanour of a rich girl with good family connections and expensive tastes.

Regaling us with tales of her conquests and the colourful web of lies that she spun, Candice would explain some of her rules for getting money without delivering the goods. She was a modern-day Scheherazade. She would tell her suitors that she was behind with her rent (usually true); the phone she relied on for their romantic late-night calls was about to be disconnected; she needed money to visit her eminently respectable parents in far-flung parts of the country; her grandmother was sick.

Those of us who shared her home life had to be particularly careful when answering phone calls; although we were often asked to lie for her to add to the intrigue and mystery, it was vital not to make any comments, or give any information, that might clash with her current story.

And there was an added complication: her boyfriend, Victor. Victor, a black pimp, was the only man who visited Candice at home. She insisted that she was his true love and the only one of his women not to be a working girl. Although he had various 'wives', Candice clung to the belief that she was number one.

Victor's appearances were unpredictable. He might arrive in his flash sports car late at night and stay closeted in the bedroom with her for two days. However, just as frequently he would tell her to stay at home and expect a visit from him but then wouldn't show up. She would wait by the phone for hours. If she was lucky, he would call and make an excuse and promise to come another day.

Sometimes, amid great excitement on her part, he would take her away for a few days, but more than once he sent her back earlier than expected. The sound of a black cab pulling up outside signalled the early arrival home of Candice yet again. An embarrassed taxi driver appeared at the door and asked if someone could help with his female passenger. Opening the door of the cab, he put his hand out to steady Candice. Her appearance came as a shock to us all. Battered and bruised, she stepped out of the taxi, obviously having difficulty walking. Her nose was bloody, her eyes black, her face bruised, her teeth broken. I and another of the flatmates helped her into the flat, demanding an explanation.

Yes, it was Victor who had done this, she agreed. No, we mustn't call the police. And no, we weren't to tell her family what had happened. She just needed to rest.

On the second occasion when Candice was beaten to a pulp by her ever-loving boyfriend, she fled the city. After the heat had died down a bit, Victor started calling to check if she was okay and using all kinds of inducements to get us to divulge her whereabouts. If any of the other girls knew, they certainly weren't telling. I genuinely did not have a forwarding address for her. The rent arrears remained unpaid.

To keep up to date with their financial obligations, the other girls turned to the classic ways young, good-looking females have of making money. It quickly became apparent that prostitution was the name of the game.

Again, Arab money was the lure. Developing a network of contacts, the Australian sisters quickly became regulars on the Arabs' social scene. This involved being invited to parties in luxury apartments, often in the Park Lane and Mayfair areas. The Arabs, who were mostly visiting businessmen, were extremely hospitable. Champagne flowed and lavish spreads of food would be laid on. A party atmosphere would prevail, with music and dancing and lively conversation. Again protocol and ritual were observed. The men would take their pick from the assembled girls and arrangements would be made to accompany them home or to meet up at a later stage. All the girls were expected to dress glamorously, act discreetly and behave beautifully.

Sometimes the invitation would involve a dinner party at a nightclub or restaurant. Those that I attended were civilised and fun affairs. The men conducted themselves with excellent manners and were generous and attentive hosts. Towards the end of the evening, couples would pair off and go to hotel rooms or exchange phone numbers so they could make arrangements to meet up at another time.

Many of the men were very attractive indeed – rich, sophisticated and exotically handsome. After a first-class dinner and generous drinks in a top restaurant, it was no surprise that men and women went home to bed together. Nor was it unusual for the female escorts to be rewarded with a little 'present' for their kind attention. Pulling out rolls of banknotes, grateful Arab businessmen paid the going rate for a one-night stand of up to £100. Big bucks back in the mid 1970s.

It was on one of these party nights that I met Sadd, a beautiful 20-year-old Saudi Arabian student who lived in America. He was related to the Saudi royal family. With his almost black skin and deep brown eyes, he was a handsome devil who knew how to flirt. He was immaculately turned out, his suits costing hundreds of pounds and his leather footwear handmade.

Over that summer he visited London several times and always took a suite at one of London's best hotels overlooking Hyde Park. He would ring me from the airport and we would meet for lunch or dinner before retiring to his hotel room.   O n one occasion he rang and asked me to meet him at the airport. I was astounded to see him in his flowing Arab robes, complete with headdress, as he came off the flight from Riyadh. He looked gorgeous, like something out of a Turkish delight advert. Talk about Arabian Nights!

Sadd declared himself in love with me and I was besotted with him. We enjoyed idyllic days walking in Hyde Park and talking for hours about the differences between our cultures. Drinking alcohol and having sex outside marriage was forbidden by his religion. We broke all the rules. We even harboured unrealistic dreams of having a life together – certainly not in Saudi Arabia, which would be impossible, but perhaps in London or America. We talked and dreamed and made love.

Tanned and fit and attractively slim that year, I took to wearing a gold chain around my waist. Sadd loved it. We would lie together on the big hotel bed, looking into each other's eyes.

His dark brown body and dark eyes offset my comparative paleness. Coffee and cream – a delicious combination.

The last time I saw him off at the airport on an early morning flight to Saudi Arabia, he promised he would be back soon. I never heard from him again.

An infrequent guest at these parties, I was more likely to be found at home making arrangements for the other girls. I would watch them getting ready to go out, bathing, dressing, taking some drugs, drinking some booze. Being older than they were, I felt responsible for them, concerned, even fearful. It was always a relief when I heard their key in the lock and I knew they were home safe and sound.

The mood on the street was changing. The novelty of beautiful Western call girls was wearing off and the game was becoming much more real. Prices were going down as more girls clambered on board the gravy train and the fun was going out of the party scene. It was now business-like – as the oldest profession always has been. And the competition was tough.

Katie, who had been such a lively, bright young Aussie, was becoming cynical and embittered. She was also doing a lot of drugs. Her behaviour became erratic and unpredictable. She was getting further from reality and it was harder and harder to reach her.

We planned a treat, a trip together. We would go to see The Rolling Stones in concert in Paris on their Europe '76 tour. It has to be said that The Rolling Stones live up to their own publicity: they really are 'the most exciting rock and roll band in the world'. The energy of their performances is mind-blowing, even after seeing the band dozens of times over the years (I saw them with some friends later that summer at the Knebworth Festival). Of course, also being one of the richest rock and roll bands in the world ensures that they put on a magnificent show as far as staging, lighting and pyrotechnics are concerned.

Katie and I arrived in Paris on the afternoon of the concert and booked into a hotel overlooking the Eiffel Tower. A combination of drink and drugs – me drunk, her drugged to the eyeballs – led to us having a monumental row and falling out. We were in a taxi on our way to the Stones gig when things came to a head; she demanded that the driver pull up. Out she got and slammed the door. I continued on alone to the stadium. She didn't show up. There was a message for me when I returned to the hotel: she had come back and collected her belongings. She said she had had enough of London and needed to get away. Her plan was to go to Germany to meet up with her parents and sister, who were touring over there.

Returning to London alone, I knew the end was in sight. Katie never did return to the flat, although she wrote to me later. She apologised and explained: 'I was strung out, exhausted, drinking too much, and I needed a few days' sleep.'

Two other girls were sharing the flat by now, although I was still the leaseholder. One of them was KC, the unstable black girl who had been there when we first moved in. She had left for a time but after a failed relationship had come back again. She was scary. Suffering from grief and rage at being betrayed by her boyfriend with her best friend, she spent her waking hours dreaming up ways of exacting revenge. The latest fantasy was to kidnap him, tie him up and cover him in cheese then bring in the neighbourhood rats to eat off him. None of us felt safe being left alone with this sad girl. She had a baby boy who she brought to stay sometimes, but thankfully most of the time he was somewhere in south London with her mother. The flat was no place for a baby. It was no place for any right-minded person.

The last survivor of the flat was a large, bouncy, pseudo-Californian who worked at one of the West End nightclubs as a hostess. Sharon introduced me to 'happy pills'. Her doctor in California swore by them to keep away her depression. When I was not sedated with sleeping pills and valium, I was flying high on 'happy pills'. All still washed down with liberal amounts of alcohol.

Somehow, through all this madness and confusion, I still managed to work. I had got so used to coping on autopilot with the drink and the drugs, I seemed to be moving into a new phase of active addiction. But burn-out was beckoning and I was heading for a crash. It was time to get some help. The flat had to go, so I gave notice to my flatmates and to the landlord.

Packing up all my belongings, I called a taxi.

CHAPTER 10

WE ARE FAMILY

Every available inch of space in the minicab was taken up with all my worldly goods. Suitcases on top of suitcases filled the boot, a stereo system complete with speakers took up the lower layer of the back seat alongside hundreds of albums stacked neatly in matching plastic bags. On top of the music section, layer upon layer of clothes, still on their hangers, stretching up almost to the roof of the car and totally obscuring all sight lines out of the back windows. On the floor, a kettle, toaster, heated rollers, hairdryer, cleaning materials – brushes, cloths, tins of polish, scouring pads – and a foot spa.

In the front seat, on my lap I had a vanity case filled to overflowing with makeup and toiletries. Between my feet was my briefcase jammed full of papers, and balanced precariously on top of that was my handbag, a black leather one almost as large as an overnight bag. This held the most precious of my personal possessions: purse, cheque book and jewellery roll, in which costume jewellery rubbed against the real stuff, mostly presents from my former husband – a strand of milky white pearls, a moonstone ring, a red garnet ring and several pairs of gold hoop earrings plus a matching gold bracelet and necklace. Nestling among them was my discarded wedding ring.

'Where to?' the driver asked yet again. We had set off from Putney over an hour ago and I still hadn't decided on my final destination.

After a quick stop at Hobbes Hotel in Victoria – where I discovered that the female manager I had been friends with had moved on – we ended up at a hotel in Sussex Gardens, Paddington. I had phoned them earlier in the day, having spotted an advert for their special weekly rates in that day's *Evening Standard*. The very provisional booking that I'd made still stood.

Looking relieved that I had found a resting place at last, the patient taxi driver began to help me unload the contents of his cab into the uncomfortably small hotel reception. It was getting dark; nearly nine o'clock on a Friday evening in October, and any driver of a central London minicab would want to be out earning money, making lots of short journeys around the West End. Being used as a removal van had lost its novelty.

While the cab driver continued to unload my possessions, I asked the uninterested but not entirely rude young male receptionist to show me the room I was to occupy. Reluctantly tearing himself away from the TV set perched on the end of the reception desk, he collected a key from the rack behind him and told me to follow him up the narrow staircase.

If the state of disrepair of the public rooms had upset my sense of the aesthetic, as we ascended the staircase I began to have serious concerns. Redecoration alone would not have solved the major problems of scruffiness and general decay.

Somewhere up in the heights of what once would have been

the attic of a splendid old Georgian house, a place where the domestic staff slept, he stopped outside a shabby door and tried the key in the lock. The cracked wooden door creaked open to reveal a small, shabby, single room. Peeling wallpaper, damp patches, grubby curtains, grubby bedding and a filthy washbasin.

The sight assaulted my eyes, the smell made me catch my breath, and the loud music and sounds of quarrelling coming from adjoining rooms almost made me break out in a sweat. I couldn't spend a single night in that foul place. Fearing for my safety and sanity, I made a quick decision.

'It's not a bad room,' he remarked, obviously seeing my apprehension, 'and you can lock it from the inside. The toilet and shower are just one floor down.'

'No, forget it,' I said, turning and walking quickly from the room and down the first few stairs.

As I reached the reception, which was now crowded and noisy as students stood watching the television and waiting for the return of the concierge, the minicab driver looked relieved. Anxious to be on his way, he decided to offer me a good price. 'Call it £25,' he said, holding out his hand for the money and simultaneously gesturing towards all of my belongings lining the walls of the tiny corridor.

Close to tears, I had to throw myself on his mercy.

'Please don't leave me here,' I pleaded. 'I can't stand it. Take me somewhere else.'

He started to protest, frantically trying to find a way to dump me and my possessions and get the hell out of there, but his better nature prevailed. There could be no doubting my obvious distress.

Not for the first time that night, the minicab driver showed himself to be a decent, caring and thoroughly kind human being. With a sigh of resignation and some rude muttering under his breath, my hero of the hour picked up the nearest suitcase and headed back outside to reload the cab.

Settled back into our by now familiar positions in the front seats of the taxi, surrounded by all the paraphernalia of a home from home, he asked again: 'Where to?'

This time I really was going home. I gave him my parents' address in south London.

Closing time, 11 o'clock, and merry males spilled out of public houses as we passed through the London streets on our way to Balham. Mum and dad were happily settled into a lovely new purpose-built flat on a small estate behind the High Road.

Although totally unprepared for my arrival, they welcomed me and all my worldly goods with open arms. The minicab driver had by now became a supportive travelling companion and he was charming as I paid him and added a generous tip for all his help and support – he had gone beyond the call of duty. We parted on friendly terms and he assured me that he would sleep easy in his bed knowing that he had saved a young lady in distress.

I thank God for those special people who restore one's faith in human nature, instead of taking advantage when we are at our weakest and most vulnerable.

Mum and dad had settled into a cosy, domestic routine. Mum went out to work part-time in a supermarket where she was well respected and liked by her colleagues and dad stayed home as a househusband doing all the shopping and cooking. Age had mellowed them and, after having celebrated their silver wedding anniversary, they now seemed to accept that they were destined to stay together. Both of them were less volatile and more comfortable with each other.

Since I'd left school and got married, they had come more

and more to rely on me to sort everything out for them, so having their grown-up daughter back was a blessing. It was a comfortable arrangement and they indulged some of my worst excesses. At weekends I was allowed to sleep till noon, then mum would wake me with a cup of tea before running me a bath. Bizarrely, dad took to painting my toenails for me as I sat watching TV. He would fetch booze, cigarettes and dry cleaning for me and act as my social secretary, taking phone messages and booking my daily taxis. In return, I would provide extra financial support and cover household expenses. Also, I would keep them entertained with tales of where I'd been and who I'd seen.

I was still writing show business features at *Reveille*, which meant that I was in the thick of the entertainment world, especially the small-screen world of popular television. During the mid-1970s I interviewed practically every game show host, situation comedy actor, newsreader and television presenter who graced the three TV channels.

Socially, I kept busy and had my fair share of romantic encounters, though nothing serious. Sometimes work combined with pleasure. As well as the one horrendous encounter with the actor in Birmingham, I also had a more pleasurable experience with another star of the small screen. This one still appears regularly on television and it amuses me to remember our passing affair.

I had met him at a couple of TV events before the evening we bumped into each other at a nightclub in Oxford Street. It developed into a party and he invited a few of us back to his place for yet more late-night drinks. He lived in a beautiful house in south-west London, and we all piled into a chauffeur-driven car to continue the party.

His wife, a well-known actress, was away from home. We

demolished a cheesecake she had left in the fridge, poured drinks and put on smoochy music to dance to. With little preamble, we ended up in bed that night. A few weeks later we met up in the company of friends and went to a Chelsea football match. There was no return match.

The swinging sixties and the concept of free love have, in my opinion, a lot to answer for. Freed from the consequences, with the advent of the pill, women were able to act more like men. But the cost was high. What might have felt like a free-spirited approach turned out to be, for women like me at least, soul destroying. After leaving Gavin and before meeting Derek, I was footloose and fancy-free and I accepted dates, romance or adventure whenever they were offered.

While I cannot condone my past behaviour, I am thankful that later I was able to regain my self-respect and turn my life around. My morality increased in direct proportion to my abstinence from alcohol.

Being back home, I hardly took any drugs but I did drink large amounts. Vodka and bitter lemon was my preferred drink at that time. Somewhere I had heard that vodka doesn't smell – nonsense, of course. When you're drinking upwards of a bottle a day, that seems a forlorn hope, but I still pretended that people didn't know I drank too much.

Of course, mum and dad were daily drinkers, but it upset me that even they would sometimes suggest I was overdoing it.

One Sunday afternoon we sat at home listening to the Art Garfunkel hit song 'Bright Eyes', used on the soundtrack of *Watership Down*, the tear-jerker story about a bunch of rabbits. The chorus line was 'Bright eyes, how can you close and fail?' Mum bought the record for me as I had been called Bright Eyes since the day I was born.

Dad turned to me with tears in his eyes and said, 'Bright Eyes, your light is fading fast. Your eyes are dull. Do something before it's too late.' I stormed out of the house, hurt and angry. I was furious. He was a fine one to talk. Later, I went back and he tried to calm me down.

'It's too late for me, doll,' he told me. 'But you can do something about it. It's not a criticism, it's an observation. If I didn't love you, I wouldn't care so much. Don't let the light fade.' Nearly 10 years later, those words would come back to haunt me as I looked into my own eyes in the bathroom mirror and knew they were about to 'close and fail'.

I enjoyed social outings with my parents and we kept up many family traditions. Going to the races was one of them. The Epsom Derby and the Oaks took place in the same week, and it was a tradition for the three of us to go. We would find our perfect spot and spread a tartan blanket out on the grass up on the Downs. We shared a picnic lunch with strawberries and cream and teased dad for losing pounds – and often nearly his shirt – betting on the horses while mum and I enjoyed minor wins with our shilling punts.

We finished off the day with a visit to the funfair and mum would look on happily while dad and I enjoyed death-defying trips on the roller-coaster and high-speed waltzers. We persuaded her to join us on the bumper cars.

It was like being kids again and we always made our way home exhausted, exhilarated and promising to do it all again next year. For many years we fulfilled that promise, and then mum died, aged just 51, of heart failure. Although dad and I went on our own that first year, we couldn't recapture the fun times. It wasn't the same without mum. The spell had been broken.

I loved horse racing though I am not a sporty person and I certainly was not a cricket fan. However, I was delighted to be invited to a county game and lunch at the Oval by the big wigs at *Reveille*. On that same day I was also a guest at a posh breakfast party at the club Les Ambassadeurs, attended a reception hosted by London Weekend Television for critics, and had front row seats for a Paul Simon concert at the Royal Albert Hall. My life revolved around social events and work commitments – if it was happening in London on the entertainment scene, I would probably be there.

Weekends were my time for recovery. I caught up with my beauty sleep and shopped for the constant demands of a wardrobe that often had to supply half a dozen clothes changes in one day. In the office I kept outfits and jackets to take me from breakfast to dinner and all points in between.

Sometimes my carefully laid plans came unstuck, as on the occasion when I was in the office, all ready for a business lunch with one of the higher-level newspaper executives, and instead I was sent to conduct an interview on a pig farm. The lady in question farmed a rare black breed of porkers that were owned by the then Archbishop of Canterbury. I never did find out why the story was suddenly so urgent.

That day stays in my memory as a complete nightmare. I tried to be polite, professional and interested while picking my way across a muddy field in high heels and a tight skirt. I was far from amused but others in the office thought it very funny when they heard what had happened. And the executive never did buy me that lunch.

Six months after moving back in with my parents, I met Derek: the greatest love of my life, a man who would sweep me off my feet and fall in love with me as passionately and completely as I did with him. He saved my life. Mum and dad approved of my relationship with him, though I didn't go into too many details about his wife and family. They could see that, being 20 years older than me, he was a stabilising influence and they welcomed him into our family. Dad was delighted the first time Derek appeared in his local pub on a Sunday evening and introduced himself as the man who was in love with his daughter. Even before he was famous through television and radio, Derek attracted attention everywhere he went, and the fact that he was a top newspaper executive held great cachet for dad with his drinking mates.

CHAPTER 11

NEVER MIND THE BOLLOCKS

Promising myself that I'd get to bed early for once, I'd cleared my desk and was leaving the office when one of the subeditors walked past my desk. 'Fancy a drink in the Stab?' he asked. The Stab, short for Stab in the Back, was the *Mirror* journalists' name for their local pub, the White Hart.

It wasn't hard to figure out why it was called the Stab. The pub was the breeding ground for every rumour and every bit of juicy gossip pertaining to the executives and staff of the three main Mirror Group titles – *Daily Mirror, Sunday Mirror, The Sunday People* – and *Reveille*, the weekly newspaper of the stable.

Character assassinations, wild accusations and drunken treachery were the staple diet of the constantly changing cast of characters in the Stab. In the early evening the pub filled with editorial staff finishing work for the day and an assortment of secretaries and administrative workers. There were also visitors, usually PR men or publicity girls hoping to meet up with an executive in an informal setting, buy them a drink and sell a news story or feature idea. It was also a meeting place for underemployed journalists looking for casual work.

As the evening wore on, production people, the subeditors, art editors and backbench executives would pop in when they had finished their shifts or were on a late meal break. By 10.30 or 11pm, when the first edition of the paper was printed and all but a handful of production staff had finished work for the day, the pub would be heaving. Shop talk was the order of the day. Work was discussed, alliances were formed and romances were started and finished.

On 2 December 1976, it was about 7pm when I arrived with my office colleague at the Stab in Fetter Lane from *Reveille*'s office across the river at Waterloo. We were disappointed to find that most of our friends and contemporaries were not there.

'They've all gone to a farewell party over at the Princess Louise in High Holborn,' the barman told us helpfully.

'Do you want to go?' said a colleague.

'Might as well,' said I.

We finished our drinks and took a taxi to the new venue about a mile away. Sure enough, when we got there we were greeted by dozens of our friends who were packed into an upstairs room – where they got louder and drunker as the evening wore on.

The gathering was a farewell party for a *Daily Mirror* reporter, John Penrose, who was being transferred to the paper's office in Rome. I didn't know him particularly well but went over and congratulated him on landing what was considered one of the plum postings.

By 10 o'clock I was getting ready to go. The early night I had promised myself was not going to happen, but at least it didn't need to be a late night. As I stood in a crowd of people, the conversation turned to that day's *Daily Mirror* front page: SEX PISTOLS IN FOUR-LETTER TV SHOCKER.

'That story should not have been on the *Daily Mirror*'s front page,' I said.

Sensing aggro, a Scottish subeditor, one Bill Fletcher, jumped into the discussion. 'Tell that to this man,' he said. 'He's running the *Daily Mirror* at the moment. He's responsible for what goes on the front page.'

Bill broke away from the group and pushed his way with me in tow to another group just yards away across the crowded bar. 'This young lady's got something to say to you,' said Bill, as we stood before a tall, curly-haired man I had never seen before.

'Ellen Petrie meet Derek Jameson, managing director of the *Daily Mirror*.' He pushed me towards him. 'Tell him what you just told the rest of us.'

I repeated my opinion. 'That was not a *Daily Mirror* splash. That story should never have been on the front page of the *Mirror*.' It was the story of a major confrontation on the previous evening's TV news magazine programme *Granada Reports*, when veteran presenter Bill Grundy was forced to move studios to get away from the outrageous behaviour and language of the punk rock group Sex Pistols.

'Don't you tell me what to put on the front page of my newspaper,' said the executive in charge in a forceful voice. 'I was producing front pages when you were still in nappies.'

I stood my ground. Verbal sparring was very much a feature of the newspaper game and the Fleet Street pub culture.

Our eyes locked and we faced each other. The atmosphere was charged with electricity; a powerful chemistry was at work. We continued to look at each other, then, with emotions running high, I changed tack. I leaned towards him and straightened his tie. Whether I realised at the time what an overtly flirtatious gesture that was I still don't know.

'Dreadful tie,' I commented, holding in my hand the gaudy replica of an ancient Greek temple scene.

'I know,' he laughed. 'Don't know why I wore it.'

We had found something to agree on. We were standing very close together. He certainly was a powerful presence, I thought. So this was the great Derek Jameson, the ace newspaper circulation builder from the north, and at that stage the blue-eyed boy of the Mirror Group.

'I'm just going back to check the edition,' he told me. 'Come with me. Then you can see how a real newspaper is run.'

It was close to 11 o'clock. We left the pub together and as we crossed the road to catch up with a passing black cab, he took my hand.

Back at the *Daily Mirror*, he made a tour of inspection of the editorial floor and I followed. This man was an impressive operator. A larger-than-life character. He moved with complete authority down the length of the department, barking out instructions, making jokes, laughing loudly, and every now and then stopping to describe how he wanted something changed.

Derek Jameson, Managing Director, commanded total respect and was obviously well liked. His very presence set off a buzz of excitement in the atmosphere; his powerful energy swept others along with his enthusiasm and professionalism. One newspaper executive told me, "When Derek is in charge, you always know the paper is in safe hands."

After about an hour, he was ready to leave. As he walked towards the exit, he called out his final instruction: 'When the paper's off the press, send over a copy to me at the Zanzibar.'

We walked together into the Zanzibar – a trendy, private members' drinking and eating club in London's fashionable Covent Garden.

And we were together for the next 36 years.

CHAPTER 12

THE POWER
OF LOVE

By midnight the Zanzibar was packed to bursting. It was a favourite haunt of media people, who had spent the evening wining and dining in restaurants and pubs and now wanted to do some meeting and greeting. The Zanzibar was one of the 'in places' to see and be seen.

After the theatres had closed, actors, actresses, members of theatre chorus lines and backstage staff would all arrive. The out-of-work actresses and actors who were 'resting', after working their late-night shifts as waiting staff at trendy restaurants such as Joe Allen's, would also descend on the Zanzibar.

Perched on a high stool at the bar, I drank an exotic blue cocktail. Blue Lagoon was a mixture of blue curaçao, vodka and lemonade. The Zanzibar was one of the first cocktail bars in London and its list of exotic concoctions included more well-known drinks such as Piña Colada and Banana Daiquiri, which I'd acquired a taste for in American-inspired bars and restaurants like this establishment and one of my other favourite bars, the upmarket hamburger joint Peppermint Park.

As the crush of people at the bar got more uncomfortable and the noise level rose even higher, Derek and I swapped personal histories.

He never hid from me the fact that he was a married man. Pauline, his wife, had stayed behind in Manchester to pack up the home when he had moved south to take up his new position. There was also another good reason for her staying close to her family in Manchester, Derek admitted. She was pregnant with their second child, which was due in March. Ben, their first child, was four years old.

Derek was too honest to go into any 'my wife doesn't understand me' routine. And I was too naive to think that our evening together was anything more than a fling. Moral considerations did not enter my head. Although I had never made a habit of having affairs with married men, I wasn't exactly averse to the idea. I told him that I was married but was separated from my husband, who still lived in the marital home in Kent. By then I had returned home to mum and dad in south London.

We left the Zanzibar, hand in hand, at around one o'clock. Derek hailed a taxi. 'Where's it to?' he asked, as we settled in the back seat. 'St James's or Balham?'

The *Daily Mirror* was paying for a luxury flat for Derek in Bury Street, St James's – he had already told me that. In a trick that was to change the course of both our lives, he took a coin from his pocket. Repeating the options, he offered: 'St James's – heads? Or Balham – tails?' It was almost 20 years before I realised that he had already decided which it was to be. 'Heads – St James's,' he cried triumphantly.

Minutes later we climbed the impressive staircase to a well furnished flat at the top of the substantial apartment block.

There was a comfortable if impersonal living room, two bedrooms – one with a double bed, the other with two singles – a bathroom and a fully equipped kitchen.

We went straight to the bedroom. Derek was undressed and in bed in minutes. As I started to undress, he lay with his arms stretched out above his head, watching me. I took off my blouse and undid the zip on the chocolate-coloured corduroy skirt I was wearing. Stepping out of the skirt, I then pulled off the black polo neck sweater I had been wearing under my flame-coloured blouse. I stood there in my underwear and knee-high brown boots.

'Beautiful,' he sighed appreciatively. 'Come to bed.'

We made love and fell asleep wrapped in each other's arms.

Some hours later, I woke up and Derek was in the bathroom. As he heard me stir, he came out of the bathroom, drying his face with a towel. He pointed at me and said, 'You didn't have an orgasm. I'll put that right next time.'

It was strange how embarrassed that extremely intimate remark made me feel in the bright light of day. Excited, too. Here was a man who actually noticed whether a woman had been satisfied in bed.

The fact was I hardly ever had a genuine orgasm. I was so used to faking it, that the real thing was rarely an issue. Sex was something I did as a reward for whatever the man had done for me. Take me out, flatter me, and buy me a meal or a few drinks. It had become a fairly typical way to end an evening. Not that I didn't enjoy sex; it was just that I didn't care too much either way. Most men seemed to expect it. Few were very good at it.

Derek was the exception. He was the best lover I ever had – he was amazing in bed, imaginative, intuitive and adventurous. He really did ignite in me a previously untapped passion fuelled by our deep love.

The next few weeks were a frantic round of Christmas parties and events. He and I became a couple from day one; news of our affair spread like wildfire in Fleet Street. But all was not well at home.

After spending my first night with Derek, I returned home to south London to change clothes before going to work. My colleague on the show business pages, John Deighton, would cover for me, just as I would have done for him.

As it was after midnight when we left the Zanzibar, I had decided not to phone my dad. My not going home was not an altogether unusual occurrence, although I usually did phone to tell my parents of my plans.

When I arrived home the next morning, dad was slumped in the armchair. I tried to wake him but to no avail. Mum had gone to work. After bathing and changing my clothes, I tried again to move him. I had expected him to wake up when he heard me moving about the small flat.

Gradually I realised that he had overdosed on pills and alcohol. It wasn't difficult to work out. I spotted the carefully contrived scene. The empty bottle of pills by his armchair and the empty bottles of booze. As I shook him, pulled up his eyelids, talked to him and tried to get him out of the chair, he started to come to. He was mumbling almost incoherently but at least he was conscious.

From what I could gather, he had been so worried about me that he had decided – after the usual night of continual drinking – to try to top himself. I'm not sure what it was supposed to prove but I gave him little sympathy. I persuaded him to drink a cup of black coffee and after establishing that he was not in any danger, I helped him into bed.

'Have a good long sleep,' I told him. 'We'll talk when I get home this evening.'

However, the affair with Derek took off so quickly and became so all-consuming that dad and I never did have that talk. Within days I had virtually moved into the Bury Street flat. It really had been love at first sight for both of us. Each of us had found their soul mate.

Our affair was the talk of Fleet Street. Derek didn't try to hide it. On that first night he had invited me to attend a special screening of the *King Kong* remake in a cinema in Soho, the following week. The film's distributors had put on this private screening for executives and reviewers of the *Daily Mirror*. Derek made a beeline for me as I walked into the small reception area.

'I haven't stopped thinking about you all weekend,' he said as he leaned forward to give me a welcoming kiss. During the film we sat in the first row and held hands. We watched the film in a state of heightened anticipation and then headed straight for home – and bed. We were mad with passion for each other. We would be awake all night making love. As dawn came up over the rooftops of London, he would insist, 'I must get a couple of hours sleep. I've got a newspaper to run.'

Then we would try to settle down to sleep, but as soon as one limb touched another or our lips met, we'd be fired up with longing all over again. Derek's imagination knew no bounds. He would engage every one of my senses and make me feel alive.

I was deliriously happy and in love. This man had brought me to life. I was besotted with him. We slept together, travelled to work together, lunched together, met up after work, went home together, and still managed to talk on the phone several times a day, exchange love notes and presents and miss each other desperately.

It felt like we had known each other for a lifetime. If I never experience it again, I thank God for the incredible gift of an all-consuming, desperate love affair. As he would write to me in a letter some three years later, 'You have been the most incredible love of my not uneventful life. We really did fall in love, madly, desperately, totally.'

Through Christmas, the New Year and the following month, we spent every waking moment together. Although Derek travelled home to Manchester most weekends, he would dash back to me at the first available moment.

My working life was energised by our wonderful love affair and it was a time of successful stories, an exciting social life and the love of my life to admire and support the job I was doing. 'My highly clever lady writer,' he called me. I revelled in the attention and basked in the glow of love.

On Valentine's Day 1977, I headed off on my first trip to America, though not with Derek.

New York, the Big Apple, was the first stop and then a trip down to Florida was planned. My travelling companion, a fellow female journalist, had encouraged me to book the holiday some six months previously. We had been determined to start a new life for ourselves and to take America by storm, and we had chosen Valentine's Day as a symbol of our desire for romance and adventure. We found both.

She met someone and fell in love with him on the plane from Gatwick to New York. A Scottish golf professional called Bobby. He lived on Long Island, half an hour by car ride from NYC.

Our arrival at Newark airport was dramatic. I had been drinking on the flight – heavily – and the aggressive attitude of American immigration found a match in my arrogant British superiority. I was later told that they had threatened to refuse me entry – I didn't remember. But they let me into the country after my friend did a bit of diplomatic intervention.

We had booked a hotel on West 42nd Street, in the theatre district, but within a day she and I had moved into Bobby's apartment on Long Island. I went along for the ride. I had fallen head over heels in love with Derek and couldn't wait to get back to England – although I did have a minor romantic encounter with a blond all-American tennis coach who helped me fulfil a lifetime ambition of kissing and cuddling in the back seat of a convertible at a drive-in. And I had an innocent flirtation with Bobby's flatmate – a zany, spaced-out New York golfer.

The other journalist and I had arranged our trip to Florida to be interviewed for feature writing positions with the British-run but American-owned *National Enquirer*, based in Fort Lauderdale. Somehow they had devised a system for getting British journalists the coveted American work permit, the green card. We made the 24-hour journey by Amtrak; it was the stuff of American legend, that old train whistle blowing as we powered through the countryside and mountains, and all kinds of wild and wonderful characters on board. The club room was a riot of partying with a succession of travellers playing a honky-tonk piano and singing.

Derek called me and I called him several times a day. Despite the *National Enquirer* interview, there was never any question that I wasn't going straight back home to him at the first possible opportunity. Although my outward behaviour might still have been somewhat unconventional, I had genuinely fallen in love with this man – my heart was engaged.

The reunion at Gatwick airport was emotional, passionate and, after three weeks in the States, long overdue. We were ecstatic to be back together again and, apart from when we had to eat, we didn't get out of bed for several days.

Derek's flat in St James's was our love nest and refuge. But reality was around the corner. Less than a week after I arrived back, late one evening the phone rang. Derek's wife had gone into labour. He returned to Manchester to be with her.

While Derek was at the hospital, he got a phone call from his eldest son, Peter. Derek's first wife, Jackie, whom he had divorced some 10 years previously, had died. A birth and a death on the same night. Derek phoned me at the flat to break the news.

Obviously, our idyllic life in the big city was about to change.

Derek found a four-storey house for the family in Islington, north London, and I moved into a flat in Dolphin Square, Pimlico, on the banks of the River Thames.

By the summer, Derek had been made editor of the *Daily Express* and I had found us a perfect place a mile from Fleet Street near Gray's Inn Road. The living room was modern and streamlined with white carpets, glass furniture and oversized, comfortable seating units. The bedroom had mirrored wardrobes, red velvet curtains and a king-sized four-poster bed swathed in white lace.

With the proceeds of the sale of my long forgotten marital home in Beckenham, I bought the one-bedroom flat in Clare Court, a mansion block in Judd Street. Despite later owning larger and grander properties, Derek always said it was his favourite home ever.

It was a love nest par excellence. On his way from work, Derek would get his driver to drop us off at the flat, wait outside while we made love, and then take him home to Islington. Practically every night I met him straight from work, we went to dinner, waited in the pub until the paper came out, and then went home. When he could manage it, he would organise trips out of town and I would go with him.

The affair grew more intense and more passionate, and it became more and more obvious that it was only a matter of time before his wife worked out that something was going on, as he spent so little time at home. When she finally discovered the affair, Derek left home. Apart from a brief return to fulfil a family holiday obligation, he never went back again.

For the next seven years we continued to live in that one-bedroom flat. Every weekend Derek took his sons out. Like any other single father, he took them to the cinema, the park and McDonald's.

Pauline laid down the law: her sons were not to be introduced to me or allowed to visit the flat if I were there. That situation lasted for almost the next 10 years. Pauline maintained her dignity and the loyalty of her ex-husband while firmly holding onto her position as the mother of his children. It was an arrangement that worked. He had the utmost respect for her.

Derek and I were now officially a couple and we both obtained divorces from our partners. As he had eventually told me about the coin trick he had played to make sure I stayed with him that first night, I revealed a secret too. Using a spell from an ancient *Book of Enchantments*, I had performed a magic pink candle ritual to bind him to me forever. He loved that romantic gesture and he loved me all his life. A word of warning: spells are sacred and powerful. 'Forever' is a long time – we were together for 36 years and married for almost a quarter of a century.

There's no such thing as 'forever' in Fleet Street, however, and with the closure of *Reveille* by Mirror Group Newspapers in a cost-cutting exercise I had launched into a successful new career as a freelance feature writer.

Then in 1984, Rupert Murdoch fired Derek from *News of the World*, where he had been the editor for the previous two years, having left Express Newspapers in 1980. Derek also got involved in a messy libel action with the BBC. The case went against him and he lost all his savings – £75,000 – in paying costs and his own legal fees.

By the following year, 1985, he had recovered financially and was earning enough to move us into a beautiful three-bedroom garden flat in Elgin Avenue, Maida Vale. His broadcasting career took off and, after a whirlwind apprenticeship when he appeared on every game show, chat show and panel show on television networks all over the country, Derek landed his big break.

The breakfast show on BBC Radio 2 was offered to him and he jumped at the chance to become a full-time broadcaster. Within months, his show was attracting a daily audience of some 10 million.

I continued to do freelance feature writing for newspapers such as the *Daily Star*, *Sun*, *Mirror* and various Sunday supplements and women's magazines. Our life together was great. Our love grew stronger and Derek was prospering.

There was only one shadow over our idyllic life: my heavy drinking. It seemed to have been getting progressively worse and by the time Derek started the Radio 2 job in March 1986, he was threatening that he could not cope with my daily drinking as well as the demands of his new show business career.

Erratic behaviour, with violent mood swings and emotional outbursts, and a gradual deterioration in my physical and mental health eventually led me to rock bottom with my alcoholism. By a miracle, I agreed to seek help. In June 1986, I had my last drink.

Two years later, in 1988, Derek and I married in Arundel cathedral. Our wedding present to ourselves was a fabulous home on the beach in Brighton, which we named Angels' Rest. Our neighbours were Fat Boy Slim, the club DJ, his wife, television presenter Zoe Ball, and a former EastEnder's actor, Nick Berry. Many years later we later we sold the house to Sir Paul McCartney and his soon to be second wife, Heather Mills.

CHAPTER 13

LOVE ON THE ROCKS

Derek dedicated the second volume of his autobiography, Last of the Hot Metal Men, *to me with these words: 'For Ellen, who took my hand and walked into the light.' In the following extracts he described how we met – and my later problems with alcohol – from my perspective.* [The text below in this chapter is extracted from *Last of the Hot Metal Men: From Fleet Street to Showbiz: Volume II of His Life Story by Derek Jameson*, published by Ebury Press. Reprinted by permission of The Random House Group Limited.]

It was 2 December 1976. Mike Molloy, the editor of the *Daily Mirror*, was on holiday and I was in charge. Always in my element when left alone to run the paper, I was particularly pleased with that day's splash. 'Sex Pistols in Four-letter TV shocker.' The new wave punk group had forced Bill Grundy to abandon an interview on tea-time television when their behaviour and language became uncontrollable.

'That wasn't a *Daily Mirror* page one story,' said a female journalist who only a few seconds earlier I had been introduced to as Ellen Petrie, a feature writer on *Reveille*.

I had left the office early to go to a farewell party for *Mirror* reporter John Penrose who had been made Rome correspondent in the days when newspapers kept foreign bureaux all over the world. His appointment had not met with my approval. To this day I still claim that if you sent Penrose to cover the Great Fire of London, he would ask 'Where's the fire?' Still, the editor had given him this plum job and I went along to the Princess Louise pub in Holborn to bid him bon voyage.

There are always smart alecs in the pub who want to tell the editor how he should be running the paper. This particular smart alec interested me. Ellen was tall with long auburn hair and she was wearing a jumper under her blouse. Quite a looker, too.

'How dare you?' I said, launching straight into an attack. 'Don't you tell me how to run newspapers, my girl. I was producing newspapers when you were still in nappies.'

She didn't flinch. 'That story should not have been on page one,' she repeated.

The sparks were flying and already that strange phenomenon, sexual chemistry, was in overdrive. We were igniting each other. Face to face, eyes locked, we engaged in verbal battle.

When the time came for me to go back to the office to check the first edition of the next day's paper, I invited her along. To see how a proper newspaper was run.

We collected her coat, a huge fun fur which made her look like a honey teddy bear, and took the office car back to Holborn Circus. The Fleet Street gossip machine started working as soon as we left the pub together.

I had only been back from Manchester a few weeks following my promotion to managing editor, number two on the paper.

The *Mirror* had provided me with a luxury serviced flat in St James's while I looked around for a property to buy.

Ellen stayed the night with me at St James's. The following morning I had just arrived at the office when I got a phone call from my old mate Peter Grimsditch, who was deputy editor of *Reveille*.

'You wouldn't know the whereabouts of one of my feature writers, Ellen Petrie, would you?' he asked.

'At this moment she is in the ladies' loo changing her clothes,' I told him.

It should have ended there. A one-night stand. I had a pregnant wife and son back in Manchester. It should have ended there but I knew it couldn't.

By the following week when we had our first date, a trip to the cinema to see the remake of *King Kong*, we were already heavily involved.

It was one of those relationships where in a very short time you already feel as if you have been together for years.

I had never been involved with a lady writer before and enjoyed hearing all about the jobs she was doing and took a great pride in seeing her large byline on an exclusive feature.

Ellen seemed to have a genuine love for newspapers and delighted in showing me her latest efforts. She was anxious to improve her journalistic skills and glad of my experience and advice.

For the first time I had someone who understood the newspaper business and loved it as much as I did.

Extramarital affairs are a common occurrence in Fleet Street and though we were playing a dangerous game, I never hid my love for Ellen. In the long evening hours waiting for the first edition to come up, we would go out to dinner or stand around the office pub, the White Hart, known to all as the Stab for Stab in the Back, talking shop.

We were a couple and most people accepted that the relationship was none of their business. It was a painful yet exhilarating time. On the one hand I felt desperately guilty about my wife and family. On the other, I was madly in love and just couldn't keep away from Ellen. In those early days we broke up many times when I decided I had to do the decent thing and be faithful to Pauline who had now joined me in London with Ben and our new son, Dan.

For all my good intentions the partings never lasted more than a few hours before I would telephone her or make a search of the Fleet Street pubs until I found her.

There were some who tried to warn me. *Reveille* was a part of the Mirror Group and my new love had managed to capture the attention and imagination of several people in the organisation.

There were stories of her wild behaviour and these served to excite me even more.

Ellen didn't deny the stories but was always reluctant to be pressed on details of her life before me. She had been married to a Scottish journalist called Gavin Petrie. They had lived a nice middle-class existence in a semi-detached in Beckenham, Kent.

Her only explanation for walking away from all that cosy domesticity was that she had been bored. She was already separated when we met and, having spent most of the year moving from flat to flat with an assortment of other unattached girls, was now back living with her parents in Balham, south London. When the house in Beckenham was sold she would buy a flat of her own.

In her married life she had never wanted children and I was impressed and relieved that this independent, self-supporting career girl was adamant that she would never marry again.

I knew I was a failure as a husband and domestic life with my children was never a priority. I was too ambitious and consumed by newspapers to give my attention to being a husband and father.

Ellen understood and agreed that newspapers came first, though I often told her, 'I should be working my balls off to be successful at the *Daily Mirror*, not involved in a passionate and all-consuming affair with you.'

The work was successful despite my misgivings and it was less than a year later when Lord Matthews offered me the job of editor of the *Daily Express*.

For my first television appearance on *The Editors*, Ellen bought me a new shirt and tie. In brown. Colours I never wore but to please her I wore them on the programme.

I was in my first week as editor of the *Daily Express* when I arranged to meet her in the front hall of the Black Lubianka, the *Express* building in Fleet Street. Ellen had already been celebrating my appointment with my new staff in the *Express* pub next door, the Popinjay. In the front hall in full view of security men, messengers and passing *Express* executives, she fell flat on her face.

I was livid but, having helped her up, put her in a taxi to go home. 'Can't hold her drink,' I thought. Drinking is an occupational hazard in Fleet Street and at that time it didn't stand out that Ellen drank any more than other people. Long hours hanging around pubs of course meant consuming alcohol, not for the sake of drinking but just because there was nothing else to do.

A year to the day that we had met, on 2 December 1977, Ellen moved into her own flat. It was a one-bedroomed flat in a mansion block just off the Gray's Inn Road. A short taxi ride from her office in Fetter Lane and halfway between the *Express* and my family home in Islington.

She had decorated and furnished the flat before moving in.

Chocolate brown settees, white carpets and glass and chrome tables. For the bedroom she had bought a pine four-poster bed with lace drapes. Ruby red velvet curtains framed the windows. The perfect love nest.

On that first Friday night she held a house-warming party. As midnight approached and the other guests drifted away, I prepared to leave. Without warning, Ellen started a scene. Upset and crying, she held on to me and pleaded with me to stay the night.

With a wife waiting at home it was out of the question. 'You don't love me,' she accused. 'Just this once, please. I've never asked before. Please don't leave me.'

It disturbed me greatly to see her so upset and I was powerless. I couldn't just not go home. Of course I loved her, but Pauline was still my wife.

I tried to calm Ellen down and promised to stay until she fell asleep. I arrived home much later than I intended but in newspapers there are always good excuses for working late.

The next day when I telephoned, Ellen didn't mention the incident. It didn't occur to me then that she might have no memory of it. I took the view that she was emotional having got her own home again and felt sad about being left on her own.

She had always accepted that I could not walk out on my wife and children and never asked me to do it.

Her emotional outburst had disturbed and upset me. Already wracked by guilt and divided loyalty, I again tried to end the affair. It wasn't fair to put her through all this and I urged her to build a new life for herself with someone who was free.

We had a long, sad lunch and agreed not to see each other again. That evening I turned up on her doorstep. She came to the door with a towel on her head. Underneath her hair was blue. She had tipped a whole bottle of bleach over it.

'What are you playing at?' I yelled.

With a shrug she told me, 'Dying my hair blonde to start my new life.'

'Your life is with me,' I told her, cradling her in my arms. 'I don't know how, when or where but we have to be together.'

The next day she looked a fright. Her lovely, long auburn hair was the colour of straw and the same texture. A trip to the hairdresser resulted in it being chopped down to 1 inch all over.

In the next few years, Ellen's dramatic gestures became more and more outrageous. On that occasion only her hair was a casualty; later she would try to take her own life.

I continued to lead my double life. The situation at home became more and more unhappy and I made more and more excuses to be away. Pauline was convinced I was having an affair.

Unlike the *Mirror*, where everybody had known and loved Pauline, at the *Express*, Ellen was the woman most often at my side.

Being away from all those old friends at the *Mirror* and their disapproval made it easier to make my decision.

I was going to leave my wife and children and set up home with Ellen. By now, Pauline knew I was involved elsewhere and that it was not a passing affair. I couldn't stand the lying and cheating anymore or the sad and confused look on her face. Knowing that she had done nothing wrong, that she was a perfect wife and mother made it all the harder. I knew how much I was hurting her but I had to grab the chance of happiness and emotional fulfilment with Ellen.

Very few married men choose the mistress. I know why. It was the hardest thing I ever had to do. On 13 April 1978 I packed my bags and left home.

Ellen welcomed me with open arms. We settled into a cosy, domestic routine which would have been idyllic but for my terrible guilt. I took the eldest boy, Ben, out every Sunday and if sometimes when I got home Ellen had had a bit too much to drink, I put it down to her insecurity about me and the family commitments.

My position as editor of the *Daily Express* meant that we had a glittering social life. There were invitations to parties, receptions, premieres and first nights. Ellen loved dressing up and having a good time. We were out most nights of the week and when we had an odd free evening were more than glad to curl up together in front of the television.

Before leaving home I had booked to go on a family holiday to Greece. I didn't tell Ellen but I still intended to go rather than disappoint Ben, who was then six.

I was trying to work out a way to tell Ellen when she behaved in a way which made me wonder why I had ever left home for her. She disgraced herself at a family party, getting outrageously drunk and dancing suggestively with some neighbour while his wife and I fumed on the sidelines.

Despite protests from her family, I dragged her out and when I got her home I laid my cards on the table. I was blazing with anger. 'I didn't go through all the agony of leaving my wife and children to have you treat me like that,' I told her. 'I would never have left home if I had known you were a drunk. And I'm going back to take them on holiday next month.'

With the plausibility which was to disarm and confuse me so many times in years to come, Ellen owned up. 'I knew you were going to leave me,' she said. 'I could tell you had something on your mind. I guessed you were planning to go home; that's why I behaved so badly.'

We kissed and made up. Over the next few weeks I was back on the emotional see-saw. I reassured Ellen that I wasn't leaving, just fulfilling my obligations to a family holiday. Pauline was prepared to forgive and forget and saw the holiday as a way of us giving our marriage another chance.

At short notice Ellen booked a holiday to Spain so she was away at the same time as me. I drove her to the airport and returned to spend my last night at the flat alone. Late into the night I sat composing the letter I would leave for her return.

'This should be a thank-you-very-much-it-was-lovely note,' I wrote, 'but I can't do it because I love you so desperately and somehow, someway I have to get back to you. God help me, we really did fall in love properly and beautifully. Whatever happens, remember that you gave me the best 18 months of my not uneventful life.' I ended, 'Take care – and go easy on the booze.'

The next day I packed all my belongings and moved back home again. Pauline, Ben and I went on holiday in a spirit of friendly truce.

The first day back at the office after the holiday I telephoned Ellen and we met for lunch.

'When are you coming back?' she demanded. I hedged.

'If you are not back by the weekend then it really is all over between us,' she threatened. 'While you were still at home I accepted the situation of being the other woman. But now that we have been living together I am not going back to that half life.'

On that Sunday I packed my bags again and left the matrimonial home for good. Pauline started the divorce proceedings.

★ ★ ★

Being freelance suited Ellen fine. She didn't have to go to an office every day. She could work when she liked and as long as she met the deadlines everyone was happy. Sometimes meeting those deadlines meant she stayed up all night working at the typewriter with a bottle of Scotch at her side. Always a night owl, she spent most of her day in bed. She always denied she was recovering from too much drink. Her work schedule was erratic. That was the life of a freelance, she tried to convince me.

In December 1980 I parted company with Express Group Newspapers. We headed for Scotland to celebrate New Year with her family. A few days later I drove back down the motorway with Ellen, white, shaken and exhausted. She would tell me defensively, 'Everyone likes a drink – I am a party girl.' When she had a drink in her she would add, 'Everyone except boring old you, who doesn't know what having a good time means.'

1981 saw my first venture into the world of show business. Granada Television had signed me to do a pilot of a new late-night magazine programme. We worked on it for a month. It was exciting but nerve-wracking. I had appeared on radio and TV numerous times. Now I was running the show.

It was a month of working out the format of the show, gathering guests, never easy for a pilot, preparing interviews and all the time trying to get familiar with the technical workings of a television studio. Cameras, lights, autocue, earpieces with which the producer could talk to you from the control box.

I had my teeth fixed, tried to lose some weight and spent hours in rehearsal learning to be spontaneously natural on television.

The cast of characters on the show included many new alternative comedians whose hardest job was to remember not to swear on screen.

Rik Mayall, Alexei Sayle and French and Saunders made hilariously funny colleagues. We were all trying to find our feet in the world of television and all went on to be hugely successful later.

Although it had many good elements, the Granada bosses did not take up the option to make a series.

At Easter that year we joined Ellen's parents for a long

weekend in Blackpool. Worried about my future and needing reassurance, I went to one of the gypsy fortune tellers on the Golden Mile. She told me many things about my work and prospects and then asked, 'You're worried about your partner, aren't you? She's a sick person but she will get well.'

With the confidence and grandiosity displayed by so many of her kind, Ellen encouraged me to give show business another try.

'I know you can be a big, big star,' she would tell me. 'This can't be the end of the road for you. You are too powerful. You have too much to give. Don't let them beat you. I don't want you to go back to newspapers as a number three or four. You can make it in show business.'

Her enthusiasm and faith in my abilities fired me up. Her support kept me going.

Although it was difficult for someone like her who had no regard for money, she told me grandly, 'You concentrate on becoming a star. I'll pay the rent.'

Anyway, in those next months she did appear to be self-supporting. If she had money problems, she didn't burden me with them.

Ellen was working constantly, mostly for the *Daily Star*. They thought highly of her and the job satisfaction and respect she received did seem to steady her.

I gave show business my best shot. I appeared on every chat show, quiz show, panel game and discussion programme going as well as writing a twice-weekly column in the new *Today* newspaper.

The media exposure was working and the work rolled in. My big break came with a BBC2 television series called *Do They Mean Us?* It did fabulously well in the ratings and to this day my catchphrase is 'Do They Mean Me?'

Within 18 months I had earned enough to move us out of the one-bedroom flat we shared for so long.

We bought a beautiful garden flat with three bedrooms in Maida Vale. We had an office each. Sheer luxury after so long with Ellen's desk in the living room and mine in the bedroom.

'Now I will be happy forever,' she told me when we moved in. 'I'll never want for anything else.'

Ellen had freedom in her own office. She could escape from me – and I from her. She furnished her office like a bedsitter. Sofa bed, wardrobe, display unit complete with cocktail cabinet, fridge, television, telephone – and a desk.

From behind closed doors I could hear the bottles and glasses clinking. Sometimes she would 'work' late into the night and I would hear her making long, drunken phone calls. But now instead of disturbing me, she would crash out on the sofa bed in her office. She tried to avoid confrontations about her drinking and kept much of it secret from me. Still, I would have had to be blind not to notice that she rarely came home without a plastic bag clinking with bottles.

Just before Christmas 1985 I landed the top job in radio. The old Wogan breakfast slot on BBC Radio 2. I was now a powerful force in broadcasting.

We treated ourselves to a holiday in Tenerife. As usual on holiday, Ellen took the view that drinking was a normal activity and there was no reason why she shouldn't spend hours in the hotel bar.

One night she drank even more than usual. Another drunken row started.

She screamed at me, 'Look at all I've done for you. I've made you a star. You were nothing when I met you.'

If it hadn't been so painful it would have been comic. As the managing editor of the *Daily Mirror* I thought I was doing quite well for myself.

When she sobered up, I warned Ellen. 'I can't take all the pressures of this new life and you drunk all the time. This is deadly serious. It's me or the booze. You can't have both.'

When we returned from holiday Ellen informed me, 'I'm on a Drinkwatchers' course. It's like Weight Watchers. You have so many units per week.' For women it was 20 units – each unit being a single measure of spirits. With the two suggested alcohol-free days each week that meant she could have four units per day. It didn't seem much compared with the vast quantities of alcohol that she usually drank. Still, anything was worth a try.

It worked fine for two weeks. Then Ellen decided that four units weren't much use to her so she would save up her allowance for the week and have all 20 on one day. Madness. It was like a slimmer having their whole week's calorie allowance all in one go.

On 7 April 1986 I started my show on Radio 2. Ellen settled into a new drinking pattern. She wouldn't start until I had gone to bed at 9.30 in the evening for my 5.30am start.

She was getting more and more sick. Physically she looked a wreck and mentally she was anxious and sinking deeper and deeper into depression.

We were coming to the end of the road.

One morning on the radio show I had to interview a man who ran a treatment centre, Broadway Lodge, for alcoholics and drug addicts.

I asked him, 'Is it true that people can have just as much trouble giving up booze as heroin?'

'Yes,' he said, 'but at least most people on heroin know they have a problem. Alcoholics usually refuse to accept they are addicted.'

I prayed that Ellen was listening. When I got home she was

in tears. 'I phoned the treatment centre,' she told me. 'I would have to go there for five weeks and it costs £5,000.'

'I'll give you the money,' I said. 'You can have the money I was saving to have a conservatory built.'

'But it's not fair,' she cried.

'Look, Ellen,' I tried to make her understand, 'if you had cancer and it could be treated for £5,000 we would pay it. You are sick, you must get help.'

'Let me try it again on my own,' she said.

She did try but it wasn't long before she got horribly drunk.

Ellen had been missing since lunchtime without even the usual drunken apologetic phone calls. I had long since given up trying to track her down when she was on a bender.

About 10 o'clock at night the doorbell went. 'We have your wife here,' said a male voice on the intercom. Two men carried her into the hallway and she lay motionless.

'What happened? Where did you find her?' I asked. They gave the name of a local wine bar but they didn't know how long she had been in there. When she passed out they found her address in her handbag and brought her home.

They say God looks after drunks and it must be true because Ellen always found Good Samaritans to look after her. These particular Samaritans refused to take any money for their trouble and having deposited her into my safe keeping were anxious to be off.

When she came to the next day, Ellen looked pathetic. She went to have a bath and from the other room I could hear her sobs. I went into the bathroom and she was crying as if her heart would break.

Huge teardrops splashed into the bath water and she looked like something out of *Alice in Wonderland* about to be washed away on a sea of tears.

'I know you can't take any more,' she cried. 'You might as well leave me. It's never going to get any better. I'll always be like this. Just go.'

I grabbed her by the shoulders and almost in tears myself I said, 'You are very sick. They can help people like you. Please let them help you. You don't need to go on destroying yourself.'

'What are people like me?' she asked sadly.

'You are an alcoholic,' I told her. 'It's a disease. You can get better.'

For once not denying the accusation I had thrown at her so many times over the years, she sighed and some relief crossed her face. 'Okay, let's see if they can help this alcoholic,' she said. 'I'll try anything to get out of this hell.'

She had finally admitted she was beaten. The gypsy's prediction which had given me a glimmer of hope over the years came back to me. One day she will stop.

Ellen started to live her life one day at a time on 10 June 1986. It was as if the devil himself had been lifted off our shoulders.

CHAPTER 14

ONE DAY AT
A TIME

Some four years after 'the devil was lifted off our shoulders', as Derek so graphically described it, I was asked to contribute to a book, *Getting Sober ... and Loving It* (Vermilion), published in association with SHARP, a charity that runs courses for addicts.

It told the stories of recovering alcoholics from all walks of life, including celebrities such as Ringo Starr, Eric Clapton and Jimmy Greaves. In it, I told the story of my own drinking and how I stopped and discovered sobriety.

The roots of what was to become my drinking problem began when I first arrived in London. As a child growing up, I knew what the problems were. I had loving parents who were absolutely wonderful, but when they had a drink, everything changed. Our lives spiralled into chaos and so I was determined not to touch it. The joke was that when everybody else was drinking alcohol, I was drinking tea. I just didn't want anything to do with it. Then suddenly I started drinking. I was 19.

My favourite had always been Coca-Cola, and then someone

said to me, 'The Beatles put whisky in their coke.' I thought, 'If it's good enough for them, it's good enough for me.' Easy to say, but it didn't taste nice. Right up until the end of my drinking, I didn't like the taste. I was a fussy alcoholic. I was always saying 'Could I have some lemonade in this?' or 'Is there any Coca-Cola?' I never liked the taste but I loved the effect.

At the time it was all go in the pop world – lots of receptions and parties. There wasn't any question of money. We would g o to receptions where yards of whisky were poured, topped up with coke. For a long time I didn't know how much I was drinking.

In 1970, at age 20, I was married to Gavin. As journalists in the pop world, we were drinking champagne on river boats, not cider under the arches. It was a glamorous world of drinking and somehow it seemed to be okay. At that time, all my friends were in that circle and there were always some who stayed out late.

I was one of those who, when the party finished, went on to another party and then to a club and then to somewhere else. By now Gavin was editor of *Disc* magazine and it was a case of: 'Four o'clock. Right. Where are we going tonight? Polydor has got this event at such and such a place and this film company have got something on there.' There might be five events going on. 'Right. We'll look in on all of them.'

Everyone wanted to give a better party than the last person, and that involved loads of free booze. There must have been people in those days who didn't drink, but I didn't know them.

The hangovers were pretty ferocious. I remember one occasion, about four months after I started drinking, when with each step I took my head was going bang, bang, bang! One bang after another. I still didn't know. In those days I thought the problem was me. As soon as I got a drink inside me, I could talk to anybody, go anywhere, do anything.

I honestly believe that if I hadn't drunk then, I could have had a wonderful time. All those places I went to. Things would have been even better without drinking.

At the same time, drinking *was* a lot of fun. There was a lot of social drinking and it just seemed that everybody else drank as much as I did. I don't know what their heads were like the next day.

Working in journalism, you met everyone in pubs, clubs and restaurants. You did your interviews there. Talking to people and drinking, with your drinks paid for on expenses. It seemed to be an implicit part of the job. And if you went back to the office drunk, there was a good chance of concealing it. I knew plenty of quiet places where you could put your head down, or someone would put you in a cab and send you home. *Or* someone would take you back out to another drinking club. I don't recall anyone in those days ever saying to me that I had a drink problem.

Since getting sober I've often thought of the jobs I wanted that other people got. Or the title, or the promotion. I would be in the pub complaining: 'Why didn't *I* get it?' Afterwards you realise you were always in the wrong place. You weren't in the office.

As with everybody else, there were times when I said: 'Right. That's it. I'm on a diet. I'm not drinking.' I told people I was on antibiotics but I never managed to stop drinking for more than a couple of days. People watched out for me, trying to see which drink it was that 'did it'. I never got it into my head that it was the *first* drink that did the damage, that started me off.

My drinking became progressively worse. By now my marriage was over and I had met Derek. He was part of the 'Fleet Street scene' with all its heavy drinkers, but luckily for me, he hardly drank at all. Not because he particularly disapproved of it. Drink wasn't that important to him.

I suppose I knew I had a problem when, on my thirtieth birthday, I tried to commit suicide. I had always claimed that I wouldn't live past 30. The thought came from people like Marc Bolan. We all reckoned: 'I won't need this body after thirty. So it's okay to abuse it. I'll be gone anyway.'

So when I got to 30 and I was still here, I tried to commit suicide. That was just one of several attempts. And when I sobered up, I did go to a self-help group, based on the 12-step programme. I tried to find out what the problem was. I didn't think it was the drink. I thought I was 'depressed'. At the meeting I thought what nice people they were, like Jehovah's Witnesses. But it wasn't for me.

I still saw myself as a high-flier and, after a period without a drink, I poured another and stayed 'out there' drinking for another six years.

When I did finally seek help, I was in such a mess. They said, 'Why don't you go to a meeting?' I said, 'I went to one and it didn't work.' But I was ready by this time. I was sick and tired of being sick and tired.

The mental thing was the biggest problem. I was going out of my head. I knew Derek wouldn't put up with much more. I was out of touch with the real world. I used to walk around the flat with a large drink in my hand saying, 'God, what have you done to me?' I didn't want to answer the telephone; I didn't know who I'd spoken to the previous day. I didn't dare answer the door because I didn't know who I'd taken up with. I was in total fear.

At one stage, Derek said to me, 'Why do you never even apologise? Why do you pretend the next day that everything's okay?' I didn't know. Maybe I thought that if he didn't say anything I had got away with it. Now it all seems so sad.

I asked him, 'Why did you stay with me? Why did you love

me?' He replied, 'Because I knew you. I knew the *real* Ellen.' He saw that the drink was dragging me away but he was determined not to let go. That was one of the amazing things about him. When I would say, 'Just give up. Just go, for God's sake. Just leave,' he wouldn't.

Of course, I wanted a bit of freedom as well. I dreamed of staying in a little seaside hotel, where nobody would bother me; and drinking. I wanted him to let me go. But he wouldn't. He had decided he would hang in there until I got well.

Derek told me the story about the gypsy in Blackpool. She knew about the drinking and she said, 'One day she'll just stop.' It took another six years.

He waited, one day at a time. On the day I put down the drink, six years later, I came home and told him I had been to get help. He said, 'Thank God it's over.' I said, 'Well, I don't know. It sounds like a pretty tall order. So today I'm going to try not to pick up another drink.' And he said, 'No. It's okay. The storm is finished.'

A couple of months later he said to me, 'Let's get married.' I replied, 'I can't. It's suggested that you don't make any major life changes for two years after getting into sobriety.' I was very lucky because two years later he asked me again. That time I said, 'I'd love to.'

Being abstinent is the only thing that has ever worked for me and has ever given me any real happiness. When I came to London from the north, everybody else seemed so confident. I was the only one who wasn't, but with a couple of drinks I was just as confident as them. It never occurred to me that maybe they had their own fears and hang-ups. I just wanted to be part of the crowd. I didn't realise that someone like me, with a propensity for alcoholism, would get caught.

And that's what's so frightening. That the disease was there but I denied it. I used to scream at Derek: 'Don't talk to me about the drink. Let's talk about why I'm unhappy. Why am I unfulfilled? Why am I depressed? Why do I never get the jobs I want? Let's put the drink on one side.'

He always attacked the drink, but that was the very thing that I felt I had to defend. I suspect that somewhere deep down inside I knew what was wrong. I knew that only when I admitted it would I stop.

I went to a self-help group and a lady was talking about the problems her drinking had caused and it clicked. A light went on in my head; I came home and said, 'It's the drink. Why did nobody ever tell me?' I then knew that the depression came out of the bottle. The mental problems came out of the bottle and the physical problems came out of the bottle.

Only as I got more sober could I trace it further and further back to when I started drinking. I never drank like an ordinary person. I always wanted to get drunk. Not liking the taste of it, I needed the sensation. I always wanted to be high.

In those early days of sobriety there was so much fun in getting back in touch with reality and with a world I didn't really know. I used to think, 'How am I going to tell everybody that I don't drink?' It was astonishing the number of people who just didn't seem to notice, people I thought must have known I had a drink problem. When I went to their houses, they would say, 'What are you drinking?' I would ask for a Perrier and they'd say, 'Fine.' I, however, had prepared a long speech to explain everything. Really, people don't take that much notice.

On the other hand, when I hadn't had a drink for a couple of months and I was at a party, somebody came up and asked if I had started drinking again. They said, 'You're so happy.' 'Yes,' I said, 'I am. This is me without drink.' After my own wedding, somebody said to me, 'You were drinking, weren't you? You were laughing and dancing.' And I said, 'There wouldn't have been a wedding if I'd been drinking, but it's possible to do those things without a drink.'

I had never identified *alcohol* as the problem. I had identified, say, whisky or gin, or maybe that Australian wine was a bit off. Or that particular red wine gave me a headache.

In the past I had tried so often to stop drinking and be a good girl, to get Derek talking to me again, and catch up with the work. Then, 'I think I'll have a shandy' or 'I'll just have a glass of wine.' I honestly didn't realise that it was that one shandy, that one glass of wine that started the binges.

If I didn't have a drink for two days and still lost my temper, swore or dropped something, I would say, 'See. It's not the drink. I haven't had a drink for two days and yet this is still happening to me. So this is *me*. So I might as well drink because I'm like this anyway.'

Now that I'm in touch with reality, I've discovered that the three-hour traffic jams I used to get caught in have gone. Trains that didn't appear seem always to turn up now that I'm sober. I had thought the world was so chaotic, but in fact it wasn't. It was me who was chaotic. I always left somewhere an hour after I should have been at my destination, and that's why the 'traffic jams' were so bad. That's why the trains never came. That's why, if I stood on the corner for three minutes and the cab didn't come, I'd go back into the pub and say: 'You can't get a cab in London for love or money.'

I think what happened was that I spent most of my last six months drinking and trying not to drink. And so I would have three days on, two days off, a week on, a week off, and so on. On Derby Day 1986 I hadn't had a drink for a couple of days. We were going to Epsom in the car and Derek said to me, 'I hope you're not going to start drinking again.' I said, 'Oh, don't start. Don't spoil the day before we get there.' But, of course, I did drink.

We were with some friends and on the Sunday Derek said to me, 'Well?' I had woken up and everything looked fine – clothes off and hung up. Then Derek added, 'I never thought I'd see you falling out with her.' I didn't know what he was talking about. He said, 'Ellen, if you don't remember, you've got a problem.' By this stage much of my drinking was blacked out; as long as I was where I should be when I woke up, I didn't know if anything had gone wrong the previous evening. I kept trying to piece the evening together. I thought he was winding me up so I phoned my friend Lee and said, 'Did I fall out with you?' That terrified me because I had no memory of the event.

I had one more weekend of drinking. I had gone for a Sunday lunchtime drink and had phoned Derek every hour, saying 'I'll be back any minute.' By six o'clock in the evening, when I was supposed to be at home cooking a joint for our dinner, I phoned to say, 'Oh, the baby's lying on my coat so I can't leave now.' I woke in the baby's cot the next day with my boots and all my clothes on and crayon all over my face. I just cried and thought, 'What have I come to?' I went home from there and picked up a couple of cans of lager to 'straighten me up'. I stood in the bathroom at nine o'clock in the morning, forcing down a can of lager just to stop the shakes long enough to get on with some work. I thought, 'Derek's on the radio till 9.30am.' I didn't know how long it took him to get home from the station – it could have been 10 minutes or 10 hours. I just had no idea. All I knew was that if he wasn't on the radio, he might suddenly appear in the house.

Soon afterwards I came home a day later than expected. I found a note from Derek that said, 'You are a mess. The office has been phoning all day. There's no cat food. There's no food in the house. I've gone to Birmingham as arranged. I'll see you when I see you.' When Derek came back from Birmingham, I was in the bath. It was one of those days when I was covered in bruises and didn't know how they had got there.

After 10 days spent in and out of blackouts I was at rock bottom. The tears were running down my face. I thought I was going to drown in my own tears. Derek came in and I said to him, 'Just go. It's never going to get any better.'

Having a sober, long-suffering, loving partner is such a support. Derek told me I needed to get help, and within two weeks I was in recovery.

To go to a self-help group and be told 'You're not bad, you're sick', is the most miraculous thing. I was prepared to say that I was the worst person in the world and they said, 'You're not, Ellen. You're a sick girl. We can help you. You can get better.'

I came out of that meeting of recovering alcoholics and I went back to the bathroom. I got down on my knees and said, 'God, you probably don't remember me, but my name's Ellen. You've kept those other alcoholics sober. Would you do it for me? Just for today.'

And I have never had another drink. My last drink was on 10 June 1986.

CHAPTER 15

TWO'S COMPANY

Derek was offered the editorship of *News of the World* in 1981 by Rupert Murdoch. He was glad to take up the editor's chair again after a year on the show business circuit, travelling all over the country to television companies and radio stations and appearing as a media commentator on news programmes, a guest on talk shows, and a celebrity on game shows.

I also returned to full-time freelancing, having enjoyed the time as his travelling companion. Television may not always pay the big bucks, especially for one-off appearances; the money is to be made when you are hosting your own show (when Derek was given his nightly chat show on Sky, the *Sun* called him 'The Highest Paid Man in Television'). However, expenses and hospitality are generally lavish and Derek and I enjoyed a carefree existence driving from one end of the country to the other in his fancy Jaguar, staying in the best hotels and being wined and dined by the TV companies.

In many ways it was sad when it came to an end – for me at

least. On the morning of his first day back in Fleet Street, I lay in bed watching him get ready for work and asked, 'What about me?'

'Look,' he said, holding out a tiny phial of silver glitter, 'I've got you in my pocket. You won't leave my side.'

And Derek was always good to his word. He took me to work with him every day for years. I still have the phial. It's a shame he couldn't take it with him on his last journey but now I have it by my side so he is still always with me.

Our lives again became super-busy and the diary was filled with work commitments and exciting invitations. I worked at one stage for a public relations company based in Fleet Street and also for a picture agency, doing feature stories to illustrate the photographs they sold to newspapers and magazines.

However, I had to contend with a double tragedy in the family. My younger brother Gerard, 31, and my mother, just 51 years old, died within three months of each other. Mum had had a heart attack on her fiftieth birthday and the next one, a year later, killed her. Really, the cause of her death was a broken heart.

My brother, Gerard, a wonderful, lively character, always full of schemes and dreams and an inability to cope with the real world, died .

Mum never recovered and didn't stop crying from the day of Gerard's death till her own three months later. Dad lived another 18 years and died a month after his seventieth birthday. 'I've done my three score years and ten,' he announced. 'I won't hang around much longer.'

My dad and I had one of those complicated father/daughter relationships. As a child I had worshipped him and thought he could do no wrong. As I got older, of course, the picture became much clearer, but he and I were still extremely close and it's true to say that he always favoured me over my brothers.

He believed that I could do anything and achieve anything I wanted, but he was also notoriously difficult to please and his criticisms and unrealistic expectations made me fear him as much as I loved him. I feel sorry for him because he was not a bad man. He was funny, charming and extremely intelligent but suffered from his own demons. I for one will never let the booze off the hook for taking my dad away from his family and exposing him to uncontrollable emotional dysfunction. No wonder they say alcoholism is a family disease.

I honestly believe that he wanted to do the best for us and he did try, but the discipline he imposed simply added to feelings of rebellion in his children. I have always made excuses for him, and I appreciate that the way of bringing up children was very different in the 1950s from today. I don't hear many parents now trying to impose a 'children should be seen and not heard' rule. (Though perhaps they should!)

Dad wrote me a letter shortly before he died and I treasure it. He told me:

'Darling Daughter, I loved you from the minute you were born and there has been nothing, not once in those intervening years when anything you could have ever done made me stop loving you for even a minute. You are the best daughter I could ever have asked for, you are a credit to me and even if I don't deserve you, I love you with all my heart. Your Dad.'

When people ask me if I have any children, I always say, 'I was never blessed. Thank God.' Instead, I get to be a favourite auntie and great auntie to the extended family of my brother Billy. My brother Billy – the only one left now out of three – is the one with whom I always had most in common, apart from wanting to mother and marry my baby brother James.

Billy was the middle boy and he and I have always had a close relationship. In the days of grammar schools, he and I were the ones who won scholarships and so spent part of our secondary school life on the same track. He is intelligent and displays great common sense, which is something the rest of the family often seemed to lack. While I am an airy-fairy Libran, Billy is a down-to-earth Taurean; I call him my 'earth man'. He is practical, reliable and loyal. Mind you, it helps not to take yourself too seriously when he is around. Billy is quick-witted and always ready with a laugh – and a jokey put-down.

Billy is the patriarch of his family and adored by his children and grandchildren. He and his wife Mary run an open house where family members are always welcome for food, a bed and a shoulder to cry on. The family set-up reminds me of the wonderfully inclusive attitude to family and friends portrayed in the song 'Consider Yourself' from *Oliver!*

I always thought it was a cliché about the importance of family and, having lived abroad and away from them for many years, I sometimes saw family as more an obligation than a relationship to cherish. Now that there is just Billy and me left out of a family of six, I know where my heart lies. When my brother James died, Billy took complete charge. Also, since Derek's death, Billy has been there for me every step of the way. His strength, support and love through the past months have been one of the brightest lights in the darkest time.

If your family, knowing you with all your faults and weaknesses, can still love you, that is a truly priceless gift. Just don't expect them to put you on a pedestal.

When Billy and I had lunch recently in the fancy dining room at a lovely hotel in Box Hill, it was Billy who reminded me about the times I used to hang out at the bikers' café or eat in the Wimpy Bar at the top of the hill, having enjoyed a hair-raising pillion ride up and down the dangerous zigzag road on the back of a boyfriend's motorbike.

I still love motorbikes and, when in America, I got to enjoy hitching a lift on the back of a Harley-Davidson with a huge former Hells Angel. The sensation thrills me: life in the fast lane, with the wind in my hair, not a care in the world and a driver you trust, just hanging on and letting them take you on an exciting journey.

In my search for an adrenalin rush I even sky-dived at an airfield in central Florida. It was one of the most scary and the most amazing experiences I've ever had. Jumping out of the plane, even in tandem with an experienced diver, felt like the greatest mistake I had ever made. 'Oh, my God,' I thought over and over again. 'Why did I do this?'

The roar of the engine, the smell of the gasoline and the cold and discomfort were horrendous. Then, all of a sudden, the parachute opened and I floated gently to earth. The sky was blue, there was complete silence, a divine peace enveloped me and I felt as if I had died and gone to heaven. I made a perfect landing and lay in the grass in the shape of a star angel, exhilarated and full of joy.

Ever since I had agreed to the sky-dive, my one fear – apart from having to tell Derek, which I didn't do till after the event – was that I would break a leg on landing. Instead, the instructor complimented me and said I landed gracefully, like a ballet dancer. Feet together, knees bent. But it isn't an experience I will be repeating. Once was enough. I am very glad I had the opportunity and I loved the sense of achievement, but in future I will restrict my flying to the commercial airlines.

Another of the high-flying experiences I have been lucky enough to enjoy was the helicopter ride from Nice airport to Monaco. Monaco is one of my favourite places and over the years I have been lucky enough to meet and get to know a few of the famous residents who base themselves there. Having been that young, crazy Beatles fan, and still a huge fan of their music, I have enjoyed spending time in the company of Ringo Starr and his wife Barbara. I have also become friends with a beautiful Spanish princess, Beatrice.

Once, when visiting Beatrice at her apartment, I asked the mutual friend who had introduced us, 'What can I possibly take as a gift for her?' Perhaps only a princess who already lives in palaces and has fabulous jewels and an unimaginably glamorous and mega-rich lifestyle could be so delighted with the gift of a special English brand of perfumed soap that she thought had been discontinued. In return she gave me a traditional Spanish black lace fan. It still has pride of place on the windowsill in my bedroom. I hope I was able to accept the gift with the graciousness she displayed.

In many ways Monte Carlo reminds me of Miami, where I now live – a playground for the rich and famous with great weather in a fabulous setting with stunning architecture, grandeur, luxury and streets filled with Lamborghinis, Ferraris and Bentleys. They have both been described as 'sunny places for shady people'. And the café society where you can sit at a pavement café indulging in to-die-for ice cream sundaes while watching the world go by – no wonder real life in ordinary places has never satisfied me.

My passport, until they changed the format, said 'Journalist', even though I had left print journalism years previously. Journalism gave me my entry to national broadcasting, thanks to International Women's Day and the far-sighted and innovative Radio 2 controller Frances Line, who gave me my big break.

Derek, however, was far from pleased to hear that on International Women's Day 1990, in the interests of equal opportunities, he was to be given the day off and his wife would get to greet the Great British Public on the breakfast show with his famous catchphrase, altered to 'Mornin', mornin', *Mrs* Jameson here.' Perhaps he was right to be concerned, for it wasn't long before I was offered a full-time job on Radio 2 as a co-presenter. The show was to change from *The Derek Jameson Show* to *The Jamesons*.

There was a national outcry when Derek was removed from the Radio 2 breakfast show and, although Derek was accepting about most things that happened in his career, that decision upset him. He had attracted a huge audience of 10 million listeners a day, and then the BBC, in its usual arbitrary and largely unfathomable manner, decided to change a winning formula. Derek and I were used to tick a few boxes in order to 'keep the politicians happy' and address concerns that too much of the licence payers' money was being spent in the south.

The Jamesons' programme was shipped to Glasgow and handed over to an independent radio production company, Unique Broadcasting, under the excellent stewardship of Tim Blackmore, MBE and Simon Cole, fielded a highly professional and talented creative team to produce our nightly radio show. Our figures continued to grow and we were credited with attracting the largest late night radio audience in Europe. Even the Radio 2 controller – a new one now – was moved to say that the programme we hosted on the night of the Dunblane shooting, when 16 schoolchildren were killed, was one of the best he had ever heard.

But Derek had made up his mind to retire. Glasgow was a long way from our home on the south coast and he had been diagnosed with a heart condition. 'I don't want to be the richest corpse in the graveyard. I've worked all my life. Now I need a rest.'

Thinking that he would probably still want to keep working,

I asked him, 'Will you write another book?' – which he did do – but he said, 'No, I'm going to take the time to read a book and listen to music.'

On the last night of our radio show, we had a great send-off from the public, many lovely friends and colleagues and some honoured guests, including the wonderful Barry Humphries and always delightful Barbara Windsor.

A farewell article in the *Glasgow Herald* by the highly respected columnist Jack Webster said it all: 'Couple who found a place in the hearts of the nation ... Derek and Ellen had that common touch that endeared them to millions.'

While Derek continued the journalism career that had begun some 50 years earlier writing columns for his local newspaper, I set up a consultancy business on the south coast. But as the millennium approached we took some major decisions.

It was time to retire completely. We wanted to spend more time in America, we wanted to travel, and we wanted to be free of contracts, obligations and responsibilities.

The year 2000 was to be the start of yet another chapter in the roller-coaster life we had enjoyed together for 24 years. Derek had turned 70, I was 50, and our families were all settled and living their own lives. Now was our chance to live the life of leisure. New horizons beckoned.

CHAPTER 16

GOOD MORNING AMERICA

Derek's sister Jean lives in Ohio, and between 1999 and 2001 we made several trips to the States, staying with her and her family – and puppy Peanuts – and travelling around the country.

On a Christmas trip to New York, we stayed at the Intercontinental Hotel and did some serious shopping at Trump Tower and admired all the seasonal window displays at Saks and Tiffany's and Asprey's. We had a truly romantic meal at a newly opened Italian restaurant with a sky blue painting on the ceiling and romantic fairy lights twinkling everywhere.

We took in a Broadway theatre show, a version of *Smokey Joe's Cafe* with the music of Leiber and Stoller, which Derek was ecstatic about. Walking home, we watched people still skating on the ice rink at the Roosevelt Plaza at 11 at night – it is truly the city that never sleeps. We walked around Times Square and saw on top of one of the tallest skyscrapers the new Waterford Crystal ball that had been commissioned to drop at midnight to mark the millennium. The energy of New York City thrills me, though Derek was less enthusiastic.

Mass at St Patrick's Cathedral the Sunday before Christmas was a treat for me. We lit lots of candles for family, friends and absent loved ones. Later we saw a truly spectacular production of the *Nutcracker Suite* by the New York City Ballet. We were both enthralled: it was a really stunning and unforgettable Christmas treat.

For the New Year, Derek and I headed north to Niagara Falls. It took six hours to make a three-hour journey as our escort, Donna, insisted on meal stops and 'comfort' stops at places where she obviously picked up commission on sales. Jean had advised against driving ourselves as the road conditions can be really challenging.

We stayed at a modest and comfortable enough motel and prepared to celebrate the millennium with a black tie dinner at the Hilton Hotel. Unfortunately, a major security alert closed the border between Canada and America and the showcase millennium concert and many of the other planned festivities were cancelled.

Dinner was rescheduled at a Holiday Inn but we fled the noisy, cold ballroom with a Yugoslavian couple called Lozo and Manda, from Croatia via West Akron. A cab back to our motel to change out of evening clothes and into warm clothing, including thermals, then it was on to the waterfront overlooking the rainbow-coloured falls for the midnight fireworks and millennium countdown: a memorable place to welcome in the year 2000.

After a guided tour of the Falls and surrounding area on New Year's Day, we enjoyed a wonderful dinner in the revolving restaurant of the Skylon Tower. It overlooks the Falls and revolves so you can see the whole of Niagara spread out below.

We could clearly see the casino from our window, and, after dinner, the gaming tables were our next stop. The casino attracts hordes of tourists – we waited in line for 20 minutes to get in and once inside it was so busy I could hardly see anything of the plush decor, or even get a seat at a slot machine. Derek made a dive for a machine and barely moved for the next two hours. By the end he had won $100 and lost $100.

After our millennium adventure we returned to Jean's for a few days. It had become our home from home and we started to talk about coming to live in America permanently. One reason was puppy love. Derek and I loved Jean's dog Peanuts and we took her for long, glorious walks by the frozen lake at the bottom of the road. Neither of us had ever had a dog before.

We walked through powdery, sparkling white snow that crunched underfoot and shaded our eyes from the glare of winter sunshine. A real wonderland: Derek and me and Peanuts, a happy band.

On our outings we would have long and serious discussions about selling up back home and returning to live in Akron. We both thought it a splendid idea at the time. We talked about it after coming home but it needed careful thought and consideration. In the meantime, we agreed to start to clear up outstanding matters, particularly Derek's paperwork and the overstuffed cellar.

Jean really did appreciate our being with her over the holiday and she celebrated much more than she thought she would be inclined to. She and I and Derek shared many poignant and tearful moments when she was so overwhelmed with missing Jerry, her husband of 42 years, who had died in May that year. But we also enjoyed many laughs, outings and happy times together. A gift of a Christmas and the millennium. Here's to 2000!

CHAPTER 17

THE GREAT AMERICAN ADVENTURE

6 June 2001: Continental Airways. Gatwick to Cleveland, Ohio. Excellent flight; wonderful service; felt well spoiled. Arrived Cleveland and met by Derek's sister Jean and her daughter Joanne. All's well. Had a couple of days to settle in and acclimatise before Founder's Day Convention at Akron University.

Filled with gratitude and a sense of achievement and completion: I celebrated my 15 years sober anniversary on 10 June – Founder's Day. My meetings in Akron, the home of the 12-step programme that got me sober, always make me feel emotional and very well blessed.

One of the major highlights of the trip to Akron was an escorted tour and lunch at the Interval Brotherhood Home, a drug and alcohol rehabilitation facility run by Father Sam. It was such an awesome and humbling visit. Since that day I have had thoughts of working there – or, what I would really like to do, write the story of Father Sam. This Italian Catholic priest was a towering figure in the alcohol recovery movement in Akron. Sadly, he too was a flawed human being and was some years later convicted of embezzling millions of dollars of the organisation's funds. Life is so strange. No wonder God laughs at our little plans and schemes.

Met up with many old friends and made some new ones. Greatest buzz – a ride on a black Harley-Davidson to Dr Bob Smith's grave for a spiritual service. Awesome! Weather stunning. Stayed at the Sheraton Hotel overlooking Cuyahoga Falls.

Home to Jean's, where Derek had started to plan the Great Amtrak Adventure all around America. Sounds great: first leg – fly to Washington then overnight train to Miami.

15 June: Stretch limousine (white) from Jean's to Cleveland airport. First class to Washington DC where we have an appointment with an immigration lawyer.

Derek's health is not great; he's having trouble walking. I think it's overexertion on the long walking trips with Jean's dog Peanuts. I hope that now we are back on the road he will begin to get greater mobility.

Arrived DC at Ronald Reagan National Airport – men in suits and power-dressed ladies all seemed to dress in corporate black. The Foggy Bottom bar is doing a brisk business; apparently Foggy Bottom is a well-known political area of Washington.

Super shuttle to the Capital Hilton; there's a cowboy in the back seat who calls me ma'am and removes his hat because there are ladies present.

Washington attracts 20 million visitors a year. Driver Sam doesn't know his way around too well and keeps asking us 'What's the zip code?' and passing round pieces of paper for us to write down our addresses. It seems we are not the only out-of-towners.

We keep passing the same buildings again and again – Grubb

& Ellis, Real Estate, the New York Cafe, the Wall Street Deli. And the same churches – 'Repent or Perish', 'Jesus Saves'.

Finally we arrive at the Capital Hilton. The desk clerk, Mohammed, is wearing a badge saying 'Catch me at my best'. He likes a joke. With a sympathetic smile he tells us, 'The registrations desk is closed for the next three hours but the bell captain will deliver your luggage by Tuesday at the latest.' Fortunately, even after our round-Washington tour en route from the airport, we managed to maintain our sense of humour and the service turned out to be excellent.

Straight off, we enquire about guided tours of the White House. It turns out you have to join a tour at 6am or get there at 5am and line up for the 1,000 tickets given out to those waiting. The other 1,000 tickets available on a daily basis are allocated to travel operators.

After dinner, a stroll in the warm, summer evening. Behind the hotel, offices and printing presses of *The Washington Post*. On the street, 30 newspaper vending boxes including *Washington Jewish Week*, *USA Today*, *The New York Times*, *New York Post* and *Miami Herald*.

17 June: trolley tour of Washington. Awesome. Lincoln Memorial – emotional. In the evening the Eisenhower Theatre at the Kennedy Center for an English star production of *Lulu* by the Almeida Theatre Company, which is usually based in north London. A gruesome and graceless piece of theatre, though Derek enjoyed the British accents.

The next day we continued our tour, this time out of the city centre to the Georgetown historic residential district. Senators, administrators and movers and shakers live in this highly fashionable and ultra-expensive area where the smallness of the houses belies their huge price tags.

After a self-guided walking tour of Georgetown, took a cab to the Smithsonian Institution to see the Hope Diamond – the largest known diamond in captivity – plus an impressive exhibition of American Indian art and culture. Turns out the eponymous Smithson was British – like Andrew Carnegie – who although he had never visited America, left his entire fortune to endow museums and research institutes. In his honour, Washington built a magnificent replica of a Scottish castle which houses the Smithsonian Institution.

After a busy day sightseeing, we hailed a cab outside the Smithsonian. The driver, an Arab, already had a passenger alongside him in the front seat but he enthusiastically waved us into the back. 'Get in, get in. Where you going?'

We shared our journey back to our hotel with a female relative, possibly the mother of the driver, dressed head to toe in black purdah with only her eyes showing. She showed no sign of being aware of us, so engrossed was she in the information the driver was imparting in English.

Below the city streets of Washington, he assured her, was another city, a city under the city complete with streets and transport and buildings and people working – government offices all under the control of the Department of Agriculture. He had stumbled on it once when he had needed water for his radiator and somehow he had walked down a secret entrance into this underground city. He had a theory: it was, he assumed, a safe haven to which the government could retreat in the event of an enemy attack.

The next day, Monday, we took an underground train ride out to the Chevy Chase shopping mall and experienced a piece of pure American theatre. Sitting opposite us was a Washingtonian in a New York state of mind: bulging muscles, shaved head, tattooed body. He shared his stream of consciousness with all who shared the carriage, in particular a nervous-looking young black kid who had the misfortune to sit down next to him.

Referring to the numerous tattoos that covered his face and neck and hands, he declared: 'I want to be a work of art before I die. These were all done by an unlicensed tattoo artist. She took 12 hours. I'm an artist. I used to be in tattoo school but my hand shook too much. I make people nervous.

'I was also in a guitar band but I quit after two weeks. I'm also a good singer. You got a band? You got a singer? You want a new singer? I play by ear but I'm ready to go all the way. I can jam. I'm really good with my fingers. You looking for a second guitarist? You can put me on hold for backup.

'You know who I play guitar like? Jeff Hardy. Of course no one's heard of him but if I say so myself, I do sound like him. I like picking the strings. I slap the bass with my fingers. I slap like this using my knuckle and I just play the top C strings. I'm, like, really good.

'I do some acting too but I'm in medical school now. But I got to confess, this is as far back as I can move my neck. I used to be a lifeguard when I was in the Navy. That's where I injured my neck.'

He paused for effect, and to stare briefly at two girls in school uniform who got on the train at Friendship Heights. One girl was black, the other white, and they both carried lacrosse sticks. Lacrosse sticks on a Washington underground train. No wonder our loquacious and multi-talented travelling companion had been stopped in his tracks. Lacrosse, now I bet that was something he hadn't tried. But we would never know. The train was pulling into Chevy Chase.

Chevy Chase – an exclusive and seriously expensive shopping mall. I had always thought Chevy Chase was the name of an American comedian – makes sense, the prices there are certainly a joke.

Tuesday 19 June: On the Amtrak Silver Star to Miami. Amtrak lives up to all expectations. The double sleeping compartment is spacious, clean and ingeniously functional. Every inch of space is utilised. Four picture windows allow the sunlight to shine in and us to gaze out at the ever-changing vista.

Alvin, the sleeping car attendant, is an affable, unflappable middle-aged black man who has been serving Amtrak passengers for 28 years. He has four years to go before retirement.

In this age of economical and highly frequent interstate air travel, Amtrak is perceived as expensive, but our $700 fare (£510) was worth every dollar. In fact, it is a priceless experience to sit aboard this huge silver locomotive as she rides majestically across the lands of America, hooting that haunting railroad whistle and calling adventurers to 'climb aboard'. I search for Willie Nelson travelling songs on the in-compartment entertainment centre to accompany the visual delights of the foliage, waterways and small American towns of the state of Virginia.

After our first stop, Alexandria, the conductor blows the whistle joyfully as we pass by white clapperboard houses whose backyards reach down to the railroad track. Last time we visited America, we took home a wooden railroad whistle. It must be one of the most evocative sounds in the world.

Derek and I smile happily at each other as the speeding train eats up the miles. It is a shamanic journey, a call to adventure. 'Oh, wow, look at that harbour. See the sunlight reflecting on the trees. There's the sweetest house. Look, more water, a swampy pool. Look, look, the other side, a deep forest of vibrant green trees, unpopulated, majestic, rising above the train.

Vegetation, yellow, purple, blue and rust-coloured trees, red, orange and white flowers.'

We pass Quantico Marine Corps Base, Virginia – rows of military men. Their ears prick up and they turn towards the railway track as they hear the whistle blow. Most of them will have come into camp on the train, and it's the train that will carry them home. A small salute. The silver train rolls on.

Silver service dinner. Sharing our table is an elderly black lady, Vernon Lee Bee Forrester, a nurse from Pennsylvania on her way to a nurses' reunion in Jacksonville. She is gracious, softly spoken, and declares that her journey has been 'mightily enriched by meeting some folks from England'.

Back in our compartment, an apposite announcement over the conductor's intercom: 'We're leaving Richmond, Virginia. It's time to get your nicotine fix. Smoking is allowed in the lounge for the next 30 minutes. Hurry on up and light up.'

Stunning sunset: impressionistic shades of pale blue, lilac and palest pink, with a red globe in the west.

CHAPTER 18

WHAT A SWELL
PARTY

B al Harbour, Miami, is a dazzling palm- and waterfall-lined designer shopping village where even if you cannot afford the Dior gowns, Gucci handbags, Chanel shoes and Louis Vuitton luggage, you can still treat yourself and enjoy a great day out window shopping and people watching.

For the price of a cup of coffee it is possible to buy hours of entertainment just observing the beautiful, rich people indulging their love of retail therapy and showing off. It's a place to go to see and be seen, and some people, perhaps the lonely or bored ones, can be surprisingly friendly. The British accent seems to attract them. One elderly German lady, dressed head to toe in Dior and masses of chunky gold jewellery, engaged me in conversation from her café table next to mine.

'You're English?' she demanded to know.

'Yes,' I replied.

Then, without further preamble, she asked the question that was on her mind. 'How's the Queen?'

'Oh, fine,' I told her.

'And her family, how they getting on?' she asked.

I wanted to laugh at the notion that the Queen and her family and I were on such friendly terms, as if I were always popping into Buckingham Palace for tea or calling her up for a chat.

However, as it happened, I was able to tell my new friend, who was lonely and later told me she was married to an Italian ship's officer on one of the cruise liners that sail out of Miami, that I had indeed been invited to tea with the Queen. I conveniently omitted to mention that there were another couple of hundred people at one of the Buckingham Palace garden parties the Queen hosts throughout the summer.

I told the German lady that Her Majesty, accompanied by her son Prince Andrew, had stopped and talked to our small group as she circulated among her guests and asked the questions that she undoubtedly asks a hundred times at every garden party. 'Have you had some tea? How are the sandwiches? The cakes are very nice. Do try them.'

What a way to spend a glorious summer afternoon, chatting to the Queen and trying to appear nonchalant, having stepped out of a hired black limousine at the famous golden gates. There I was in the landscaped gardens of Buckingham Palace, dressed in pink and purple silk complete with a wide-brimmed hat and carrying a frilled umbrella in case of unexpected showers. Derek was dressed in his best – hired – tailcoat, wearing a top hat. Tea is served, as you would expect, on the best china; the triangular cucumber and salmon sandwiches are dainty and the delicious cakes are bite-sized.

The afternoon is one of elegance and gracious living and makes for an unforgettable experience. Even years later, each time I drive past Buckingham Palace – there's a great view from the top deck of a red London bus – I look over the high wall into the enchanting gardens leading down to the lake and smile.

The German lady was very happy with the account of my tea with the Queen and turned her attention to Princess Diana. Happily, again I was able to satisfy her curiosity. I had talked to the Princess of Wales after a musical charity event at London's South Bank and also at a charity luncheon when we had discussed one of her favourite subjects, astrology.

Having trained as a professional astrologer at the Faculty of Astrological Studies in London's Kensington, I had been commissioned to write a column in the *Sun* newspaper. I was promoted as 'The World's First Romantic Astrologer'.

Princess Diana joked about how difficult it was to achieve compatibility between star signs. Diana was a Cancerian and her then husband, Prince Charles, a Scorpio.

'Beware the sting in the tail,' she warned.

Having proposed to Prince Charles many years before he married Princess Diana, when I undertook a newspaper stunt for St Valentine's Day, I knew all about the dangers of getting too close to the heir to the throne. I was almost shot by his bodyguards. When I next met him at a Press Awards ceremony, some of the journalists present were fascinated to see whether he would stop and talk to me.

The royals are always primed by their aides with pieces of useful information and small talk to allow them to engage with their guests and make them feel acknowledged. Prince Charles and Derek talked about newspapers, and when I was introduced, Prince Charles smiled knowingly at me and asked, 'And what is your role here tonight?' I was considering whether to apologise for having proposed to him previously – but he quickly moved on. The moment had passed.

The next time I met the Prince of Wales was in Scotland when Derek and I were invited to a luncheon at the opening of the Prince and Princess of Wales Hospice in Glasgow. Conversation flowed easily that day; everyone was talking about the monumental effort needed to establish a brand new hospice and praise went to officials, medical staff, fundraisers and volunteers. Derek and I were there in a reporting, and supporting, role.

To ensure maximum publicity for their causes, organisers always invite high-profile celebrities to attend such events. National broadcasters are a very important part of the promotion of events, from charities to fashion shows to official launches. For our part, we met and enjoyed the company of some wonderful people, including royal figures and even prime ministers – and their wives – and were always more than happy to tell our BBC Radio 2 listeners all about it.

That German lady who engaged me in conversation at Bal Harbour could have heard many more stories of celebrities we had met. It's not boasting, just a fact of life that during our lives as high-profile journalists and broadcasters, Derek and I enjoyed many wonderful opportunities to walk the red carpet and be welcomed into the splendour of royal palaces, grand government residences, fabulous stately homes, country mansions and luxurious houses and penthouse apartments.

It has been an honour to meet formally and informally some of the most powerful people in the land, including prime ministers Callaghan, Thatcher and Major, newspaper magnates Lord Rothermere of the Daily Mail Group and Lord Matthews who owned the *Daily Express* and the *QE2*, captains of industry Lord Sugar and Sir Richard Branson, and media moguls Rupert Murdoch and the late 'Captain' Bob Maxwell.

Andrew Lloyd Webber, now Lord, invited us to his prestigious Sydmonton Festival at his country mansion near Old

Burghclere in Hampshire, a weekend that will go down in the annals of theatre history as the time when the world record-breaking musical *Phantom of the Opera* was unveiled. The star-studded audience was treated to the beginnings of one of the greatest musical productions ever staged. I have the distinction of being the first person to be swooped by the flying chandelier as it flew out over the pews in the All Saint's Church. A piece of the chandelier broke off and I keep it as a trophy.

Colm Wilkinson was the Phantom and Sarah Brightman sang the role of Christine. She and Andrew were newly married and at that first-ever production when the Really Useful Group was recruiting 'angels' to help finance the show, it would have been the perfect opportunity to get in on the ground floor as an investor.

Lifelong pensions and successful investments were the rewards for those who did sign up as backers that weekend. Derek, in an unforgivable lapse of financial judgement, decided that no one would be interested in going to see the reworked tale of the Phantom set in a turn-of-the-century Parisian opera house.

The Sydmonton weekend also featured terribly English country pursuits such as the Festival cricket match and one offering that does not feature on my list of memorable moments, a talk entitled 'An appreciation of edible fungi'.

However, a lively after-dinner debate, 'Sydmonton fears for the future of the press', featured principal speakers Robert Maxwell, David Frost, Andrew Neil and my own Derek Jameson.

I had just one moment of personal worry. Arriving in the car park in a flapper-style, black-fringed dress covered in diamante, one conservatively dressed fellow guest saw me climb out of the car, legs flashing through the fringes, and declared, 'My goodness, I do think you are most awfully brave to wear that *here.*' Thanks for the confidence boost – or was she just jealous? The dress certainly attracted a lot of attention, and in a good way! Still, as I always say, and Derek certainly encouraged me, 'You only get one chance to make a first impression.'

'Knock-out drops,' he would say

At swanky events and glamorous occasions, inside my head I would be singing that show-stopping song from the musical *Sweet Charity*, 'If My Friends Could See Me Now'.

While living in America I got to meet, on two occasions, my all-time hero, President Clinton. At a Florida reception for the launch of his book *My Life*, I enjoyed flirting with him and managed to stop him in his tracks.

When we were introduced, I put on my best smile. 'And where are you from, ma'am?' he asked, returning my smile. When I told him, he said happily, 'I love your country.'

'And we love you,' I told him, adding, 'Mr President, I am so glad you chose to go bowling.'

He looked puzzled and I reminded him that on a trip to Belfast, on what he would later describe as the worst day of his life – the day the Monica Lewinsky story broke – he told a press conference: 'I am reminded of the words of one of my favourite country songs, "I don't know whether to kill myself or go bowling".'

Bill Clinton laughed uproariously and gave me a kiss.

'Remember those words, ma'am,' he said. 'They make a good philosophy for life. You've made my day.' How could I forget them?

Like God, President Clinton loves a laugh.

Back in London, one event we always endeavoured to attend was Sir David Frost's annual summer party at his home in

Chelsea. A highlight of the London season, David always attracted a stellar list of interesting and famous guests. It was a *Who's Who* of the rich and famous and we always enjoyed ourselves enormously.

Derek and I were in our element meeting old friends, being introduced to new ones and knowing that we were also a well-known celebrity couple on the London media and social scene. It felt good. We saw so many people we knew and talked to an amazing range of individuals, all of whom were welcoming, friendly and interesting. The very cream of London society attended.

Prince Andrew and Sarah, Duchess of York were there *en famille*, with their two daughters, the Princesses Eugenie and Beatrice. We chatted and shared some laughs. Princess Michael of Kent and her husband were also there. Derek knew the Princess from when she and he hosted a Press Awards ceremony. She had been on our table and was most gracious and knew how to laugh at herself and her relationship with the press. (They used to call her 'Princess Pushy' and claimed that her husband was so impoverished that the couple would go anywhere for a free meal. She seemed to find it quite amusing – at least on that occasion as a guest of the London Press Awards.)

On one occasion at the Frosts' party we met the late Lady Thatcher. Derek had been to Downing Street several times on official newspaper business, and we had also attended charity functions there. When Derek was editor of the *Daily Express*, Lady Thatcher paid a visit to the newspaper offices. We chatted briefly to her, although it would be more accurate to say that Britain's first – and still only – female prime minister generally talked while others listened.

We had fun conversations with Sir Elton John and his civil partner David Furnish. Derek always addressed Elton as that 'great British museum' (instead of musician) and, although he smiled politely, I'm not sure if he was much amused. Sir Michael Caine, accompanied by his always stunning wife Shakira, was a different matter. David told Derek, not for the first time, 'When I turn on the radio and hear your voice, it's like listening to me!'

We talked Pakistani politics with Imran Khan, who at that time was still best known as a cricketer and in the process of getting divorced from Jemima Goldsmith, daughter of the late businessman Sir James Goldsmith. Jemima later took up with actor Hugh Grant, after he separated from actress Liz Hurley and before she too married and divorced an Indian businessman and was later involved and separated from Australian cricketer Shane Warne. Talk about the social merry-go-round. The world really is a small place on the London celebrity scene.

Meeting actor Richard Wilson, best-known for playing Victor 'I don't believe it' Meldrew in *One Foot in the Grave*, reminded us of the episode when he was stuck in a traffic jam and, reaching a fever pitch of frustration, turned on the radio to calm himself down. When he heard the presenter's voice, he shouted 'Not bloody Derek Jameson' and promptly turned it off. Derek loved that episode.

Legendary musical star and singer Elaine Paige was a celebrity I certainly can't claim as a friend but I was a massive fan and we always greeted each other warmly when we met on the party circuit. I knew her from way back when Gavin and I attended her first-ever West End performance in Andrew Lloyd Webber's *Evita*. Elaine is talented, charming and always ready to impart backstage stories and gossip from the shows. As divas go, she is right up there with the best of them.

As Derek and I circulated around the vast Chelsea gardens where David Frost's annual summer party was held, we joined in congratulating Greg Dyke and commiserating with Alan

Yentob – the former had learned he was to be the new director-general of the BBC, a poisoned chalice if ever there was one.

We swapped fashion notes on the other guests with Shakira Caine and Mary Parkinson, wife of chat show host Michael. Photographer Terry O'Neill told us about the renovation work he was having done at his villa in the south of France.

Rolf Harris and his wife talked animals and we enquired about the hairless cats they breed and had brought into our BBC studio for an interview. Rolf – long before his recent troubles – was busy working on television shows including *Animal Hospital* and he promised to send our animal-mad god-daughter some photographs.

We attended the Frosts' summer parties for more than 20 years, and Sir David remained one of the greatest broadcasters who ever lived until his death in 2013, a media giant on both sides of the Atlantic. It was a great honour that, when Derek died, he agreed to read from Derek's autobiography *Touched by Angels* at the thanksgiving service in the journalists' church, St Bride's, just off Fleet Street.

No doubt Derek and Sir David are indulging in some lively debates 'up there'. I can think of no two better-informed pundits with the ability to make God laugh.

As a journalist, there were plenty of times when I was aware that it would be inappropriate to report the proceedings at events to which I had been invited. The outrageous parties thrown by Playboy UK boss Victor Lownes were a good example.

Victor, an American, came to London and made a huge impact on the nightclub, casino and party scene. He was a most generous host. Away from the London headquarters of the Playboy Club he held extravagant parties at Stocks, a mansion in the Hertfordshire countryside.

Mirroring the image of the Playboy Mansion in California, Stocks became famous for attracting party-going celebrities, beautiful models and members of the media. There was an unwritten law about what elements of the parties could be reported, usually by the gossip columnists, with some activities distinctly off limits.

I was invited as Derek's 'plus one', when he was editor of the *Daily Express*, so I considered myself very much off duty. Derek wasn't likely to be reporting stories or giving tips to the gossip columnists either, but his own diarists would be covering the event discreetly.

Name badges would have been far too vulgar for parties that were considered to be for purely social reasons, not hosted as promotional events. However, there was a distinct policy in operation that meant that not everyone was permitted entry to the higher floors. 'Access all areas' was reserved for some of the most high-profile celebrity guests and high rollers who frequented the Playboy Club in London. In private, at the top of the house, Victor could often be found playing backgammon with these guests. At a time when recreational drugs were all the rage and cocaine was the drug of choice, partygoers often wore a small gold spoon on a necklace. It was not difficult to make connections with those who enjoyed the same indulgences. A knowing nod to a friend or acquaintance would signal that it was time to retire to the bathroom and snort a few lines together. However, stories of excesses such as glass bowls of cocaine being offered around freely with the peanuts seemed exaggerated – drugs tended to be enjoyed discreetly, behind closed doors.

One highlight of parties at Stocks was the late-night pleasure of partying in the fabulous indoor Jacuzzi. At a New Year's Eve party, Derek and I ended up in the Jacuzzi and a story appeared in *Private Eye*. *Daily Express* owner Victor Matthews was not amused to read that his editor had been frolicking naked in a Jacuzzi with Playboy bunnies. 'Outrageous lies,' Derek assured the proprietor. 'I was not naked. I kept my underpants on.'

On another occasion, 'getting naked' caused problems for me in another *Private Eye* story. For one extravagant party, Victor erected a roller rink in the grounds of Stocks. Having been quite a good ice skater in my younger days, I thought roller skating would be a breeze. However, I had not allowed for the flimsy boob tube I was wearing, which insisted on sliding down in a wardrobe malfunction that left my boobs fully on display.

A photographer snapped – and so did Derek. He yelled at me to get off the skating rink. Friends were amused by my mini exposé in *Private Eye*; my employers at *Reveille* were not.

Another enthusiastic party host was film and TV director Michael Winner, now sadly passed on. In the days when he was producing big-budget movies he would throw glamorous parties at his antiques-filled mansion off Kensington High Street after the first showings of his films. At one memorable dinner after the première of *The Wicked Lady*, we were guests sitting alongside the movie star Faye Dunaway and guitarist Jimmy Page.

Michael did not go in for the crowded receptions held in clubs such as Tramp or Harry's Bar or in the function rooms of large London hotels. The bon viveur favoured discreet, stylish dinner parties at home with a beautifully laid dining table with pristine white tablecloths, shining glass, silver cutlery and fragrant flowers bathed in the glow of glittering chandeliers. Dinner was served in the ornately furnished dining room and the select guest list was treated to a menu of exquisite haute cuisine dishes and rare wines. The opulent surroundings were reminiscent of a lavish film set.

Michael Winner knew how to treat his guests – he was the perfect host. Certainly, in his home there were no displays of the bad temper and insufferable behaviour he often employed in public.

On one of Derek's Thames Television shows, *Headliners*, Michael, a celebrity guest, walked out of the studio minutes after arriving because his car had been late, stuck in traffic, and then the producers had explained that he was scheduled to appear on the second show being recorded that day. He would need to wait in the green room for at least an hour. He recoiled in horror as someone offered him a curled-up cheese sandwich and coffee in a polystyrene cup.

I was Derek's manager at the time, so, together with producers and researchers, I tried to persuade our reluctant guest to stay. I jokingly reminded him of our friendship, which included having had the honour of sitting on the heated golden throne that was the centrepiece of the lavish downstairs bathroom at his home. Michael refused point blank and stormed out, leaving us with a gaping hole in the programme's line-up and adding to his reputation as an unreliable television guest.

Another high-profile celebrity whose hospitality we very much enjoyed was the novelist Jeffrey Archer. Jeffrey and his wife Mary live in a stunning penthouse on London's South Bank overlooking the Thames and, across the river, the Tate Gallery. A private elevator to the top floor opens onto a breathtaking home straight out of a glossy interiors magazine. Jeffrey is very proud of his art collection and delights in showing off to guests his latest acquisitions. The walls are lined with paintings by world-class artists such as Picasso, Chagall and Monet, displayed in delicate frames with strategically placed lighting, and priceless sculptures sit on shelves and side tables.

Perfectly located on a bend of the Thames, the illusion is that the river is flowing right through the enormous reception area. A wall of mirrors leads to a balcony, completing the effect and giving an amazing view over Lambeth Bridge and downstream to Westminster.

Jeffrey makes no secret of the fact that he is hugely proud of his success and his lifestyle, so it must have been a huge shock to him when he had to serve a prison sentence in a British jail. If any man has paid the price for hubris, he has.

Jeffrey infamously sued the *Daily Star* newspaper for libel and collected a quarter of a million pounds in damages. Years later, in a dramatic about-turn, he stood trial and was found to have lied in the libel case and colluded with a friend, Ted Francis, to commit perjury.

However, being Jeffrey, after the shame of going to jail, being stripped of his title Lord Archer and being forced to step down as chairman of the Conservative Party, he went on to write a West End play, *The Accused*, based on his experiences and to resume his career as a hugely popular best-selling author.

Jeffrey's downfall started at a party he was hosting at his London penthouse when he made what he may have meant as a jokey remark to the man who had given him an alibi in a damaging story involving Jeffrey and a female prostitute that had been reported in the *Daily Star*.

Jeffrey made his remark and moved on to mingle with his other guests, but the offended man made a decision to own up to his part in the conspiracy to mislead the jury in the *Daily Star* libel case.

Jeffrey had phoned Derek the day after the first story broke about his alleged relationship with a known prostitute, Monica Coghlan. Derek was a former editor of the *Daily Star* and Jeffrey asked him to act as an intermediary. Derek asked him straight out: 'Do you know the woman, Jeffrey?' Jeffrey's answer was inconclusive but he implied that he did know her but not in the context to which the newspaper story was referring.

MAKING GOD LAUGH

The serving editor of the *Daily Star*, Australian Lloyd Turner, was forced to resign when Jeffrey was awarded libel damages. The press were outraged, but little did we know at the time that, like a good Jeffrey Archer novel, the story had many more twists and turns ahead. Jeffrey would not get away with it – he was forced to return the money and went to jail.

That chance remark at a cocktail party cost him dearly.

Not such a swell party.

CHAPTER 19

LET ME ENTERTAIN YOU

In the wings of the Theatre Royal, Brighton, I waited anxiously to make my debut in the *Babes in the Wood* pantomime as Spirit of the Greenwood. The wonderful *Hi-de-Hi!* actress Su Pollard, one of Britain's best-loved comedy stars, was principal boy, Robin Hood, and as she rushed off stage after her opening number she kissed me and shouted in her usual exuberant manner 'break a leg'.

A puff of smoke and a multi-coloured twinkling spotlight announced my arrival as the good fairy and maker of magic. I held my wand up high – in the left hand so it connects to the heart, which is where the power of the good fairy comes from – and raised my voice to make myself heard above the cheering of the excited opening-night audience.

Panto has to be one of the most enjoyable and interactive theatrical experiences available to a performer. The audience, mostly children but also parents, grandparents and kids from two to 92, are determined to enjoy themselves and are up for a good time. They love to shout back, cheer and boo, and make their voices heard and their feelings felt throughout the show. As the 'goodie', I was off to a flying start. The audience were on my side – oh yes they were.

Goodness knows what they would have thought had they seen the Spirit of the Greenwood make her first exit, float back into the wings and, raising her dress, put her bum in the air as Friar Tuck reached under her glittery greenwood skirt and grabbed the radio mike he needed for his next number.

The glamour of show business – and I loved every minute of it. Some of the young dancers in the show convinced themselves that I really did have magic powers and they would queue up in my dressing room before the twice-daily performances waiting their turn for a tap on the head from my glittering wand – and a gold chocolate coin for luck.

As a BBC presenter on a nightly live radio show, my job had been to be as natural as possible on air. When I became part of *The Jamesons* radio programme, Derek gave me very clear instructions: 'Be yourself. You can't keep up an act and pretend to be a different person for two hours a day five days a week.'

One of our most respected actors, the Oscar-winning Sir Anthony Hopkins, told me the same thing when I happened to meet him with some mutual friends days before Derek and I launched the BBC show. 'Act naturally,' Sir Anthony told me when I admitted I was nervous. As an afterthought, he added, 'And breathe. Breathe deeply and your nerves will disappear.' He was right; if you focus on your breathing, your nerves are steadied.

Taking my place alongside Derek, who had been called by Sir Terry Wogan 'a great natural broadcaster', I quickly learned the art of being natural. It is amazing how insincerity is picked up in an instant by listeners and viewers.

Now I was to learn that, as a stage performer, acting requires a subtle blend of becoming a different person and yet retaining your own integrity. Still, in my acting debut I wasn't playing King Lear, just a good fairy who loves and is loved and whose job it is to see that good triumphs over evil. I can't argue with that.

Live performances had always been my favourites: outside broadcasts for radio or television shows, concerts and personal appearances. They are the lifeblood of performance to me. It is all very well being in a radio studio surrounded by equipment, technical crews and producers and talking to invited guests, but I love to experience that live audience reaction.

As a performer you are required to project your energy from the stage and the reaction comes back from the audience, giving you more energy to redirect back to them. It's a two-way street. Live theatre requires a commitment from the audience; it is not about being a couch potato slumped in front of the television. It is about being engaged and involved with what is happening on stage.

Comedians talk about 'dying' on stage. If an audience does not laugh or respond, you are immediately aware that you are not on their wavelength. However, you can't blame the audience; as the performer up there on stage, you need to be performing at the peak of your abilities. You need to work harder, and when you win their approval and applause, it is the best feeling in the world, a natural high that is difficult to replicate – except by going out there and doing it again the next night.

Derek had made the decision to retire, but he knew that was not what I had in mind. For a while I ran my astrological consulting business and began to make a reputation for myself in the corporate field. I was invited to speak at conferences in Europe and America and also to contribute to a business astrology book.

I had it all planned out and had even chosen the best time to be establishing my business based on the alignment of the planets and how the transiting cycles of Saturn and Jupiter were impacting on my personal natal and progressed chart. This was what I wanted; it was in the stars, the time was right, and it was my destiny.

Was that God I could hear laughing? Our lives were to change again completely and in an unpredictable but exciting way.

Derek and I both loved America and we travelled extensively in the States. We loved rural Ohio, where his sister Jean and her extended family lived, and the fast pace of New York always energised us, although we wouldn't want to live there.

Instead, we went on holiday to Miami Beach and settled there. It calls itself the most thrilling 16 blocks on the planet, and the fusion of South American style, European chic and the American go-getting attitude made us decide that this was the place to establish ourselves. To be fair, I was always more of a Miami Beach babe than Derek, who to the end of his days preferred Worthing, but we were both excited by our new life and the endless possibilities.

Anyone who complains about a lack of culture or sophistication in America hasn't been to Miami Beach or the vibrant downtown area of Miami. The city boasts its own world-renowned ballet company, Miami City Ballet; classical music with Michael Tilson Thomas's New World Symphony Orchestra housed in a architecturally splendid state-of-the-art concert hall with outdoor viewing screen showing concerts and movies for free; the magnificently restored art deco theatre, the Colony; international concerts at the former Jackie Gleason Theater, now renamed the Fillmore; the world class Adrienne Ardsht Centre of Performing Arts; Florida Grand Opera; the globally acclaimed contemporary art festivals, Art Basel, and one of the largest annual book fairs in America; film festivals and street performers; and all the retail attractions of high-end designer shopping, award-winning restaurants, the glamorous beach and jet-skiing on the bay. What's not to like?

We became the proud owners of a waterfront property in one of the most fashionable resort-style buildings, on Belle Isle Avenue, with a million-dollar view overlooking Biscayne Bay and downtown Miami, on a residential island with swimming pools, jacuzzis, a gym and, the ultimate in luxury, valet parking.

My heart would sing with delight driving my silver convertible towards home over the Venetian Causeway, which has been described as being one of the top 10 views in America. Derek donned sunglasses and a baseball cap as he drove his Jeep Cherokee to the News Café on Ocean Drive to get his daily fix of the English newspapers. The café's right alongside the old Versace mansion, where the designer was gunned down as he went for his morning coffee.

We settled into an enviable lifestyle of relaxed days by the pool, outings to other towns along the Florida coast, shopping trips, theatre or cinema visits and eating out in the English-owned Balans restaurant on pedestrianised Lincoln Road.

Miami Beach also provided me with the perfect opportunity to take classes, attend auditions and connect with the theatrical community and work to develop an acting career. The acting community was active, and, with their trademark enthusiasm, many fellow actors introduced me to opportunities and pointed me in the right direction to meet directors, agents and teachers through organisations such as the Theatre League of South Florida.

One of my first major roles, playing the Beryl Reid character in Joe Orton's classic black comedy *Entertaining Mr Sloane*, was a dream come true for me. I auditioned at the theatre in Lake

Worth, some 100 miles north of Miami, and nailed the part. Later, the director, a female Brit, told me she had already chosen the actress she wanted for the part even before auditions began. Walking through the waiting room, the director spotted me and told the producer, 'If she can do an English accent, she's got the part.'

It was one of the happiest – and worst – times of my acting career. Let's call it 'artistic differences' between the director and myself. In some scenes where the toy boy lover of Kath physically abuses her, I ended up with some unsightly bruises. I take the blame for not being trained well enough in stage combat to block the blows.

Getting a show ready for the stage nearly always produces tension, conflict and fallings-out. The stakes are high, the process is tiring, frustrating and frightening, and it can be difficult to get everyone singing from the same hymn sheet.

The rewards, though, are amazing. When the show comes together and you get out there on opening night, all the hard work, tantrums and tensions are worth it. You just have to develop a thick skin, refuse to take criticism personally and believe that ultimately everyone is working for the good of the production – even when to all intents and purposes some people seem to be doing all they can to sabotage things.

Ultimately, the act of creation is a challenge and a struggle, but hopefully in the end a triumph. *Entertaining Mr Sloane* certainly proved to be so. The audiences loved it and I would speed back down the I-95 highway to Miami late at night after the performance with rock music blaring on the in-car system and a feeling of complete and utter exhilaration.

During the day I walked on the beach, learned my lines, attended rehearsals and lived the character of Kath, who had grown up in a modest terraced house in north London but always said she would one day live somewhere 'where there are palm trees'.

Derek had returned to England briefly and he sent me a card: 'You go, girl.' As always, my husband was my chief cheerleader.

However, he was not so happy when he witnessed me being seduced on the sofa by a handsome young actor in his twenties. When the rough stuff started and Kath's leather-clad young lover beat her up, friends later claimed that Derek had to be physically restrained. 'No one treats my wife like that,' he told them angrily, as he got ready to storm the stage.

The run of *Mr Sloane* came to an end and, like all actors, I was reluctant to return to a life more ordinary, so looked around for another part.

It couldn't have been more perfect. I was introduced to one of the most dynamic and well respected British artists on Miami Beach, Liverpool mime artist Jude Parry, who had been running the Gold Coast Theatre Company in the city for 25 years and was looking for British actors for a pantomime. The star was Miami Beach resident Mike Winters, one half of the famous British television double act of the fifties and sixties, Mike and Bernie Winters.

Working with Jude was a complete education. She knew so much about theatre and she allowed me to become her production assistant and an executive helping to promote the only British panto in Florida. We toured every year with various pantomimes that Mike wrote. I often played several parts, getting to change my costume and character up to half-a-dozen times in any one show. Each production, whether *Cinderella*, *Babes in the Wood*, or *Mother Goose Goes to Mars*, would involve special guest artistes, sometimes Brits visiting from England and sometimes those living in the States.

There was great excitement and we attracted large audiences

to ever bigger venues when Jude secured the services of a legendary British pop star Davy Jones of The Monkees. He lived on a ranch in north Florida where he rode and trained horses. He met and married his wife, Jessica, a flamenco dancer, when she appeared in the panto.

Sadly, Davy died in 2012, just after returning from a British tour with The Monkees. At the time I felt great sympathy for Jessica and thought how awful it must be to lose your husband to a sudden heart attack and become a widow overnight. In the morning everything is normal – and by the time you go to bed that night your world has been shattered. Within months, my husband too would die of a heart attack and I would know exactly what she went through.

The sheer fun, slapstick and family-friendly humour of the traditional panto meant that we attracted lots of amazing professionals to work on the shows. One year we had a British director from the Florida Grand Opera, then a director from the actors' university degree programme at one of Florida's top universities – he happened to be married to a British lady. Jude always gathered a cast of high-performing international artists from South America and Europe.

One year, Derek agreed to be the king in our production of *Babes in the Wood*. British fashion icon Barbara Hulanicki, who lives in Miami Beach, designed the costumes and the whole British community came out to help us teach the Americans what panto was all about. Christmas is not Christmas to the Brits without a panto.

Like most good things, Florida's only British panto has now come to an end, but our *Panto in Paradise* will always rank among my favourite holiday shows. Straight out of drama school, young actors learn their craft on a wide variety of acting jobs, all of which add to the sum total of their experience. I learned my craft by taking parts or opportunities wherever and whenever they were offered.

Being on the books of Florida's largest central casting agencies meant that I could appear in an advert walking my white poodle down a Miami street in my underwear (in a television advert to sell Mitsubishi air conditioning to Europe); appear as a red carpet guest in a Virgin mobile phone ad featuring the rapper Missy Elliott; stay up all night filming scenes at a medieval monastery for a South American soap opera; learn to talk chimpanzee for a cereal advert; or join *Frasier*'s Kelsey Grammer at a multimillion-dollar waterfront mansion to film scenes for a television Christmas special called *Mr St Nick*.

My mobile phone would ring at any time of the day or night and an energetic and enthusiastic agent called Sal would ask, 'How do you fancy auditioning for a Miss Moneypenny part in a pilot for a new police series called *Miss Miami*? Dress like a CIA agent. Be there in an hour.'

It has always been my philosophy that you should never turn down a job or part, however small, because you never know where it will lead or who you will meet. My life was exciting, fun and unpredictable. I loved it.

Standing on stage in the Hollywood Boulevard Theatre during the annual Shakespeare Festival playing Lady Capulet in *Romeo and Juliet*, dressed in a medieval gown, bejewelled and masked for the famous ball where the star-crossed young lovers meet, inspired and humbled me every night.

Another part that allowed me to act outrageously and dress glamorously was the character of Nessa in the play *Fit to be Tied* by Nicky Silver. Nessa is an impossibly rich and overbearing attention-seeking mother who humiliates her son with her dramatic and unconventional behaviour, including having an affair with a beautiful male angel. I appeared on stage in my underwear and a flimsy negligee – thank goodness Derek was not there to see that one, especially on the night that I remember as being this actor's worst nightmare.

Anxiety often makes performers dream about appearing naked on stage, usually also having forgotten their lines. But this was not a dream – this was real. And it was the audience who were naked. It seems it is a Miami Beach tradition among mostly gay men – the ones who also fly off on nudist holidays and stay in clothes-free hotels.

The other members of the cast promised to support me and the director insisted it would be a unique experience. The things we do for our art! By the time I told Derek years later about the 'Special Naked Gala Show' it was too late for him to do anything other than laugh at the ridiculous concept. It gives a new twist to the famous John Lennon quote at the *Royal Variety Performance* when he told those in the cheap seats to clap and the posh front-row audience to 'rattle their jewellery'!

Derek was not in America at that time as we were in the middle of a family crisis and he had more pressing matters on his mind.

While I was building an acting career for myself in the States, serious events were taking place back home in England and Derek had been getting homesick and missing the family. He felt he should be there for them as our beloved daughter-in-law faced a battle with cancer. After being in remission for seven years, she died, leaving a husband and two young children.

Dr Siobhán Kilfeather was a Professor of English Literature at Queen's University Belfast and the whole family had moved to her native Belfast when Siobhán took up what was her dream job.

In a book that Derek and I wrote called *Siobhán's Miracle* (John Blake Publishing) we told the story of how the cancer from which she was suffering disappeared after she and I made a trip to the Shrine of Our Lady of Lourdes in France. She had been diagnosed with secondary cancer in the lungs and given a date one month later to go into the Royal Marsden Hospital to have a 'very aggressive' form of chemotherapy. She was in a terrible state physically and emotionally and Derek paid for both of us to go to Lourdes on the Feast Day of Our Lady, 11 February.

We had a beautiful and spiritually uplifting time there and attended masses at the grotto, candlelit processions and prayers and penance, including climbing up a flight of marble steps on our knees to the statue of the cross. We both came back lighter in heart and mind and spiritually refreshed. When Siobhán went to her appointment at the Marsden, the cancer that they thought might have grown to the size of a grapefruit had all but disappeared.

They sent her home – no hospitalisation, no chemotherapy. A miracle. We praised God and Our Lady and thanked them for their mercy.

We were wrong about that as we had been about so many other things. After seven years in remission, during which we really felt Siobhán had beaten the disease, it returned with a vengeance. Only a truly cruel God would laugh at that.

* * *

After working with Jude Parry at Goldcoast, I had gone on to produce my own original shows. Again, I had fabulous opportunities. As well as performing, I directed and undertook all the planning and organisation of running a successful theatre company. One of our best-loved shows was an original fractured fairy tale, a Miami twist on Cinderella called *Sobe Wonderland* where the lead character, Chicabella, needed to go to the ball to meet the Prince, marry him and get a green card. It was an over-the-top musical fantasy – pure Miami.

In contrast, *Don't Hug Me* was a uniquely crafted, award-winning musical comedy with a long-running history off Broadway, a cast of zany characters, crazy songs and a touching message about love, loyalty and location. This love story was set in Minnesota, and my British accent had to be completely transformed as I played Clara, a former beauty queen whose husband wants to move from the hunting, shooting, fishing snowbound lifestyle of Minnesota to the sunnier climes of Florida.

Singer and actor Charles West, who starred as my husband in the play, was a seasoned Broadway performer who in real life had made the switch to Miami with his Wall Street financier boyfriend. He is now back in New York performing on Broadway – with a wonderful new partner, another highly successful Broadway performer.

The opening night of our *Don't Hug Me* production, which had had very good sales and attracted a large amount of publicity, was due just days after Hurricane Katrina, which had stormed though Miami Beach and gone on to wreak devastation in New Orleans. In our building we lost power for just hours and stayed safe and protected in our lockdown room in the apartment with food, water, candles and supplies. Surrounding areas did not fare so well and some homes and businesses were without electricity for weeks; the hurricane had taken down the power and telephone lines. Hurricane season starts in July and ends every year on Derek's birthday, 29 November. The hurricanes are named in alphabetical order as they form, and so Katrina was halfway through the season.

Much of the time, hurricanes blow themselves out and became tropical storms, but we still would make all the preparations, including plans to evacuate. Often the storm blows over and we experience nothing more than heavy rain, winds and perhaps some minor leaks on the balcony doors of our apartment.

The television news channels, as with so much of the America media, would have constant updates hyping up the tension. Seasoned hurricane dwellers know to take the warnings seriously, but not to over-react or panic.

Despite the problems of the Minnesota accent and having to find theatres that were still operational and still had power in the aftermath of Hurricane Katrina, one of the biggest challenges of that show was a prop.

With so much disruption and damage to the city, it seemed a forlorn task, but I set out determined to finish dressing the stage for our show. But where was I going to find a giant pair of antlers in Miami? I remembered the props company that all the film companies used for their productions – including the iconic *Miami Vice* police series – a company specialising in boats, anchors, chains and all manner of vintage nautical artefacts. Their warehouse was down by the still swollen Miami River.

The staff were bailing out the premises when I arrived and they greeted me like a long-lost friend; I was the first customer they had had for days. They came up trumps and I proudly carried to my car a giant pair of deer antlers.

We could easily have cancelled our performances, but, despite all the complications, the show did go on – but there was a message there for me.

The conflict between Clara and her husband revolved around the fact that he wanted to move to Florida and she wanted to stay in the frozen north with her family and friends. She was also forced to admit that the main reason she wanted to stay was because every year as a former homecoming beauty queen she was invited to ride on the lead vehicle in the winter carnival and experience again the applause of the crowd and the sensation of being a star, dressed in her tiara and snow queen gown.

Making the difficult decision to be true to her marriage vows and accompany her husband on his journey, she finally faced reality.

'I guess it's time to hang up my tiara,' she said.

As I said the line on stage, I almost cried. It was time to hang up my tiara and go home with my husband. When Derek told me he had made the decision to return home, I was sad but not surprised. He was reluctant to take me away from my life in Florida, but it was the right decision.

Derek had tired of America and wanted to come back home to England. Here he could again be Derek Jameson. He could walk down the street and people knew who he was. He could ring directory enquiries and the operator would ask, 'Is that *the* Derek Jameson?'

Every week some newspaper, radio or television programme would ring to ask Derek's opinion on a wide range of subjects connected with the media and Fleet Street. He even managed to revive his television career when he appeared on one of the BBC's most talked-about television series of recent times, *The Young Ones*. A scientific study into the ageing process featured Derek and half a dozen other senior citizens, including *The Royle Family* actress Liz Smith, dancer Lionel Blair and cricket umpire Dickie Bird. The team was locked up in a house in the suburbs near Reading, which had been decorated to recreate the 1970s. They were to have no contact with the outside world, not even a phone call. The aim of the programme was to see if older people can be made to reclaim their youth and vitality by living in the past and undertaking mental and physical exercises.

Derek told the programme makers and the great British public that after the experiment he would be glad if he could just bend down and put his socks on. By the end of the series, he had achieved that small task.

Although he complained about being locked up in a house and the communal living – and privately we called the programme *I'm an OAP … Get Me Out of Here!* – Derek actually enjoyed it and missed the series when it was over. It did give him a new interest in life.

Derek was happy to be home. We moved out of the small seaside cottage we had owned in Worthing for almost 30 years – it had been an ideal place to come home to from America, but not really large enough to live in long-term. Derek and I enjoyed our new home in Worthing and he supported me when I saw an opportunity to run my own company, a children's theatre school called Razzamataz, which had featured on the BBC television show *Dragons' Den* and attracted investment from multi- millionaire entrepreneur Duncan Bannatyne.

God allowed me to complete my plan to run the school successfully and also be there for my husband. I sold the school just a couple of months before Derek got seriously sick and his health began to cause real concern.

His heart was failing. He and I had enjoyed 24 years of marriage since our lavish wedding in Arundel cathedral, we had been together for over 30 years, and I think we sometimes surprised ourselves by our ability to work through issues and always consider the marriage and our life together as a priority.

The Jamesons were a team and we worked well together. Now we were entering a new and possibly final act.

Derek's allotted time on earth was running out. I became his carer and, as in so many other times of our marriage, we were together 24/7 supporting and loving each other. That last year of Derek being ill was probably the hardest of our entire lives together. He hated being a patient and I had never been a full-time carer, never even having had any children, but together we got through it.

We organised a reunion in a local seaside hotel and every member of the family was there, including our American relatives. Derek made a speech at the large lunchtime gathering and said something positive and appropriate about every member of the family and what they meant to him. Derek thanked me for saving his life. Just like years before he had saved mine.

God may have laughed at us many times when we told him our plans, but I thank him for Derek's life, which was extended and was abundant right to the end, and for allowing me to share it.

Derek was mentally robust until the end; he was engaged with life and still interested in what was happening in the world. If his mobility was slower than he would have liked, that really was only to be expected as he was well into his eighties. He lived to see the Queen's Golden Jubilee, the London Olympics and Andy Murray winning the Grand Slam.

As I delivered the eulogy at his thanksgiving service at St Bride's church off Fleet Street and scattered his ashes as he had requested, I thanked God for our lives. Derek's life was complete.

As a joke, knowing that God likes a laugh, I challenged him: 'Tell Derek to send me a sign that I have done everything as he wanted and he is okay.' The next day I opened a copy of his book, *Touched by Angels*, and found a yellowed piece of notepaper.

It read: 'I swear my lifelong love, care and fidelity to the person it was my honour to nurture back to a full and worthwhile life, my beloved wife Ellen.' – Signed, Derek Jameson.

God will have the last laugh, as he always does, but as I contemplate the next stage of this amazing life, I am learning to trust and not take myself so seriously.

Have you heard this one, God? The entire world is a stage and we but players, until they ring down the curtain.

Would the last person to leave the theatre please switch off the light.

THE LAST LAUGH

It was no secret to Derek that my heart was still in Miami Beach. He always urged me, 'Soon as I'm gone, get you back to America.'

That was the plan, but little did I know that I was about to be hit with the 'triple whammy'. Excuse me for saying so, but I think it's time God got himself a new court jester.

Climbing a mountain in Norway during an excursion from a 'Strictly Dancing' cruise, I had a severe attack of breathlessness. It wasn't a big mountain, more a very steep hill on our way to a white water rafting experience on a fjord. I honestly thought I would have to be airlifted to hospital.

Instead, an angel appeared in the form of an amazing Nepalese Cunard cruise liner employee. He took care of me, climbed a fence to get ice-cold water from the fast-flowing glacier stream, and encouraged me to breathe and not panic. He also made a truly phenomenal promise: if I wasn't able to walk down the mountain, he would carry me on his back. 'In my village, we carry people and heavy loads all the time,' he reassured me. 'You are in safe hands.'

The breathlessness abated and, with him by my side, I climbed up to the glacier and he hitched a lift down for me on a passing tourist buggy. Not that I doubted for a minute he wouldn't have carried me if necessary. The incident was a warning but I had already begun to suspect that all was not well with my health. I was fatigued but put it down to being a full-time carer. The cruise was a welcome break away and Derek was adamant that I and our beloved 22-year-old goddaughter Michelle should go and enjoy ourselves.

Derek stayed at home and was there at our front gate as the Olympic torch passed through our town. That gave him more pleasure than a cruise because, as a young reporter, he had covered the last London Olympics – in 1948.

When I told him what had happened on the mountain, he insisted that I make an immediate appointment with the doctor. The fact was that I had put his medical needs first and had rescheduled a request from the surgery that I attend for an annual check-up.

Derek had already suffered his heart attack and died before conclusive results from my blood tests were available. There was a problem with my blood count: white cells, red cells and platelets were giving cause for concern.

The GP referred me to a consultant who, after several scans and biopsies, made his diagnosis. Chronic liver failure. He had to report that I had what is commonly thought of as the drinker's disease, cirrhosis of the liver. Almost 27 years after I had my last drink.

Thanks, God. Glad you think it's funny. Though the chronic disease needed urgent and prolonged treatment, it did provide an opportunity to rest and restore my body. Thanks to highly professional medical interventions and a sophisticated treatment regime, in just less than one year I was given a clean bill of health. Now I feel well recovered and after a delayed start I have relocated to my favourite city, Miami Beach. I have no plans with which to Make God Laugh but I am looking forward to the next stage of my life.

Did I hear God laughing?

MAKING GOD LAUGH